Gays, Lesbians, and Their Therapists

Studies in Psychotherapy

By the same author

A Family Matter: A Parents' Guide to Homosexuality
The Joy of Gay Sex (with Edmund White)
Man to Man: Gay Couples in America

A NORTON PROFESSIONAL BOOK

Gays, Lesbians, and Their Therapists

Studies in Psychotherapy

Edited by
Charles Silverstein, Ph.D

W. W. Norton & Company
New York • London

Library of Congress Cataloging-in-Publication Data

Gays, lesbians, and their therapists : studies in psychotherapy /
   edited by Charles Silverstein.
      p. cm.
   "A Norton professional book"—P. facing t.p.
   Includes index.
   ISBN 0-393-70116-6
   1. Gays—Mental health—Case studies.   2. Psychotherapy—Mental
health.   3. Psychotherapist and patient.   I. Silverstein, Charles.
   [DNLM: 1. Homosexuality—psychology.   2. Physician—Patient
Relations.   3. Psychotherapy.   WM 615 G288]
RC558.G39 1991   616.85'8340651—dc20   90-14320

W. W. Norton & Company, Inc., 500 Fifth Avenue, New York, N.Y. 10110

W. W. Norton & Company, Ltd., 10 Coptic Street, London WC1A 1PU

1 2 3 4 5 6 7 8 9 0

To Dave Ellison, a young psychologist and my supervisee, who bravely fought against the AIDS virus until no energy remained, and to James Black, the life partner of Harold Kooden, who taught his family of friends to live life to the fullest.

Contents

About the Contributors

Kathleen A. Brehony, Ph.D., is a licensed clinical psychologist in full-time private practice with Greenwich Psychological Associates, P.C., in Virginia Beach, VA. She has specialized in clinical interventions for a number of issues of importance to women including agoraphobia and panic disorders, problems of self-esteem, and issues related to loss and separation. She is the coeditor of the textbook *Marketing Health Behaviors* and sits on the editorial board of the journal *Women and Therapy*.

Laura S. Brown, Ph.D., is a clinical psychologist in private practice and clinical associate professor of psychology at the University of Washington. She has written extensively on the topic of psychotherapy with lesbians, feminist therapy theory, and ethics in psychotherapy. She is a past president of the Society for the Psychological Study of Lesbian and Gay Issues, Division 44, of the American Psychological Association.

Robert P. Cabaj, M.D., is a gay psychiatrist who works exclusively with gays, lesbians, and people with AIDS, with a special interest in substance abuse. He is currently the Medical Director of Mental Health Services at Fenway Community Health Center, Boston, MA. He is also an instructor and clinical associate in psychiatry for Harvard Medical School at Massachusetts General Hospital and is in private practice. He is a past president of the Association of Gay and Lesbian Psychiatrists. He is on the American Psychiatric Association's Committee on Gay and Lesbian

Issues and the AIDS Education Project and is co-chairperson of the Advisory Board for PRIDE Institute, Minneapolis, MN.

Armand R. Cerbone, Ph.D., received his doctorate in counseling psychology from Notre Dame. In 1985 he organized the Midwest Association of Lesbian and Gay Psychologists. He has also served as national chairperson of the Association of Lesbian and Gay Psychologists. He is in private practice in Chicago.

Dianne Elise, Ph.D., is a psychoanalytically oriented psychotherapist in private practice in Oakland, CA. She has worked extensively with lesbian clients, both in individual and in couples therapy. Dr. Elise was trained at The Wright Institute, Berkeley and at Mt. Zion Hospital, San Francisco. Her theoretical orientation is based on object relations and separation-individuation theory. She is deeply interested in issues of gender as they affect personality development, love relationships, and the practice of psychotherapy.

John C. Gonsiorek, Ph.D., received his doctorate in clinical psychology in 1978 from the University of Minnesota. He is a Diplomate in clinical psychology from the American Board of Professional Psychology and works as Director of Psychological Services at Twin Cities Therapy Clinic in Minneapolis. He is currently on the faculty of the Minnesota School of Professional Psychology. Dr. Gonsiorek has written extensively in the areas of psychotherapy with gay and lesbian individuals, professional ethics and boundaries, quality assurance in mental health, and other areas.

Marny Hall, Ph.D., a psychotherapist in private practice in the San Francisco Bay Area, is the author of *The Lavender Couch: A Consumer's Guide to Psychotherapy for Lesbians and Gay Men* (Alyson, 1985). She has contributed articles to several anthologies and periodicals, including the *Journal of Homosexuality* (1977, 1986, 1987), *The Sexuality of Organization* (Hearn et al., 1989), *Lesbian Sex* (Loulan, 1985), and *Women and Mental Health* (Bayes & Howell, 1981). Recently intrigued by the influence of cultural differences on coupling styles, she has begun to interview lesbian partners in Amsterdam and London.

Patricia A. Hunter, Psy.D., is in private practice in New York City and in Mount Kisco, NY. She is also a staff psychologist at the Northern

Westchester Guidance Clinic in Mount Kisco, where she specializes in treating children who have been sexually abused. Her professional interests include treating children and adolescents with anxiety disorders and adults who have experienced trauma during childhood.

Patricia I. Zibung Huffman, Ph.D., a clinical psychologist, has an independent practice in Seattle and is a clinical field supervisor for graduate students at the University of Washington. She is currently the co-chairperson of the Committee on Lesbian and Gay Concerns of the Washington State Psychological Association. Dr. Huffman has been working with lesbians and gay men since her own coming out in 1984.

Rochelle L. Klinger, M.D., is an assistant professor of psychiatry at the Medical College of Virginia and director of Consultation/Liaison Psychiatry Education. Her interests include psychotherapy with gays and lesbians, medically ill patients, AIDS, and interdisciplinary work with other mental health and medical clinicians. She is actively involved in teaching students and psychiatry residents about gay and lesbian issues and is a member of the American Psychiatric Association Committee on Gay, Lesbian, and Bisexual Issues.

Harold Kooden, Ph.D., is in private practice. He is a fellow of the American Psychological Association and co-chairperson of the New York City Federation for Mental Health Citywide Committee on Lesbian and Gay Issues in Mental Health. He is chairperson of the American Psychological Association Task Force on the Status of Lesbian and Gay Male Psychologists. He is a founder and board member of the National Gay Health Foundation, NY AIDS Task Force, the Foundation for Integrative Studies, American Psychological Association Division 44 (Society for Psychological Study of Gay and Lesbian Issues), and the Association of Gay and Lesbian Psychologists.

Gregory Lehne, Ph.D., received his doctorate in psychology from Cornell University. He is assistant professor of medical psychology in the Department of Psychiatry and Behavioral Sciences at The Johns Hopkins University School of Medicine. At Hopkins, he has worked with Dr. John Money in the Psychohormonal Research Unit and with the Sexual Disorders Clinic. Since 1978, he has maintained a private practice in Baltimore, MD where he specializes in treating gay men for a variety of problems and in the evaluation and treatment of all types of sexual concerns. He has published in the areas of homosexuality, homophobia, micropenis, and sex offenders.

April Martin, Ph.D., received her doctorate in clinical psychology from New York University in 1975 and completed the NYU Postdoctoral Program in Psychoanalysis and Psychotherapy in 1980. She is in private practice in Manhattan, and is also on the supervisory faculty of Yeshiva University's graduate program in psychology. She has published and spoken on therapy with gay men and lesbians and on lesbian motherhood. She lives with her lover and their two children.

Donald L. Mosher, Ph.D., trains clinical psychologists at the University of Connecticut. Don, a past president of the Society for the Scientific Study of Sex, has published over 90 scientific papers. His research focuses on sexual guilt, macho personality, and script theory. A fellow of several scientific societies, Don is also a diplomate in multiple clinical specialties: clinical psychology, psychotherapy, marital and sex therapy, and sexology.

Gerald Perlman, Ph.D., received his doctorate in clinical psychology from the City University of New York in 1970. He holds a certificate in psychoanalysis from the William Alanson White Institute and a certificate in behavioral psychotherapy from New York Hospital—Cornell Medical Center. Dr. Perlman is Director of Internship Training at Manhattan Psychiatric Center. He is a former president of the New York Association of Gay and Lesbian Psychologists and a Site Visitor and Peer Reviewer for the American Psychological Association.

Esther D. Rothblum, Ph.D., is an associate professor in the Department of Psychology at the University of Vermont and editor of the journal *Women and Therapy*. She is currently a Kellogg Fellow and has traveled to Africa to study women's mental health. Her research and writing have focused on mental health disorders which predominate in women, including depression, the social stigma of women's weight, procrastination and fear of failure, and women in the Antarctic. She has written about lesbian issues and coedited the book *Loving Bodily: Issues Facing Lesbians*.

Michael Shernoff, CSW, ASCW, is founder and codirector of Chelsea Psychotherapy Associates in Manhattan. He is a board member of the

National Lesbian and Gay Health Foundation and past member of the National Committee on Lesbian/Gay Concerns of the National Association of Social Workers.

Charles Silverstein, Ph.D., editor of this volume, a fellow in the American Psychological Association, is in private practice in New York City and is a supervisor at the Institute for Human Identity. He is the founding director of both Identity House and the Institute for Human Identity and is the founding editor of the *Journal of Homosexuality*. His writings concern the ethical and moral considerations of diagnosis and treatment.

Edward J. Tejirian, Ph.D., practices psychotherapy in Manhattan and teaches at Queens College. He is the author of *Sexuality and the Devil: Symbols of Love, Power, and Fear in Male Psychology*. His current research focuses on homosexuality and heterosexuality as related, normal components of male psychology and explores the hypothesis that significant meanings and feelings are at the heart of all sexual imagery and action.

1

CHARLES SILVERSTEIN

Psychotherapy and Psychotherapists: A History

THE THOUGHTS LEADING TO this book arose from a series of conferences in New York City attended by gay therapists. Each year the Institute for Human Identity, a counseling center for gay people, holds a conference with dozens of workshops about psychotherapy for gay people. Four years ago, Clare Coss and I proposed a workshop entitled "Erotic Countertransference," the purpose of which was to examine therapists' erotic fantasies toward their patients. It is common for therapists to analyze the sexual fantasies their patients have about them, but seldom do they analyze the situation when it's the other way around! This is uncharted territory, filled with fears of a therapist's own neurotic needs and vulnerabilities, and I wondered if the workshop would be attended.

Not only was it visited by other therapists, but "Erotic Countertransference" was the conference's most heavily attended workshop. Chairs were borrowed from nearby rooms to seat all the participants and dozens were turned away. Every psychotherapist in attendance was asked to write out an erotic fantasy that he or she had had about a patient. We asked that these accounts faithfully reflect the content and affect of the fantasies. The written fantasies were to be placed into a box. When everyone was finished, each account was to be read aloud; our task during the discussion period was to understand how these fantasies exposed the therapist's need for love and affection.

The participants asked no questions and made no comments. In response to my unique request they went to work, some writing at their desks, others leaving the room to work in a quiet corner. I was certain that some of them would leave the room and march into a different workshop, one less likely to bruise the ego. Fifteen minutes later they all returned to the room and dropped their "homework" into the box.

One by one the fantasies were read aloud. They varied in content from lyrical expressions of love and romance, scented with flowers and pastel-colored skies, to the pornographic, with the odor of sweat and dingy surroundings. However, whether poetic or hot and horny, a common theme emerged. Therapists, it would seem, take care of their patients even in their erotic fantasies. This discovery led to a lively discussion about how dependent therapists can be upon their patients for love and affirmation.

The most interesting aspect of the meeting was the universal appreciation of the participants for the opportunity to reveal their erotic needs in an open and safe forum. Some were surprised to learn that other therapists also fantasized about their patients. At workshop's end, the participants left humming with energy. Later that day, the entire conference buzzed with gossip about the goings-on in our room.

Since then, the workshop on "Erotic Countertransference" has become a regular part of the Institute for Human Identity's annual conference. Each year the room is filled to capacity by therapists wanting to learn more about how their own erotic needs are expressed during psychotherapy.

It's no wonder that our workshop was so successful. In New York City, as in most other places in the country, therapists seek better training in therapeutic techniques specifically for gay men and women. Once, only therapists who were gay themselves sought further training in these techniques. Now, more and more heterosexual therapists want to be retrained to be better able to serve the needs of the gay community. The AIDS crisis has produced an urgent drive to serve this once hidden group, which is suffering this hideous plague without emotional support from our homophobic society.

I recently surveyed the psychotherapy literature about gay and lesbian people. While some books and articles have become more insightful over the years, there's almost nothing published to aid therapists in tuning their therapeutic techniques. There are no courses in any university or medical school that teach the skills of psychotherapy with gay clients. Later we will discuss the extant literature on this subject. At this juncture, a review of the history of psychotherapy by gay therapists and their patients would be helpful. By explaining why training has been so inadequate, I hope to lay the foundation for this book.

GAY THERAPISTS

The First Generation: The Pre-1970s

The period between the Second World War and 1970 is known in the gay community as the "pre-Stonewall" era. The term derives from riots at the Stonewall, a seedy, Mafia-controlled bar in New York City's Greenwich Village that was frequented by hustlers and transvestites. These riots, which occurred one weekend in 1969, are commonly viewed by historians as the origin of the modern American gay liberation movement.

Professionals did not participate in these riots. In fact, we have every reason to believe that gay therapists were horrified at the violence in Greenwich Village, not to mention the sight of transvestites beating police over the head with their high heels. Most of my colleagues, who were closeted within the established institutions of our society, thought those involved were sick homosexuals. The "helping professions," including clinical psychology, psychiatry, and social work, were peppered with homosexuals at the time, but they felt threatened by the rioting of street hustlers and transvestites. They feared that the stereotype of homosexuals as deficient men and women would be reinforced by this rioting. Every hospital, clinic, and analytic institute probably had its share of gay therapists outwardly paying homage to the orthodox ideological line that homosexuality was a mental illness. How sad it seems to us today that many of these closeted homosexual therapists spent their days trying to "cure" homosexuality in their patients, while practicing it themselves at night. One wonders what price they paid for this duplicity between their professional and personal lives.

Back then, gay students in psychoanalytic institutes took a particularly high risk because there was always the possibility that an instructor or supervisor might discover their sexual orientation and expel them. The greatest danger was the training analysis in which the student was required to submit to years of psychoanalysis by a member of the institute's staff. Astoundingly, some gay analytic students were able to avoid detection by merely substituting pronouns when they discussed their romantic experiences.

In those days, gay professionals still called themselves "homosexual." The word "gay" referred to the radicals: people who demonstrated in the streets, faced the television cameras, and fought against bigotry. "Gays" were outside of the mainstream of society. They refused to remain in the closet. Their intention was to change society, not submit to it. One of their primary objectives was to attack the established psychiatric institutions that were, in effect, the "gatekeepers" of society's attitude toward gay people. Homosexual therapists employed in the established institutions kept their distance from these boisterous gay liberationists.

There was always gossip, of course, and some of it was very juicy. There was talk about Harry Stack Sullivan, a leading light in American psychiatry, and his "homosexual inclinations." We now know that he was indeed so inclined. During his last twenty years, Sullivan lived with a former teenage hustler. There were worse rumors. Why hadn't Anna Freud ever married? A child devoted to her father, answered the fathers of American psychiatry, failing to note that Anna did not live with her father but lived with another woman for over forty years (Fine, 1985; Gay, 1988).

There were a handful of well-trained gay therapists in New York who were open about their sexual orientation during the pre-Stonewall era, but many of them were barred from employment or analytic training. The originators of Gestalt therapy, Fritz and Laura Perls, lacked the puritanism of American psychiatry and psychology. As they themselves were deviant in their therapeutic approach, they apparently saw no reason not to train those who were also diagnosed as deviant. Some Gestalt students came to their training institute in New York City with an academic background in psychotherapy but many did not. Very few would have been acceptable to the establishment, and fewer still had completed the requirements necessary for licensure when that became required. But they were open about their sexuality, and they were the first in our profession to call themselves "gay." They were a resource, albeit a small one, for those gay people who didn't view themselves as mentally ill and who didn't want to change their sexual orientation from gay to straight.

To sum up this pre-Stonewall period, there were two groups of gay therapists: the high status psychiatrists and clinical psychologists who were in the closet and the low status professionals and paraprofessionals who were open and affirmative about their sexual orientation. These two groups didn't sing from the same hymnbook. It is this latter group of therapists that I consider to be the first generation of gay therapists. One wonders whether each of these groups envied what the other had to offer.

The published literature of this era stated that homosexuality was a mental illness. I remember that literature well. During the 1950s, as a teenager attending high school in Manhattan, I was struggling with my own homosexual desires. One day in class, while my mind wandered, I looked out the window to a clock across the street. There was a sign above it which read, "It is time to seek the Lord." I was sure it meant me! From then on I spent every lunch hour at a nearby library reading what doctors had to say about people like me. It was a dreadful experience. There wasn't a book that didn't tell me how depraved I was or that I was doomed to a life of misery and that my only salvation was to seek the services of a good psychoanalyst (at least three times a week) who would help me change my abnormal sexual orientation. However, I was cautioned, I really, really had to be highly motivated or it wouldn't work, and I would be condemned to a life of depression and, ultimately, suicide.

There were no alternative ideas published in those days. Not a single professional book published before the 1970s contradicted the accepted idea that homosexuality was a serious and obdurate disorder. Would they have been published? One wonders. The psychoanalytic establishment had closed the book on this particular "disease."

The Second Generation: The 1970s

The 1970s were galvanized by the excitement of the Stonewall riots. The ideology of gay liberation was in the air, and a younger generation of gays joined radical organizations to fight oppression. The new ideology was leftist in flavor: It espoused egalitarianism, participatory democracy, and self-empowerment. "Gay is good" was its slogan, and the Greek sign "Lambda" was its emblem. Gay liberationists were furious at the professional establishment and its theory about the pathology of homosexuality. Professional judgments were rejected, and gays put their faith and trust in peer counselors and a few trusted professionals.

The early 1970s also saw the rise of gay counseling centers in the United States that were staffed by gay peer counselors. Centers were opened in New York, Boston, Philadelphia, Pittsburgh, and Seattle. These self-help groups offered an alternative to the oppressive goal of reversing the sexual identity of gays practiced by established psychotherapists. In those days, we viewed role models as an important part of the counseling process. While gays flocked to our services, established professionals, who earned their living by "curing" gay men and women, saw us as a cabal of reckless incompetents who, when successful, doomed our clients to a life of misery.

This second generation of gay therapists rejected the pathological model of gay life. Gay activists and a handful of young professionals proclaimed that homosexuality was an acceptable alternative life-style. These therapists implored gays to reject the psychiatric establishment and seek services at peer counseling centers. However, these centers were much more than a place where emotionally distressed gay men and women could seek relief. They also served as meeting places for gay professionals and graduate students. These professionals, many of whom provided supervision for their peers, were the most dedicated of their kind and ultimately would produce a new professional literature that proclaimed the healthiness of homosexuality.

Now "the love that dare not speak its name" wouldn't shut up. Peers and first generation professionals held demonstrations at psychiatric and psychological meetings. The established APAs hardly knew what to make of these bold demonstrators who carried large signs, yelled, interrupted, were often outright rude, and always angry. This wasn't going to stop, and something had to change.

What changed was the removal of homosexuality as a diagnostic category by the American Psychiatric Association in 1973. The psychiatrists said that homosexuality wasn't a mental illness *if* the person accepted his or her gayness. On the other hand, it was an illness if the gay person was depressed about his or her sexual orientation. The battle that resulted in the removal of homosexuality from the *Diagnostic and Statistical Manual* is accurately documented in Ronald Bayer's *Homosexuality and American Psychiatry* (1981). By the time *DSM-III* was published, homosexuality had been removed completely. The declassification of homosexuality as a psychiatric disorder helped begin the break-down of the walls of prejudice against gay people. It also provided incalculable support to a vast number of gay therapists who were on the brink of coming out. And come out they did.

The body of published literature was altered immediately. The first positive book by a professional was Weinberg's *Society and the Healthy Homosexual* (1972). The very idea of a "healthy" homosexual had been unthinkable only a few years earlier. Then, in 1974, Silverstein edited the first issue of the *Journal of Homosexuality* (Haworth Press, 1973/1974). Devoted to publishing scientific papers about homosexuality, the journal's editorial board was composed of openly gay professionals and straight sex researchers who were sympathetic to the gay cause.

The traditional psychiatric establishment was shocked to learn how many gay professionals there were. The coming out process sometimes led to humorous encounters. In 1973, for example, I came out on the floor of the annual meeting of the American Psychological Association. An old friend, who was on the panel to which I made my announcement, was shocked and confused to hear me say that I was gay. That evening when we met at a cocktail party, he told me that he had given some thought to the statement about my sexuality. He concluded that I was lying, and that I planned to use my professed homosexuality to get women to relax in my company so that I could seduce them! Such examples demonstrated how difficult it was for my colleagues to face their own prejudice. At least he communicated with me. Others avoided me completely. But because other gay psychologists were emboldened by my statement, I made a whole new set of friends.

New authors emerged: gay professionals writing on gay themes for a gay audience. Whereas once a gay author had to hide his or her sexual orientation, the new breed proclaimed theirs, often describing in detail their coming out experiences. It was no longer necessary for the protagonist in a novel to commit suicide as the penalty for loving someone of the same sex. A number of books written by gay professionals were published during this decade. Most sold well, some approaching best-seller status. About half demonstrate an enduring appeal by remaining in print today.

Some of those books from the 1970s were rather shrill in tone. It was as if a poison from the past was being ejected by the authors and directed toward the perceived enemies of church, state, the family, and, of course, the psychiatric power base. Taken as a whole, these books represented a wave of defensive statements designed to offset the hideous psychoanalytic literature. However, they did not yet provide a positive literature about the treatment of gay people in emotional distress. That goal was not realized until the present decade.

The openness that resulted from the removal of homosexuality from the *DSM* and the activities of gay liberationists caused profound changes in professional practice. A few graduate schools of psychology searched for openly gay students as Ph.D. candidates. Many professional organizations formed "interest groups" devoted to gay concerns, where gay professionals from around the country could meet and discuss common goals. In California, the Physicians for Human Rights, a group of gay physicians and psychiatrists was founded. The Association of Gay Psychologists was organized at the 1973 annual meeting of the American Psychological Association and more than 100 psychologists attended their first meeting. Even the behaviorists with their hated aversion therapy turned around and allowed gay professionals the time to argue the case against trying to turn gay people straight. The Association for the Advancement of Behavior Therapy joined the two APAs by announcing its support for gay rights.

Gay professionals weren't coming out, they were galloping out.

The Third Generation: The 1980s

The 1980s has been as different from the '70s as the '70s were from the postwar years. Students who were in training during the '70s are now fully qualified, and many have devoted themselves to enlarging our knowledge about the psychological needs of the gay community. Counseling centers serving gays and lesbians also changed with the times. Only qualified professionals are appointed to staff positions, and gay students in social work and clinical psychology are placed at these centers for training by their universities. These students have become catalysts for change. Peer counseling has become a thing of the past, perhaps regrettably so.

The American Psychological Association approved the inclusion of a gay division (Division 44) as an official part of the organization, a remarkable achievement for the gay psychologists who had fought for its inclusion. A lesbian was elected president of the American Psychological Association and gays have been president of the New York State Psychological Association. Psychiatrists at the other APA formed a power base that influenced policy decisions in the organization. Some of them were even psychoanalysts, which was a source of confusion to some of their colleagues. "Gay is good" was no longer proclaimed; it wasn't a lack of retention on the part of professionals but rather a lessening of the need to speak defensively and to pound one's chest in defiance against the formerly rigid attitudes toward gay people. To the chagrin of a trio of New York City psychiatrists who had built their reputations on reinforcing the pathology model of homosexuality, gay psychiatrists became part of the establishment and effectively silenced the troika forever.

Gay Professional Literature

All these changes have been reflected in the books published in the 1980s. Professional books about homosexuality have been almost exclusively written by gay professionals. Previous books asked two questions: What causes homosexuality and how can we change it? New ones discussed the lives and daily problems of gay people. The most common themes were love and sex, coming out (especially to family), religion, discrimination and gay rights, and lesbian experiences.

Psychotherapy books no longer advocated changing one's sexual orientation. The new authors were firmly against the idea and recommended instead that a therapist's job was to help gay people lead productive and happy lives. But the new books written by gay therapists were themselves rather ideological, chastising the zeal with which a previous generation of professionals ignored the needs of the gay community.

Of six important books published in the 1980s (Coleman, 1987; Gonsiorek, 1982; Hetrick & Stein, 1984; Paul et al., 1982; Ross, 1988; Stein & Cohen, 1986), all but one list the word "psychotherapy" in their titles. Every one of them can be recommended as a valuable addition to one's professional library, because each of them discusses social and psychological variables that influence gay people's mental health. Yet not one of these books is clinically oriented, and not one of them uses a case study approach to teach the skills of psychotherapy. What the current books do is talk about psychotherapy—but they don't teach it. In short, there is a paucity of clinical case material in the professional literature.

There are a number of reasons why the literature lacks clinical studies. In the first place, case studies are more difficult to write than reviews of literature or opinions on therapeutic topics. Case studies must demonstrate that the therapist has an understanding of the developmental issues leading to the personality problem. One must further formulate personality defenses and a therapeutic approach. This is far more difficult than writing about psychotherapy from a global perspective because it exposes the writer's therapeutic ability to one's colleagues. There have simply not been enough skillful gay therapists willing to do the job in previous years.

A second reason for this lack is fear. There are still therapists who are afraid to write for publications that implicate their sexual orientation. Some skilled therapists stay away from clinical case material, fearing the opprobrium of their colleagues. Many established professionals collude with colleagues who assume they're heterosexual in the hopes that promotions and financial rewards will be forthcoming. In short, publishing case studies blows their cover.

Protectiveness toward the gay movement is another reason why there is a poverty of clinical material in the current literature. It should be perfectly obvious that gay men and women suffer from many of the same disorders as the rest of the population. We suffer from psychosis, borderline and narcissistic conditions, depression, obsessive behaviors, disasters in our search for love, and the whole gamut of emotional hurdles in our complex society. But the war against oppressive psychiatry has not been completely won and some gay professionals feel that to expose the real therapeutic needs of the gay community might reactivate discrimination against gay people. To report the sufferings of gays, some believe, would only serve to reassert the claims of bigots that homosexuality is an illness and a scourge to society, further encouraging them to fight antidiscrimination laws. Therefore, the reporting of emotional distress in gay people is interwoven with worry about its effect on the political issue of gay rights.

The fears of gay professionals are not without merit. Any publication about gay life has political consequences, as has been well documented in Halleck's *The Politics of Therapy* (1971). Gay people are still unprotected under our Constitution. They are beaten in the streets, discriminated against in corporate America, and considered second class citizens in the American courtroom. Herek (1989) has shown that homophobic attitudes still permeate our society, and the AIDS crisis has added a new dimension to these fears. Even in New York City there are examples of gay men with AIDS being discriminated against in hospitals.

Fears of political consequences have resulted in a serious void in the professional literature. The decade of the 1990s will, I believe, fill this void. It will be the time for the fourth generation to exert themselves, and their voices are already being heard. They are convinced that the time is ripe to produce a clinical literature that will directly address the emotional needs of gay men and women.

THE PLAN AND PHILOSOPHY OF THIS BOOK

As a young graduate student, I remember listening to the case presentations of my professors. I was always impressed with their professionalism, their uncanny sensitivity to unconscious motivation, and their ability to keep their own emotions at bay. They always discussed their patients' transference, and we learned that transference was the most crucial behavior in psychotherapy because it represented our patients' distorted perceptions of us. Freud (1910, 1915) believed that patients projected upon their therapists the unresolved conflicting feelings they held toward their parents. From a Freudian perspective, a major goal of therapy is the elimination of these distorted perceptions.

We also learned something about countertransference (Freud, 1915), which our professors briefly described as the same projection of conflicting feelings toward one's parents, but this time, projected by the therapist upon the patient. Both these concepts seemed reasonable to me, but while we were treated to endless examples of transference, I cannot remember a single example of countertransference in any of my professors' presentations. We students followed the model set by our teachers: We carefully worked out the transference problems of our patients and ignored the countertransference. In other words, we made every attempt to pry open the Pandora's box of fears and conflicts in our patients, while at the same time nailing our own box tightly shut. That tradition has carried over into the practice of generations of psychotherapists.

The concept of countertransference has a long history. Freud believed that transference was unique to the analytic situation. "Every psychoanalyst," Freud wrote (1910, p. 145), "only gets as far as his own complexes and inner resistances allow." Sullivan (1953) proposed the term "parataxic distortion" as a substitute. He suggested that our distortions are ubiquitous and that they appear whenever people interact. Stekel (1938/1950) observed that "There is no transference without a counter-transference" (p. 177). Singer (1965) suggested that those therapists who are loathe to learn new things about themselves "will avoid investigating their own reactions to the patient lest their own fond dreams be disturbed" (p. 300).

In time, the term "countertransference" came to be used in a more general sense. Today, most therapists use it to refer to any feeling or attitude on the part of a therapist that distorts their perception of the patient. From this perspective, the term need not be confined to describing unresolved feelings toward one's parents. Liking or disliking patients, extreme attentiveness or daydreaming, and sexual interest or sexual repulsion are all often noted as examples of countertransference. So is homophobia, internalized and otherwise.

Here are a few examples from my own practice. I once treated a young man whom I disliked, though I still don't know why. I started bungling our sessions, sometimes by arriving late, sometimes by mixing up the day. Once I even left town an hour before he was due to ring my bell. I was running out of excuses—that is to say, I was running out of lies. One day he demanded to know why I had missed our previous session. Embarrassed, I said the first thing that came into my head, which was, "I was trapped in an elevator." The lie clearly showed my unwillingness to take responsibility for my dislike of this man. The problem was cleared up when he had the good sense to drop me as his therapist.

Most therapists don't like narcissistic patients. I'm no exception. I am offended by their self-absorption, their blindness to the suffering of others, and their endless complaints. I remember once wanting to walk the few feet between me and a narcissistic patient and smack him in the face. I saw him successfully getting what he wanted from others by acting like a petulant child. But why did it make me so angry? Affectionate feelings also get in my way. Like the members of my IHI (Institute for Human Identity) workshop, I have sexual and romantic feelings toward patients. The most intense fantasy is the one in which I assume the role of loving mentor protecting a lonely and depressed young man from harm. Not for a moment would I question that my delicious fantasy is an expression of unresolved feelings between me and my father.

It's hard to believe there are therapists without such feelings intruding in their work. After two decades of practice, I've learned that those without these neurotic feelings toward their patients are seriously disturbed. They're a menace because they cannot distinguish between their own feelings and those of their patients.

Young, aspiring therapists in graduate schools should be told the truth: *Being a therapist is hazardous to your emotional health*. Someone needs to tell students that therapists carry the demons of childhood into the consulting room as often as patients do. We feel sad about troubles in our own lives, we try to cope with feelings of inadequacy or incompetence, and we feel guilty about our errors. We indulge in fantasies, either grandiose or masochistic. And after years of supervising young therapists, I've concluded that fears of abandonment in therapists are at least as severe as they are in their patients. To suggest that these feelings don't influence therapy is absurd. And although every therapist will agree with that statement in principle, no one ever wants to talk or write about *their* countertransference.

What is left out of the books about psychotherapy, then, is the emotional frailty of the therapist. Most books refer to patients as if their emotions are actually different from our own. They are not. What *is* different, or at least what one hopes is different, is our willingness to expose our emotional needs to ourselves, and in so doing, learn about our own inadequacies. I believe that by doing so, we become better therapists. Note, however, that I am not suggesting that therapists necessarily "share" this information with their patients. This would be an intrusion into their lives, a narcissistic demand on our part that they love us for our accomplishments.

This book was conceived to be about "us," the therapist and his or her patient. I hoped it would demonstrate how both patient and therapist influence the therapeutic process, hence the title, *Gays, Lesbians, and Their Therapists*.

The next step was to ask colleagues to join me in this venture. I told them that the book was meant to demonstrate how experienced therapists view particular therapeutic problems. The book would emphasize the fact that psychotherapy is a process in which two (or more) people interact amidst feelings that can either aid or impede the therapeutic process. While all the patients discussed in the following chapters are gay or lesbian, the therapists are both homosexual and heterosexual. Fortunately, every member of the group of professionals who contributed to the book is secure enough to "think out loud" about the process of psychotherapy, their patients, and at times, their own feelings of inadequacy and failure. This approach makes the book unique in either the gay or straight professional literature.

As editor, I did everything possible to encourage the contributors to write about themselves. Sometimes we had lunch together; we traded computer disks, notes, letters and long-distance phone calls, and always I asked—even cajoled—for more. I urged them—and myself as one of them—to be bold and not confine themselves to standard clinical case histories. I reminded them that we were starting to build a new clinical case literature that would be invaluable as a teaching device. Here was an opportunity to discuss the kinds of problems customarily revealed in supervision, but hardly ever in print.

Here is the book. Readers will judge for themselves how well our contributors have presented their case studies and how well they have illuminated the emotional rewards and hazards of being a therapist. I would like to think that this collection represents the fourth generation of gay and lesbian therapists.

REFERENCES

1. Bayer, R. (1981). *Homosexuality and American psychiatry*. New York: Basic Books.
2. Coleman, E. (Ed.). (1987). *Psychotherapy with homosexual men and women: Integrated identity approaches for clinical practice*. New York: Haworth.
3. Fine, R. (1984). Anna Freud (1895–1982): Obituary. *American Psychologist, 40*, (2), 230–232.
4. Freud, S. (1910). The future prospects of psycho–analytic therapy. In J. Strachey (Ed. and Trans.), *The standard edition of the complete psychological works of Sigmund Freud* (Vol. 11, pp. 141–151). New York: Norton.
5. Freud, S. (1915 [1914]). Observations on transference-love. In J. Strachey (Ed. and Trans.), *The standard edition of the complete psychological works of Sigmund Freud* (Vol. 12, pp. 159–171). New York: Norton.

6. Gay, P. (1988). *Freud: A life for our time*. New York: Norton.
7. Gonsiorek, J. C. (Ed.). (1982). *Homosexuality and psychotherapy: A practitioner's handbook of affirmative models*. New York: Haworth.
8. Halleck, S. L. (1971). *The politics of therapy*. New York: Science House.
9. Herek, G. (1989). Heterosexual's attitudes toward lesbians and gay men: Correlates and gender differences. *The Journal of Sex Research, 4*, 451–477.
10. Hetrick, E., & Stein, T. (Eds.). (1984). *Innovations in psychotherapy with homosexuals*. Washington, DC : American Psychiatric Association.
11. Paul, W., Weinrich, J. D., Gonsiorek, J. C., & Hotvedt, M. E. (Eds.). (1982). *Homosexuality: Social, psychological and biological issues*. Beverly Hills: Sage.
12. Ross, M. W. (Ed.). (1988). *Psychopathology and psychotherapy in homosexuality*. New York: Haworth.
13. Singer, E. (1965). *Key concepts in psychotherapy*. New York: Random House.
14. Stein, T., & Cohen, C. (Eds.). (1986). *Contemporary perspectives on psychotherapy with lesbians and gay men*. New York: Plenum.
15. Stekel, W. (1938/1950). *Technique of analytic psychotherapy*. New York: Liveright.
16. Sullivan, H. S. (1953). *The interpersonal theory of psychiatry*. New York: Norton.
17. Weinberg, G. (1972). *Society and the healthy homosexual*. New York: St. Martin's.

2

LAURA S. BROWN

Therapy With an Infertile Lesbian Client

WOMEN'S IDENTITIES AND sense of self are often bound up in certain socially constructed roles that, while related functionally to female biology, are neither innate nor inherent in female gender. In contemporary Western cultures such roles include those of wife and mother. The further a woman strays from these modes, the more likely it is that she will face difficulties both in valuing herself and being valued by others, difficulties that may be distressing enough to merit psychotherapeutic intervention. Many people will find a woman who is neither a wife nor a mother unnatural, pathological, or disturbed in some way, and it can be hard to resist applying these views to oneself. Being a lesbian is a role that is considered "unnatural" for a woman; so, too, is not being a mother.

The role of wife in a heterosexual marriage is often incompatible with a lesbian identity. Being a mother is possible although not always easy. Lesbians who have been heterosexually married and had children in those relationships often face an odd form of dual discrimination: They are treated with suspicion in some parts of the lesbian community because of past marriage and heterosexual identity, and they also risk the rejection of the heterosexual community and the loss of their children (Pollack & Vaughn, 1987). Traditionally, the identity of a lesbian mother has not been a secure one, and no socially approved women's roles were easily open to lesbians. Yet lesbians have always been mothers.

In the past decade or so, a new generation of lesbian mothers has come into being. These women have become pregnant or adopted children as lesbians, usually while in lesbian relationships. Their status as mothers is more secure because they are not dependent on a relationship with a man and thus are less vulnerable to challenge by another legal parent. Alternative means of insemination, including both professionally assisted and self-help forms of artificial insemination, or heterosexual intercourse engaged in with a man who is not a partner (and may not always be aware that he is being brought into the transaction as a potential sperm donor) for the sole purpose of impregnation, have led to the births of growing numbers of children within the lesbian community. It is no longer uncommon to encounter women with pregnant bellies or nursing infants at all-lesbian events, nor is it odd to have local lesbian and gay pride parades led by scores of recent lesbian mothers pushing baby strollers.

As with their heterosexual peers, many lesbians in their thirties—the "baby boomer generation"—are now contemplating and actively pursuing motherhood. Being a lesbian and being a birth mother are considered easily compatible options, especially in certain lesbian communities in which many women are becoming mothers. Several lesbian writers have noted that by becoming mothers, some lesbians find themselves being accorded the social privileges of "good womanhood," e.g., familial acceptance and access to experiences that make them more similar to heterosexual women (Murphy, 1987). Thus, for the lesbian who wishes to become a mother, the rewards are both intangible and personal in her experience as a parent with her child, while at the same time, they are tangible and visible in the context of the greater society in which the role of mother assigns greater value to the woman acting within it.

But as with their heterosexual peers, lesbians who wish to become pregnant are also occasionally faced with the possibility of fertility problems. Women normally become decreasingly fertile as they age, thus increasing the difficulty of achieving a pregnancy for the over-thirty group of lesbians who seem most likely to be trying to conceive. Also, some women are infertile because of various malfunctions in their reproductive systems such as polycystic ovaries, blocked or scarred fallopian tubes, hormonal insufficiencies, or an intrauterine pH that is incompatible with sperm motility. Although the popular media tout technological advances for combatting infertility, such techniques are both prohibitively expensive (and are rarely covered by medical insurance) and likely to fail. For many women with fertility problems, becoming a birth mother will never be an option. Being told "you can always adopt" is little solace to any infertile woman, and not necessarily an option for open lesbians in the many communities that are hostile to lesbians becoming parents. For any woman who wants to conceive, infertility is a blow to her self-esteem (Hendricks, 1985). For a lesbian, whose attempts to become pregnant and give birth are more complex, this can be especially problematic.

The literature on lesbians as mothers, however, does not reflect this possibility. A careful review of the many clinical papers and personal accounts now available shows that there are stories of lesbians experiencing miscarriage and stillbirths (Mayer, 1987), of lesbians taking a long time to become pregnant (Hill, 1987), and of lesbians experiencing the SIDS (sudden infant death syndrome) deaths of their newborns (Martin, 1989). But no one speaks for or about the lesbian who wishes to become pregnant and who is permanently blocked from that option by infertility. Yet the experiences of an infertile lesbian woman who wishes to be a mother are unique among those of infertile women.

In 1986, I began to work with Carla, a lesbian who came to see me in an effort to work through her feelings about her fertility problems and the process that she was undergoing in an attempt to become pregnant. Bearing a child and becoming a mother had always been an important part of her identity, and had shaped her relationship and career decisions, as is the case for many women whose life plans include becoming mothers. But when she had begun the process of monitoring ovulation in preparation for donor insemination, she found that she did not ovulate, even though she had experienced menstrual periods, albeit irregular ones, since puberty. At the time she commenced therapy, she had just started to participate in the lengthy and tedious medical processes for making a possibly fertile woman out of a questionably fertile one.

In our work together, we have had to confront the meaning of Carla's increasingly undeniable infertility and her inability to be a birth parent as they relate to her personal history and her current sense of identity. We have struggled together with her and her partner's decision for the latter to become pregnant and with Carla's feelings during Susan's pregnancy and the birth of their son, Carter. We have dealt with Carla's attempts to claim an identity as Carter's Mom, which now includes initiating the painful process of second-parent adoption as a lesbian co-parent, so that she may legally become his mother and have rights traditionally accorded the non-birth giving parent (e.g., fathers) in this culture. Along the way, we have had to struggle with the impact of heterosexism and homophobia on what is already a painful process. We have dealt with the grief at the loss of a sense of oneself as a fertile, and therefore whole, woman and the loss of the child never to be born. We have also had to learn how to maneuver in a context in which people ask Carla and Susan who the "real mother" is, and in which Carter's attachment to his mother Carla is suspect in everyone's eyes including, at the hardest of times, her own. While Carla has addressed a variety of issues in her work in therapy, her infertility has been a theme to which we often return. It will be the focus of my discussion of our work together.

HISTORICAL ISSUES

Carla is the youngest of three children born to older parents in a lower-middle-class white family from the Southeastern U.S. As the picture of her family has become more clearly defined during our work together, several elements have emerged that have become especially salient for the therapy. Carla's family is a distant and disjointed one in which children were the recipients of emotional neglect and disinterest. As the youngest by many years, Carla was especially stigmatized for her youth. Her normal developmental childlikeness was interpreted as "clumsiness" and "stupidity," and her behavior and needs were constantly compared to adult standards rather than age norms. Children in this family were supposed to be neither seen nor heard; the job of the child was to blend in and bother her parents as little as possible. Talents and intelligence, of which Carla had plenty, were ignored or punished, for example, she was accused of "making her sister feel bad" when she outshone her older siblings academically. One of Carla's strongest legacies from her family of origin is a sense of herself as bad and wrong and the cause of problems.

The family is extremely conventional in its values regarding gender and the roles of women. As a girl in this family, Carla learned that no matter how well she performed academically or artistically, she would always be better rewarded for conforming to the part of woman-as-caretaker and childbearer. Carla remembers always feeling that if she could give her parents a grandchild, she would be more loved by them and closer to their standards of acceptability — she would be doing something that would make her more "normal."

Carla was sexually abused repeatedly and severely by a family physician, who was also a much loved and highly esteemed family member, from about the age of eight until late adolescence. This abuse was enabled by the emotional neglect and disinterest of her parents, who would deliver

Carla for visits with this man because they did not want to be bothered with entertaining a curious and active child. In addition to other forms of abuse, he performed dilation and curretage (D and C) operations on her twice, to abort pregnancies that he told her he had detected. Carla thus had good reason to believe that she was fertile, and this was interwoven with a terror of receiving medical care, especially gynecological care, since she had suffered sexual abuse in the guise of medical treatment. The discovery that she might not be fertile was doubly painful because of the price she thought she had paid to confirm her status as a fertile woman.

When I first started working with Carla, she was in her early thirties, had been out as a lesbian for several years, and was comfortably settled in a relationship that both she and I saw as solid and supportive, with a partner who liked the idea of having children. She had come out into a lesbian feminist community after having briefly been heterosexually married. Her graduate school experiences had exposed her to feminist thought and values, and she had eagerly made them her own. She was a social services worker and political activist who was often at the forefront of her town's lesbian feminist community. She had chosen me as a therapist because she knew my work and writings and assumed (correctly, as it turned out) that I would share her values and be able to deal with the complexity of the issues that she was presenting. I was also in my early thirties when we began to work together, similarly settled in a solid relationship, also a feminist, and, like Carla, visible in my lesbian community. Those similarities were important for us in creating the beginning of our working relationship. Carla knew that it was hard for her to trust people, given her history of familial abuse and neglect; she needed to have enough information about me to assume certain attitudes and values on my part so that she could expose her vulnerabilities.

However, there was one important difference. One of the issues I contemplated when she called me with her primary concern was the question of how, despite all the apparent similarities, I would be able to be empathically available to this woman who was struggling with a desire to parent. Such a goal was the opposite of my own life and choices. Unlike many of my friends and peers, I have never wanted to either bear or raise children; rather, I made a series of emphatic statements throughout my childhood and adolescence that I would never be a mother. With each new pregnancy among my women friends, lesbian and straight, I reevaluated that decision and found it to be a good one. I enjoy visiting friends with children, and I enjoy playing with children—I like kids but genuinely want none of my own. There was going to be no empathic resonance in me for Carla's distress.

I then began to wonder why I was worried about this difference when I was so comparatively blasé about other dissimilarities between myself and my clients. After all, I lacked the history of abuse or addiction that characterized most of the women I worked with, and I rarely saw Jewish women in my therapy office. Other clients of mine, both lesbian and heterosexual, were already parents, and I did not see that as a source of dissonance. So why was this difference so meaningful to me, why did it raise questions for me about my ability to work with Carla? I also wondered whether I should share the details of this difference with her, perhaps it would be important for her to see a therapist who was already a mother or was at least seriously contemplating or pursuing motherhood. I had plenty of good lesbian colleagues who fulfilled these criteria. But I didn't raise the issue and, interestingly, Carla has never questioned me about it, despite her sophistication about being a psychotherapy consumer. (After she read the first draft of this chapter, Carla told me that she knew when she first called—via the community grapevine—that I had no children and did not plan to become a mother; she *wanted* a therapist who could model being happy and fulfilled as a woman this way. This is a powerful reminder that what we think will be important for our client's growth and change may be, in fact, exactly what they do not wish to have!)

I now think that a powerful source of my self-doubt was my own lingering fear that my desire not to be a parent was in fact some sort of pathology. The motherhood mandate in this culture is a strong one. The popular press is full of stories of women in their thirties regretting their earlier, "misguided" decisions not to have children and who are now abandoning careers to stay home and raise babies with the same dedication previously given to their professions. At the same time, an emerging strain of feminist thought, which has had profound influence on the theory and practice of feminist therapy, posited that mothering was a central aspect of female personality from which flowed our capacity for empathy and nurturance (Chodorow, 1979; Miller, 1976). I was, in essence, fearful of revealing something shameful to Carla, although I did not come to that realization until I found that I could evaluate my own decision about parenting in the same way I was supporting Carla to. As we worked together, it became clear to me that I had been as much affected by the image of the role of motherhood as being "natural" to women as had anyone, even though I consciously believed I was secure in my childfree status.

I think that I also sensed the tentativeness of Carla's feelings of entitlement to becoming a mother. In essence, she was communicating to me, at a nonconscious level, her fear that her infertility was deserved, that her desire to be a mother was perverted. My own need to soothe her and to be a more perfect mirror to her (a mirror which I could not provide in my own life) also led me to doubt my usefulness to Carla as a therapist. With other clients, dissonance had been helpful. No one aspires to the status of incest survivor, for instance, and so there is less need for an embodied affirmation of experience. Carla felt truly alone in her strivings, and I could not join her. My own sense of inadequacy gave me a hint of what she was feeling and by resonating to her in this way, I was able to move past my need to be her perfect therapist and move with her into our work.

What has emerged over time is that my tendency as a feminist therapist toward explicitly valuing and holding sacred the choices made by my clients has been more essential to the success of Carla's therapy than my feelings about myself and motherhood. My feminist analysis of the process that she was in the midst of has also been essential: Without understanding the meaning of being a fertile woman in a culture that still overvalues such fertility, without comprehending the ways in which the value of motherhood and the devaluation of lesbians go hand in hand, our work might not have been so fruitful. Feminist analysis was the fabric out of which I could stitch a holding environment. Carla had to learn that she was valuable although she was incapable of conceiving a child, while I needed to learn that my decision not to utilize my apparent fertility was neither unnatural nor a slap in her face. Both of us had to move through our own internalized homophobia to join in a therapeutic coalition with each other.

THE THERAPY PROCESS

The initial stage of therapy was marked internally by testing and externally by Carla's going through a myriad of painful and complicated surgical procedures and drug trials. As emerged later in the therapy, Carla's nonconscious expectation was to be tolerated, minimized, and when possible, ignored by me, much as her family had. Carla was verbally adept and psychologically sophisticated and had been able to "shine on" several previous therapists and deflect them from probing too deeply into territories that she had declared "handled." If she was to prove herself worthy of being a mother, she needed to have no dependency needs.

Carla was confused when I did none of this, but instead explicitly acknowledged and made space for the wounded and needy little girl inside of the adult woman who had walked into the office. In particular, she expected me to swallow, without challenge, her initial bland statements about her relationship with her family of origin and her breezy assertion that she had revealed her sexual abuse history to a previous therapist and that this had "taken care" of any residual feelings she might have about it. When I challenged these stances and indicated my deep concern and interest in her past and the effect that it might be having on her current struggles with fertility, I think she was both pleased and frightened.

She did not wish to be vulnerable—her survival strategy for coping with her distant and unavailable family had been to adopt a counterdependent, emotionally withheld stance in which she used her considerable intuition and verbal skills to engage others by caring for them. The only person she had been known by and vulnerable to had been the man who sexually abused her, and she both consciously and unconsciously equated vulnerability with exploitation and shame. Yet she wished to be known, to have the depth of her pain taken seriously and resonated to and to have the child within noticed and nurtured. But she also feared the loss of my respect and was ashamed of her fear that I might exploit her in some way. In fact, my decision to ask Carla to discuss our work together in this chapter could not have been made at the earlier stages of that process, as it would have been a type of exploitation that, while conducted with her apparent consent, on a deeper level would have replicated the pattern of use and abuse by someone that she was trying to trust. I am still a little uncertain about having made this request, and I wonder how this process of writing has affected and will affect our work. (Again, after Carla read the first draft of this chapter, our work did change. Carla described herself as unable to deny the reality of her pain or the horrors of her childhood after seeing herself in print, and we have moved to some powerful and deeper levels in therapy together. I am now less uncertain than when I first wrote this piece.)

While this layer of therapy was progressing, we were dealing at a more overt and conscious level with her fertility problems and the emotions they evoked. Carla is somewhat lucky in that she lives in a major metropolitan area where there are female fertility specialists, including those who will work with lesbians. In the late 1970s, my attempts to find information about physicians who would artificially inseminate lesbians led to resounding dead ends; this had changed not long before Carla had begun to deal with her infertility. Had she been unable to see a woman physician, she might never had pursued her attempts to become pregnant after her initial discovery of her presumed failure to ovulate because her terror of male health care providers is enormous, in keeping with the severity and intensity of the abuse she experienced. Even with a woman physician, Carla found each visit frightening and evocative of nightmares. This resurgence of post-traumatic symptoms, after many years of keeping them to a minimum by avoiding all but the most necessary visits to health care providers, also made it more difficult for Carla to deny that the sexual abuse she had suffered had had a lasting effect that required attention. She felt even more exposed and shamed by the emergence of these symptoms and increasingly dependent on me in ways that she did not know how to encompass. She was intensely uncomfortable with the fact that the supposedly simple issue of her infertility had opened the door on her history of sexual abuse. Again, testing ensued within the therapy, because to be dependent on someone was to be hurt by them. And Carla did feel quite dependent on me as I was often the only witness to the emergence of this material that she purposefully kept hidden from everyone in her personal and social network.

As work progressed, and Carla still did not ovulate, she began to explore her fantasy that her infertility was somehow the result of being sexually abused. Although intellectually she could reject this notion (her form of infertility is not caused by disease or injury, and several of the women in her family may share it), emotionally she could not escape this sense that she had been permanently and irrevocably damaged by her abuser, feelings that she had been able to avoid as long as she though that she was normally fertile. She began to wonder about the two D and Cs that had been performed on her and to question for the first time whether she had really been pregnant or whether her offender had simply been acting out his sadism on her body. Her feelings of bodily lack of integrity and out-of-controlness were exacerbated by the multiple invasive medical procedures she underwent and by the effects of the fertility drugs she began to take in the hope of producing viable ova. She spoke of her rage at her body for "betraying" her; first, by being vulnerable to sexual abuse and now by being incapable of performing those most female of functions, conception and pregnancy. The dynamics of the sexual abuse began to become intertwined with those of her infertility. The shame and self-blame at having been raped and abused were difficult to separate from the shame at her "unnatural" status as an infertile woman.

During this time, we never questioned the soundness of her decision to be a parent; however, we did explore its roots in her family of origin and its meanings in the context of her life here and now. From the perspective of feminist therapy, this is an important distinction. The client's basic values are respected, while at the same time the origins of those values are made known so that the client herself is freer to examine and challenge them. In retrospect, this stance turned out to be very important. Carla herself felt totally committed to motherhood, yet simultaneously she was highly critical of her feelings. She wondered whether they were only a manifestation of some pathological urge to prove her worth to her family or to give to some fantasy child the childhood she wished she had experienced. Although she had years of professional experience working with children and families and knew what constituted good parenting, she was self-doubting and feared that she would repeat her family's pattern of abuse and neglect. She feared the loss of friends and the support of her lesbian community, which did not yet contain many women who had become pregnant as lesbians. She wondered if anyone could understand her pain and confusion—she saw herself as choosing to go through the process of trying to achieve fertility and thus "at fault" for her own distress. Ironically, Carla and I were asking ourselves the same kinds of questions about the normalcy and "naturalness" of our respective, though opposite, decisions about becoming parents. It was as though our being lesbians, that most "unnatural" of states, made it impossible to simply feel good about being or not being mothers.

Again, a feminist therapy perspective proved invaluable in helping to sort external realities and internal experiences. Some of Carla's feelings of intense isolation were genuine aspects of her situation. While infertility support groups are available for heterosexual women and men, no such programs can be found in the lesbian communities of the Pacific Northwest (that is not to say that they do not exist elsewhere. I have simply never heard of them). Carla feared, I believe realistically, that the homophobia she might encounter in such a setting would outweigh any support she might receive for her infertility. Some of her friends were indeed uncomfortable with her desire to be a parent. They could neither comprehend nor support her decision to attempt to become fertile against the odds, although they would have been relatively comfortable with her simply getting pregnant with no fuss and pain. Yet it was clear that Carla's fear of being known (e.g., exploited) made it difficult for her to begin the process of networking that she would need in order to find some kind of community for her parent identity.

Finally, Carla reached the point in her infertility treatment where she could go no further. A period of intense grieving ensued in which she mourned the loss of her fantasy child. This grief was a catalyst for more intense and self-confrontational explorations of her own childhood experiences, and she began to find her anger toward her parents who had ignored and belittled her and toward the man who had sexually abused her. Her ability to be emotionally expressive grew, and she initiated some tentative moves toward self-disclosure with some close friends. In the midst of this grief, she and Susan decided that Susan would go forward with attempting to become pregnant. Carla was now faced with new challenges. She had to find a way to feel a legitimate part of her lover's pregnancy and childbirth, and she had to come out to her family of origin if she were to ensure her child's place in that family. She wanted her child to be accepted as a member of her family, and in order to do that, she had to explain how she was the mother of a child Susan was bearing and also mothering.

As each of these life tasks was approached and accomplished, Carla and I had to steer through the maze of complicating issues that arose from the interaction of infertility and life as a lesbian in a homophobic context. For example, during the process of infertility treatments and fertility testing, Carla always had to anticipate having to explain to yet another person where her husband wasn't and who Susan was. Even though her health care providers were for the most part respectful and caring, this anticipating of being more visible and vulnerable was painful each time it occurred. Carla was an intensely private person in many ways. Although any infertile woman becomes exposed at the level of her most intimate self, Carla was more exposed as a lesbian. This issue arose again when Susan began to inseminate. While her fertility was not in doubt, AI (alternative insemination) pregnancies can take a number of months to achieve; this meant multiple trips to the physician's office, often at inconvenient times, so as to perform the procedure during Susan's ovulation. Carla and Susan decided that Carla needed to be a participant in the AI process, if only as an observer and support person, so that Carla would feel herself more a real part of Susan's pregnancy.

During the AI process, and later as Susan suffered with the normal discomforts of pregnancy, Carla's grief and rage over her infertility were compounded by guilt over "making Susan go through this for me." This scenario is a uniquely lesbian one: Fertile heterosexual men cannot become pregnant in place of their infertile partners. Apart from those rare and highly publicized cases where women have borne children for their infertile sisters and daughters, there is rarely an intimate preexisting relationship between an infertile woman and the fertile one who bears a child that the former may eventually parent. Only in a lesbian relationship is the choice made by Susan and Carla truly a possibility for an infertile woman. This raised questions for Carla and, to some degree, for me, questions that can be asked at a meta-level in most relationships, but which had unique meaning in this particular context. What can we ask of our partners? What, if any, will be the costs of such an agreement, even when freely made by both women? How does the lack of legal status of our relationships as lesbians affect our verbal and emotional commitments to one another at the nonconscious level? And if we have no legal relationship to our children, as Carla would not to the child Susan would bear, what effect does this have on the parent-child relationship?

A related fear that Carla faced, and one that is unique to her status as a lesbian, was that Susan, as sole legal parent, would leave and take the child with her. For the infertile woman in a heterosexual relationship, legal adoption is an option that secures parental rights. At the time that Susan began to inseminate and well into their son's first year of life, there was no legal precedent for a nonbiological lesbian mother to adopt without the biological mother's terminating her own parental rights. Carla did not feel that she could ask Susan to give up her parental rights (nor did she), although the couple did make an agreement about sharing the parenting of Carter should their relationship end.

Once Susan's pregnancy was confirmed, Carla began to contemplate coming out to her family. She decided that as long as she was making herself vulnerable by this revelation, she needed to tell the story of her sexual abuse as well and discover, if she could, what her parents had known of what she had suffered. Like many lesbians, Carla lived far from her family. Suzanne Pharr (1989) has commented on how many of us have gone into exile in order to freely live our lesbian selves, and Carla was no exception to that rule. She missed her southern home, but did not feel free to return to a more openly homophobic setting, and she feared her parents' reaction to learning of her lesbianism. But these self-revelations were an important step for Carla in resolving her grief over her infertility. She was, in effect, declaring herself to be whole and good to a family that had always ignored or dismissed her and, in making that declaration to them, she said things she needed to hear herself say in her own voice. She was proving the statement that her worth as a woman, a human being, and a family member as not contingent on her fitting into the social roles of good womanhood. Working to heal the wound of infertility gave Carla an opportunity to confront her internalized homophobia and see how the various forms of her self-hatred were linked to one another at the root.

The nine months of Susan's pregnancy, which was medically uneventful, allowed Carla the time and space in which to look differently at what her fertility had meant to her. Now that there was no denying that she would not be pregnant, our work focused more on the connections between fertility and self-worth. Carla was and is angry that her infertility served to reopen the door on her history of sexual abuse. Her rage at herself for being infertile has its roots in her earlier rage, which was turned against herself, at being abused. Perhaps because this internalized rage had so long been a cornerstone of Carla's psychological functioning, it was more difficult for her to be compassionate with herself about her infertility. The two issues repeatedly spiralled into one another.

Carter's birth signalled an entrance into new layers of Carla's healing. She delighted in her son and resented having to go to work and leave him at home. As she began to see how relatively easy it was for her to love this baby, even on the nights when he decided to stay up till all hours, she felt the contrast between her experience as a parent and her own painful childhood. It became harder for her to cling to her rationalizations about her family's emotional neglectfulness. Even though she had not borne this child, she was strongly and deeply attached to him. How, she began to wonder, could her parents, who were related to her by blood and childbirth as she was not related to Carter, have not felt the same with her? It is my sense that, in this small way, the fact of Carla's infertility, which she had feared would be an obstacle to loving her child as fully as she wished, aided her in clarifying what is normal and usual for parents and what was in the realm of neglect and inattention.

In mid-1989, another lesbian couple in our state, known slightly to both me and to Carla, were successful in effecting the second-parent adoption of their daughter without the birth mother having to give up parental rights. Carla and Susan decided that they wished to pursue this option. Again, Carla was being forced by her infertility and by a homophobic culture which does not automatically recognize the right of the same-sex second-parent to her child, to become exposed and vulnerable. Carla was asked by the social services agency to complete a lengthy questionnaire and autobiography. She struggled with the question of how open to be about her sexual abuse history, her political beliefs, and her true self. My validation of the basic craziness and unfairness of her situation was, I think, a necessary element of my support for the adoption. When Carla berated herself for supposedly overreacting to the intrusiveness of the adoption process, I would remind her that she had every right and healthy reason to be angry at a system that did not recognize her relationship with her son as a valid one. "Carter knows you're his mom even if the court doesn't," was a frequent statement from me in sessions where I would contrast Carla and Carter's living reality as a family with the socially constructed legal reality in which Carla had no relationship to her son. But Carla worried that if she lacked the legal contract with him, Carter would someday see its absence as more meaningful than the history of their relationship.

As of this writing, Carla, Susan, and Carter are waiting for the right judge to come on the bench. The social services worker has recommended in favor of Carla's becoming the legal mother of her son because it is so clearly in the child's best interest. But the first judge to whom the case was assigned told their lawyer that he would rule against them, simply because he didn't think that lesbians should be doing this. As a lesbian, Carla pays a higher price for her infertility than do heterosexual women. Her feelings of loss of control of important aspects of her life are constantly restimulated by incontrovertible realities. This social context makes the process of therapy immeasurably more complex and convoluted, old wounds are constantly reopened by events in the here and now. Carla's experiences are testimony to how essential it is that those of us who are the therapists of lesbians and gay men acknowledge the very real effects of that homophobic social matrix in which we attempt to heal homophobia's wounds. (A note at editing time: the adoption went through!)

CONCLUSION

Although much of the content of our work has not directly addressed infertility, it is my sense, especially in the last year and a half since Carter was born, that infertility has been the theme of our work no matter what the manifest content. Infertility is about the body; it is about shame, loss, and being out of control. It is about being betrayed by that most intimate of entities, oneself. It is about sexuality, about grief, and about being a real, valued woman. Until she was faced with her infertility, Carla had been able to put away her other parallel experiences. While she had suffered grief, alienation, and violations of her body and self, she had been able to some degree to place them outside of herself and go on in ways that were not only functional, but quite admirable.

Infertility erased the distance between Carla and her feelings. It reunited her with her body and the memories of pain that she carried there and required her to confront her life and see it in a new light. This task is still in the process of being accomplished. If Carla were not a lesbian, she would have found her road easier and, paradoxically, harder as well. Because Carla was already well into the task of establishing a positive lesbian identity, she possessed the emotional template for loving, within herself, that which others rejected and despised. Had she been more insecure in that identity or more in the grip of internalized homophobia, her internal struggles would have been greater. This has been the case especially as regards her work on recovery from sexual abuse, even though Carla finds it extremely difficult to apply her own feminist standards of care and fairness to herself at these times. But, ironically, because she is proud of who she is, her path to legal parenthood, which will go far toward healing the grief of her not giving birth, is unfairly steep.

My own positive lesbian identity has been a part of this process as well. I can know from experience the meaning of having my intimate relationships disenfranchised in the medico-legal system. At times when Carla struggled to allow herself her anger, she knew that she could see its honest reflection in me. Ours has been a relationship in which the mutuality between us has been equal in importance to the boundaries framing treatment.

Carla's experience in therapy is unique to her and yet prototypical of the issues she has confronted in treatment. My experience as her therapist runs parallel to hers. Our relationship is the only one of its kind, and yet it is powerfully illustrative of the tasks faced by a politically aware lesbian therapist working with a lesbian client. The process of balancing and juggling, sifting external and internal realities, allowing for resonance while maintaining clear boundaries, offering safe space while continuing to honor the capable adult woman that she is, and all the while bringing the experience of knowing how life is lived as a lesbian to the work of therapy have each, in their particular ways, been present in my process with Carla.

REFERENCES

1. Chodorow, N. (1979). *The reproduction of mothering*. Berkeley: University of California Press.
2. Hendricks, M. C. (1985). Feminist therapy with women and couples who are infertile. In L. B. Rosewater & L. E. A. Walker (Eds.), *Handbook of feminist therapy: Women's issues in psychotherapy*. New York: Springer.
3. Hill, K. (1987). Mothers by insemination: Interviews. In S. Pollack & J. Vaughn (Eds.), *Politics of the heart: A lesbian parenting anthology*. Ithaca, NY: Firebrand Books.

4. Martin, A. (1989, August). *The planned lesbian and gay family: Parenthood and children.* Invited address presented at the Convention of the American Psychological Association, New Orleans, LA.
5. Mayer, J. (1987). The one we lost. In S. Pollack & J. Vaughn (Eds.), *Politics of the heart: A lesbian parenting anthology.* Ithaca, NY: Firebrand Books.
6. Miller, J. B. (1976). *Toward a new psychology of women.* Boston: Beacon.
7. Murphy, M. (1987). And baby makes two. In S. Pollack & J. Vaughn (Eds.), *Politics of the heart: A lesbian parenting anthology.* Ithaca, NY: Firebrand Books.
8. Pharr, S. (1989). *Homophobia: A weapon of sexism.* Inverness, CA: Chardon Press.
9. Pollack, S., & Vaughn, J. (Eds.). (1987). *Politics of the heart: A lesbian parenting anthology.* Ithaca, NY: Firebrand Books.

3

ROBERT PAUL CABAJ

Overidentification
With a Patient

THE PATIENT, TOM, WAS a 34-year-old gay white male referred by a psychiatric colleague who was a friend of the patient. His presenting problems were anxiety, depression, and insomnia following a diagnosis of AIDS and his subsequent inability to work.

The patient was a medical professional in a field that required the careful use of his hands and called for excellent hand-eye coordination. While at work with a patient, he suddenly had a seizure and collapsed. After being taken to an emergency ward, he underwent multiple medical tests and examinations. A diagnosis of a brain lesion was made and presumed to be a toxoplasmosis fungal infection, which was later confirmed by study of the spinal fluid. He was given a presumptive diagnosis of AIDS as he had no other indications of an opportunistic infection, but no confirmation of this was made using the HIV-antibody test. Antifungal treatment began and Tom responded very well. (At the time, AZT was still experimental and was not automatically considered as part of the medical intervention.)

Tom recovered quickly, having been in very good health prior to the seizure. He was anxious to leave the hospital and return to work.

Tom felt he had been misdiagnosed and believed he did not have AIDS, and his remarkable recovery helped support his denial. In attempting to return to work, however, he found that his coordination was off and, at times, he was slightly confused. Tom did not tell his colleagues about the diagnosis. He had a lover, Mark, of several years, who was apprised of the presumed diagnosis. Tom did not confide much in his lover, and they did not discuss his problems with work.

A colleague who noticed Tom's behavior felt he might be putting patients in danger and recommended time off, thinking the coordination problems were an aftereffect of the seizure. Tom agreed, but had a difficult time staying away from work and continued going in to do administrative and other paper work. He noticed he was becoming very restless, sad, and depressed, and also had trouble sleeping. He decided to confide in a psychiatrist friend, who recommended that he speak to me.

Tom was an attractive man from an Eastern European background. He lived with his lover in the Boston area and was very excited to be finally starting his career and living comfortably. He had completed his medical training two years before, had worked briefly in a clinic, and then joined a group private practice. He was doing very well and was considered one of the bright stars of the practice.

He knew he was gay from about age ten but did not know what to do about it. He had grown up in a small town in rural New England and was the oldest boy of three children. His parents were working-class people with limited education. He had had a strong Catholic upbringing. Tom was very bright and successful in school and became the first family member to go beyond high school, but he felt his family did not know how to relate to him or understand his successes. He was very proud about working and paying his way through school and his earnings and scholarships helped him get through medical school.

Tom had had a limited social life and had felt both awkward about himself and uncertain about how to act on his gay feelings. Eventually he had a gay affair in college and a few very limited sexual encounters before meeting his current lover at the start of his graduate training. His lover, also a very independent person, was in a business that allowed him to be away often, which very much suited Tom. Tom felt they clearly loved each other, but he said that they were not physically intimate nor overtly emotional with each other. Their sexual life was limited from the beginning, consisting mostly of mutual masturbation, and even that faded away after a few years.

Tom did not want to bother anyone and always tried to do everything himself, his way. He and his lover learned to live fairly separate and independent lives, together. He had felt alienated from his family since he had moved away, and he had not told them that he was gay. His younger sister was the only family member he felt close to and the only one he told about his gay life.

Tom was very confused about his AIDS diagnosis. He didn't think he had had any sexual contacts that could have led to infection in the last several years, and he did not use IV drugs. He felt he probably did not have AIDS but did not want to take the HIV-antibody test, fearing it might challenge his belief. However, he did feel weak and undertook a course of IV vitamin treatments.

Tom appeared to have a reactive depression with anxiety, as a result of the diagnosis of AIDS. He was a young man, just beginning his life as a professional, out on his own. He had obsessive-compulsive traits and an ability to delay gratification and deny discomfort. He did not have a good view of himself and was not completely accepting of his homosexuality. He had grown up not expecting much love or acknowledgement from his family and did not expect much from his lover, friends, or therapist.

THE THERAPIST

This chapter will focus on overidentification with a patient. To be able to explore this problem with this patient, I need to describe myself in relationship to him. At the time we started therapy, I was 37 years old, ten years out of my psychiatric residency training, and three years in a full-time private practice.

I come from a Polish-American working-class background, and—like my patient—I was the first in my family to go beyond high school. My parents were proud and excited about my going to medical school, but they were not fully able to understand what it all meant or could not fully relate to my achievements. I also had a strong fundamentalist Catholic background and was the oldest of three children. I worked my way through school, with some scholarships and some help from my family, and I like to be independent. I learned to do as much for myself as possible, and I resist getting help or depending on others.

Although I knew I was gay as a preadolescent, I did not "come out" until college. I only came out to my family when I began my practice and was speaking publicly on gay and lesbian issues. When I started working with Tom, I was in a four-year relationship that was troubled. My lover and I had begun to spend less time together. We had never communicated well about emotional needs and rarely turned to each other for support, but used friends, family, or colleagues instead.

THE THERAPY

The initial therapy focused on Tom's adjustment to not working in his clinical capacity and on helping him to gradually confront the reality of his health. In addition, a powerful internalized homophobia emerged during the first few sessions and difficulties in his relationship were discussed.

As I began therapy with Tom, I recognized the possible pitfalls of our similar backgrounds, ages, and—except for his health crisis—current life situations. He was not very talkative and often seemed uncertain about what to say. I found that I was beginning to fill in the blanks or tell him things about his family and upbringing as I thought they were, rather than having him tell me directly.

I was soon allying myself with his denial and hoping that the brain infection was, in fact, a fluke and that he would be able to return to work. We geared therapy towards broader expectations, rather than looking at and trying to accept some of the limitations imposed by his health. As he talked more about his lover, I "heard" him describing my lover and began to develop a strong dislike for the man, though we had only met once. I resisted seeing his lover, because I felt he would be just like my own—difficult to talk to and not interested in what was really happening.

Tom did attempt to return to work but found he was too weak and uncoordinated. I convinced him to get regular medical care, to stop working, and to begin to accept that he did, in fact, have AIDS. In a somewhat superstitious resistance, he still refused the antibody test which would make the diagnosis definitive. However, he started taking AZT.

Tom was getting weaker and more withdrawn, but I was overlooking these physical and emotional changes; I filled in more blanks and urged him to try and do more socially. He felt, though, that he was physically and emotionally better and did not have much to say. I colluded with his denial and we agreed to meet every other week.

As we continued our work, he talked a bit about his parents; I began to "hear" him describe my own family and started to ally myself with his negative views of them and to see them as unable to understand him or be there for him. In effect, I was disliking his lover and his family in the same way I disliked my own.

During one session, he was quiet, as usual, but then complained of weakness and insomnia. He had developed an infection in his arm from the IV vitamin treatment. His lover had had to drive him to my office that day, as Tom felt he was now too weak to drive himself. Suddenly, through the combination of medical complaints and the reality of his arm infection, I began to see him as he was, listen to him, and reevaluate his mental status. Then, with his permission, I asked that his lover join us.

Although we were awkward at first, we were able to start talking directly to each other. They were both able to describe Tom's physical decline at home and acknowledged they had both been trying to ignore and deny the changes. Mark was very reluctant to think Tom had AIDS, but he was able to use this couples session to reassess the situation. To my surprise, I found that I liked Mark; he was not aloof and uncaring. In fact, he was very concerned about Tom but uncertain as to how he could help.

In that session, all three of us were able to confront our denial and see how much had changed. Tom then admitted that much of the social activity he had described to me were things he made up to please me because he felt I would be disappointed if he did not get out and do more. In fact, he only left the house to see me. He had come to count on our visits and had wanted to go back to weekly sessions, but felt embarrassed about letting me know that he felt dependent on me.

Our work together suddenly changed. We returned to weekly psycho- therapy. Tom agreed to regular medical follow-up. I started him on antide- pressant medications and low dose, intermittent antianxiety medication, mainly to help him sleep. We had alternating couples work, and Mark became an active participant in Tom's care. Mark was also very indepen- dent and did not like to help unless asked or it became absolutely neces- sary, but he certainly cared very much for Tom.

Eventually, I was able to convince Tom that letting me visit him at home when he was too weak or tired was not a sign of emotional or moral weakness. By letting Mark be part of our work, Tom was also able to look at his internalized homophobia more easily. The antidepressant medications began to have a beneficial effect and Tom became more talkative and insightful.

Over the next few months, we were all able to adjust to his declining health and make preparations in anticipation of his worsening health and eventual death, which included making a will and assigning power of attorney. He counted on my visits and hoped to live long enough for a cure for AIDS to be discovered. He also hoped to return to work, and, in fact, his position was held open for him until his death.

We talked further about death and the preparations he had made. We were able to review his accomplishments and the frustrations over what he did not get to do in his life. He continued to try and block any overt demonstration of his feelings — there were no tears or pained expressions —

but he seemed moved as we went over photographs of old friends and of trips he had taken with Mark. Near the end, he was unable to speak but used his eyes to communicate.

We said good-bye at the beginning of a weekend when I had to travel, because we both knew he would not survive; he died on that Sunday afternoon.

Tom's family had begun to take a more direct role in his life and his care near the end but were problematic in their attempts to deal with Tom and his illness. They had difficulty accepting his gayness and would not relate to Mark. They blamed him for Tom's illness. They did not want to speak to me unless they absolutely had to because they strongly believed that no one is supposed to need a psychiatrist.

I made attempts to meet with them, planning home visits when I knew the family would be there. When I arrived, the father usually left the room, and the mother complained about the poor living conditions and Mark's failure to keep the apartment clean. Tom's perceptions and my original projections about them were, in fact, in alignment.

After Tom's death, his family was angry, withdrawn, and refused to abide by the will. They took his body with them back to the rural town, did not allow the funeral to follow Tom's plans, and refused Mark access to any of Tom's personal belongings. I was shocked and disbelieving, and tried to intervene, but they would not return my calls. I met with Mark a few times to try to deal with our mutual anger and frustration, but he felt resigned and defeated and eventually moved away from the area.

DISCUSSION

The issue of overidentification is a crucial one. It is clearly a form of countertransference and though it may not necessarily harm a patient, it may lead to a delay in improvement because the patient himself is not being treated, only the patient projected and imagined by the therapist. The potential for overidentification in the clinical situation described in this chapter is obvious from my description of myself and this particular patient, but such obvious matching factors and traits are not necessary.

Many gay people seek therapy from gay therapists. There may be an assumption of acceptance or tolerance and a shared set of beliefs or common knowledge base. There is, however, no uniformity among gay people and each gay person has his or her own level of homophobia (Cabaj, 1988).

The needs to be heard, accepted, and loved seem to be universal. Gay men and lesbians may have particular problems having these needs met if there is a strong component of internalized homophobia—the belief that being gay is bad or sinful or makes one less deserving or valuable.

Many gay people I have seen in psychotherapy present backgrounds such as the one described by Miller (1981). These people relate childhoods in which their true needs or longings were not acknowledged, because the parents were either unable or unwilling to see them. Rewards were given for what the parents wanted to see or hear and not necessarily for what the patient had to offer. Many gay men recall early longings for father or other men, of both an affectional and sexual nature, which they learned were "wrong" and either suppressed or denied (Isay, 1989). The "true self" had to hide and the patient learned to seek acknowledgment for what others expected.

If either the gay patient or the gay therapist had an upbringing in which the "true self" could not emerge and the "false self" was rewarded, the need to have the real self acknowledged may be extremely powerful. When combined with homophobia, this could lead to overidentification, either as a transferential or countertransferential therapeutic situation. The therapist may look to patients for validation, just as the patient may turn to the therapist for the same need.

In the case described, I needed to see the patient as being healthier than he was. I started to see him as being so much like myself that I stopped hearing him and projected onto him my own needs and expectations for acceptance and approval. Through my own personal psychotherapy at that time, I was discovering the "false self" I had created to please my own family after learning that my parents could not see the "real" me or recognize my needs. My attempts to be recognized and accepted were often doomed by my inability to deal with my real needs and desires; I ended up pleasing others and matching their expectations while often ignoring my own. I saw that I tried to have my patients like me, and wanted them to be healthy and get better quickly.

In retrospect, I should have sought supervision sooner for this clinical situation or used my own therapy to focus on the issues of my own troubled relationship and emerging sense of self. I recognized that my own fear of illness and disability was stirred up by this patient but only after I could finally see how ill he had become. I saw that I feared that the same thing could happen to me—that I could be struck down with a fatal illness as I was finally coming into my own both personally and professionally.

When I was a child, I was sick with rheumatic fever. I was in the hospital for six months and not allowed to walk for almost a year. The need to deny and suppress that horrible time in my life clearly blocked me from seeing my patient's disability.

With some of these new insights and awarenesses, I was then able to see and use the patient's lover as an ally and not as an interfering, uncaring, or indifferent obstacle. The patient's strong need to be accepted as he was could finally be expressed, and this opened up a new world of discussion, insight, and growth in his final months. He said he was dying happier and freer than he had ever felt in his life.

Identification is a normal ego defense mechanism and is a natural part of development in all children and adolescents (Freud, 1966). Gay children have had few gay role models and rarely have the freedom to discuss their sexual feelings or desires with teachers, parents, or peers. The incorporation of traits from admired people in the developmental process may be distorted for many gay people because of the difficulties in fully relating to others in the heterosexual majority.

In therapy, identification may also be a normal part of the process (Luborsky, 1984; Roth, 1987; Tarchow, 1963). Many people feel that there is benefit in a gay person seeing a gay therapist, in that the patient may have someone to model him or herself after. The acceptance by the therapist is, I believe, much more important than the potential modeling. The therapist needs to see the patient as he or she really is and not as an idealized image. The patient may imitate or even pick up traits of the therapist, but these usually go away once the true self emerges and is acknowledged and accepted.

Overidentification is almost always a distortion, with the patient or the therapist projecting his or her own traits or needs on the other. This variation on transference or countertransference will probably lead to problems similar to those that I have described above, which are mostly related to the inability to see the person for who he or she really is. Proper supervision, peer supports, and personal psychotherapy are the best weapons the therapist can use to fight this problem.

If overidentification develops as a transference in the therapy, it is hoped that the therapist will be able to acknowledge it and use it in the therapeutic work. The therapist must be prepared to deal with the hurt and disappointment a patient may feel when he or she learns that love and acceptance come not from being like someone else, but from loving and accepting oneself. The patient may feel angry and betrayed at not getting the rewards in the therapy through the technique he or she had used in the past, that is, by living up to the expectations of others or for being like the person from whom he or she wishes to receive caring. The therapist will need to bear the anger and "ride out" the storm in order to help the patient's true self emerge.

Gay patients and gay therapists must always remember that everyone is gay in his or her own way and that everyone uses words and experiences uniquely. A therapist may opt to refer a patient if he or she sees the potential for a very difficult or confusing transference or countertransference early on or, if that option does not exist, he or she should, as I failed to do at first, line up extra help and support in the form of supervision or personal therapy.

REFERENCES

1. Cabaj, R. P. (1988). Homosexuality and neurosis: Considerations in psychotherapy. *Journal of Homosexuality, 15,* 13–23.
2. Freud, A. (1966). *The ego and the mechanisms of defense* (rev. ed.). New York: International Universities Press.
3. Isay, R. A. (1989). *Being homosexual: Gay men and their development.* New York: Farrar, Strauss & Giroux.
4. Luborsky, L. (1984). *Principles of psychoanalytic psychotherapy: A manual for supportive-expressive treatment.* New York: Basic Books.
5. Miller, A. (1981). *The drama of the gifted child.* New York: Basic Books.
6. Roth, S. (1987). *Psychotherapy: The art of wooing nature.* Northvale, NJ: Jason Aronson.
7. Tarchow, S. (1963). *An introduction to psychotherapy.* New York: International Universities Press.

4

ARMAND R. CERBONE

The Effects of Political Activism on Psychotherapy: A Case Study

To be gay in this society is to be political. And that's a message people need to take in: that they can make their contribution in a wide range of ways.

—Urvashi Vaid,
Executive Director, National Gay and
Lesbian Task Force, in an interview
with *Windy City Times*, January 25, 1990

IT WAS THE DAY AFTER the Gay Pride Parade, 1986. The six gay men were meeting for the fifth session of a twelve-week psychotherapy group. Members were reporting how they had spent Pride Day.

Greg exploded, "What good is the parade? It's nothing but a circus. It does no one any real good. It's just a bunch of queens entertaining each other."

With increasing passion he excoriated gays for wasting their energies on frivolities while there were people dying of AIDS. The parade did little to address issues seriously, and it changed nothing. "It's just a chance," he went on, "for people you never see doing anything for anybody else to get some attention. It's a complete charade."

I lost my temper, saying, "You're not including me in that number are you, Gregory?" Greg was stunned, and became silent. The other five men tensed and retreated to the sidelines of a conflict they wanted no part of.

Even as I spoke, I knew this was a wrongheaded thing to say. Nonetheless, I pursued the attack. "I was out there, too. I was there because a lot of people like you can't be because it's too risky to show your faces. I thought it was important to get psychologists out there to support our rights. I was scared, too. I had never done anything like this before, but I was determined not to let fear rule my life." My final salvo was, "What are you doing?"

By the session's end, the group had become polarized. Greg told me that I may be a good therapist with individuals but I was terrible with groups. Others said that I was a nice guy but my politics were "bizarre." I felt I had seriously damaged my relationship with the group. But I was particularly worried that I had undercut the work I had been doing with Greg in individual therapy.

PATIENT HISTORY

This incident occurred one and a half years into his therapy. I had suggested group therapy as a strategy to break down Greg's social and emotional isolation. Previously, a similar group experience had briefly eased his loneliness and lifted his self-esteem.

Greg began therapy with me in August 1984 and worked with me until June 1987 when he moved to another city. At the time he began therapy he was 34 years old and worked as a counselor in a substance-abuse program within a large urban hospital. He came in suffering from severe depression, suicidal thoughts, and low self-esteem. In addition to these problems, he complained of deep loneliness and feelings of hopelessness.

His family history was marked by a series of unusual tragedies. Greg was the youngest of four children. When he was eleven, his father died of a heart attack. Just months prior to that, the family home had burned to the ground. His older sister, who suffered from encephalitis, was suspected of setting the fire; she had recently been suicidal and homicidal. She died seven years later at the age of 21 of myesthenia gravis. Nine years later, his 24-year-old brother died of an overdose of Seconal. The death was ruled an accident, but there were suggestions of suicide.

When we began working together, Greg's mother was dying in a nursing home in a distant state where his oldest brother lived. Greg's relationship with both his mother and brother was strained. His mother died eight months later. He and his brother remained distant and uninvolved, though not without the occasional confrontation by Greg about his brother's lack of caring.

Greg's social life consisted of frequent visits to gay bars where he usually got drunk. He was close to a straight woman at work who married and moved away shortly after he began therapy with me. This deepened his isolation. His closest male friend was another colleague, a straight married man, with whom Greg would enjoy long conversations and whom he trusted deeply. The relationship was not sexual but there seemed to have been ambiguous sexual strivings on both parts. The only gay friends he had were two couples he saw infrequently and some drinking buddies. This isolation and the need for friends remained a central issue throughout his therapy.

Greg had had several disappointing romances prior to this therapy. His last relationship had ended in heartbreak when his lover in New York City cancelled plans to have Greg move from Key West only days before Greg was to join him. Instead, Greg moved to Chicago to start anew. About three months into therapy, Greg met a man whom he dated for three months. They discussed moving in together, but this relationship ended abruptly, and shortly after that Greg made a suicidal gesture. This deepened his self-doubts and fears of abandonment and also exacerbated his criticism of other gays as unstable and self-centered.

In August 1985, Greg was diagnosed with Kaposi's sarcoma. He was a victim once again. Understandably, his depression deepened. He saw his attempts to improve himself as vain, and future efforts seemed all the more painful and pointless.

By his own admission, Greg abused alcohol. He had occasional blackouts. At times, he saw himself as alcoholic and admitted needing help. But to seek treatment would have cost him his job because requirements dictated that a recovering alcoholic be sober for at least 18 months before counseling other alcoholics. And, more realistically, Greg resisted giving up alcohol—it was too much of a comfort in his loneliness and too much of a support for his anxiety in social situations. After he was diagnosed with AIDS, entering treatment for alcohol abuse became moot because he had to keep his job to keep his health insurance benefits. AIDS made him effectively unemployable elsewhere and uninsurable anywhere.

What is significant to the discussion at hand is that Greg was often homophobic. Though he had lived an openly gay life for years prior to his arrival in Chicago, he was largely closeted in his present job. He frequently worried that exposure would jeopardize his standing at work. AIDS intensified these anxieties. While he was out to a few peers, these relationships did little to encourage his building a healthy gay lifestyle. Moreover, Greg complained of the emptiness of gay life and the superficiality of gay men. He considered the failure of these men to engage with him around anything but sex or alcohol as evidence of this. Suggestions that he seek out gay social-service organizations only aroused his contempt.

INTERNALIZED HOMOPHOBIA

Chief among my concerns in this case were the severity of Greg's depression with its suicidal component, his alcohol abuse, and his internalized homophobia. It is this last issue which is most central to this discussion, for it is here that I blundered in his therapy.

In some ways it was difficult to see Greg as internally homophobic. He certainly did not regard himself as such. To the contrary, he believed he had long ago accepted that he was gay. His family and friends had known of his sexuality for years. He had pursued and enjoyed sustained relationships of considerable intimacy with other men. His social life, while limited, was spent largely in the company of gay men. He had lived and worked openly as a gay man for years in Key West. Even in Chicago the only people from whom he hid his homosexuality were his superiors at work. He regarded these superiors as being homophobic and punitive. Further, it was possible to view his depression as a chronic reaction to repeated childhood traumas and adult disappointments. His low self-esteem, periodic irascibility, and isolation were consonant with alcohol abuse. Superficially, Greg showed many of the characteristics attributed to fairly well-adjusted gay men. What pathologies he did exhibit could be due to other conflicts.

Nonetheless, much of Greg's despair and alienation were due to negative impressions of gay life (Jacob & Tedford, 1980; Malyon, 1985). His admitted sabotage of relationships was as much a consequence of his homophobia as of low self-esteem and fears of intimacy (Isay, 1989; Malyon, 1985). Further, he enjoyed no gay friendships of an intimacy similar to that shared with his straight friends. To the contrary, he criticized gay men as empty, irresponsible, and insensitive with an intensity and despair that suggested more projection than reality (Fein & Neuhring, 1981; Malyon, 1985; McDonald, 1982). The powerlessness he had distilled from a lifetime of tragic losses only heightened his fears of further victimization because of his homosexuality (Wingrove & Rodway, 1985). His drinking was also in many ways a self-directed indictment of his gay life (Kus, 1988).

THERAPIST'S HISTORY OF ACTIVISM

The year I began treating Greg was the year I introduced a course on homosexuality into the curriculum of the professional school where I was teaching. At the time I believed it was the first such course taught anywhere in Illinois. Because it meant coming out to my colleagues, it was the biggest step I had taken in my resolve to rid myself of my professional closet. Previously I had been visible only within the gay community, volunteering in local health and service organizations.

It was also the year the American Psychological Association established a division for lesbian and gay studies. In 1973 I had stood in the shadows of the APA convention in Montreal where gays and lesbians formed the Association of Gay Psychologists, the organization which pressed recognition of our concerns upon the APA. This time, I resolved to stand on the sidelines no more. If I didn't press forward, I would be acceding to my own internalized homophobia.

That fall I began organizing lesbian and gay psychologists in the Midwest. We held our first meetings on Gay Pride weekend, just days before the incident with Greg took place. At the conclusion of our meetings, I invited my colleagues to become the first psychologists to march in Chicago's Pride Parade, but only three women joined me under a makeshift banner reading "Psychologists."

Despite the exhilaration the parade and crowds afforded, I worried. How would this affect my clients? Would it expose any of them by their association with me? How would I stand in the eyes of my professional peers? A few had already criticized me privately: What did this have to do with good therapy or psychology? Would referrals dry up? Privately, I saw myself joining the ranks of movers and shakers while fearing I would turn to find no one marching behind me. Coincidentally, in a keynote address I had given at a gay conference earlier that year, I had chided those who criticized the parade. I had invited them to improve the parade rather than damn what they disliked about it, and I had to accept the challenge for myself as well. Thus my marching fulfilled another promise I had made to myself.

TRANSFERENCE AND COUNTERTRANSFERENCE

Until the time of our confrontation, Greg and I had enjoyed a solid working relationship. I believed there was a good match between our interpersonal styles (McConnaughy, 1987; Stein, 1988). Greg trusted my support and guidance; he looked to me for the constancy of nurturance and affection that repeated tragedies had denied him. At one point he asked if I would be at his bedside should he die of AIDS. Moreover, Greg saw me as a positive gay figure, well-adjusted and successful in ways he wanted to be. In important ways his perceptions of me approximated elements of his idealized self (Seligson, 1977). In this way, my growing activism and visibility in the gay community provided an attractive role model for him (Rochlin, 1985). Within this climate of trust and mutual regard, Greg could accept my confrontations and interpretations. Though initially resistant, he eventually saw them as helpful and caring (McConnaughy, 1987). These were all evidence of the positive transferences in our relationship.

What the conflict between us brought to the surface was the dark side of Greg's transference: his anger and disappointment that I was not the well-adjusted gay professional I had led him to believe I was. To the contrary, I could be arbitrary, self-absorbed, and dependent on the approval of others. I was no more developed than any of the other gay men who had hurt or disappointed him. How could *I* help him? Our clash also uncovered aspects of my own countertransference in two principal ways. First, I had played into his defense system (de Montflores, 1986), allowing him to rationalize his own homophobia. My demonstration revealed a critical and vindictive parent accusing him of inadequacy and cowardice. The manner and content of my criticism suggested he was not worthy of my esteem (Moses & Hawkins, 1982). My display of anger implied that concerns for myself were more important than my concerns for him and that when these concerns were threatened I would attack. In this way I became as self-centered and insensitive as other gay men from whom he should withdraw. The reassurances I had offered earlier that life for gays was improving because of the efforts of activists merely stiffened his resistance to me now.

Secondly, I had overidentified with Greg (de Montflores, 1986). I often forgot that Greg had no formal training as a counselor beyond his bachelor's degree. Because of his years of work in substance-abuse programs, he was psychologically attuned and sophisticated but not to the extent I gave him credit. I sometimes imagined him as a successful psychotherapist in private practice. The confrontation also unmasked a covert assumption I made that we were gay brothers all suffering the same oppression from a homophobic society. At a deeper level I regarded my activism as a form of caring for him and others like him. Didn't I march to secure a safer world and happier future for those who couldn't march? I personalized Greg's criticism of the parade, feeling its sting deeply. It stirred unrecognized fears of self-interest and self-promotion in my activism. On another level, it suggested that I was allowing the gay rights movement to engulf me (Lee, 1977). Certainly, my clinical judgment and skill were compromised.

My response to Greg's anger was damaging to him and the therapeutic relationship. If empathy constitutes the most important factor in determining the ultimate effectiveness of the therapeutic endeavor (Stein, 1988), then certainly I should have accepted his expressions of hostility to the parade. Instead, I challenged the legitimacy of his feelings and inadvertently pressured him to match my own standards of conduct (Anthony, 1985; Stein, 1988). My attack did more than shake his confidence in me as someone who could provide emotional safety; it suggested that I might also be internally conflicted, interpersonally uncomfortable with feelings, and unskilled as a therapist (McConnaughy, 1987). The damage to the relationship did not stem from my being angry or even from confronting Greg with it. Rather, it followed from my failure to keep professional boundaries intact. The insistent character of my intervention co-opted his and the group's attention to address my injured feelings in such a way as to effect a role reversal. Greg and the group needed to attend to their therapist's needs first.

There were any number of responses I could have made to Greg that would have respected his feelings yet opened doors to exploration of them. Had I not already overidentified with him, I would have probed beneath his angry words to empathize with the hurt that gave them such force (Seligson, 1977). Had I understood that my marching the day before was, in good measure, to vindicate fears of my own internalized homophobia, I would not have taken Greg's complaints as accusations. Instead of rebutting, I would have acknowledged the differences in circumstance and development between us (Coleman, 1978; Sophie, 1987; Stein, 1988). I could then have attended to his struggles with homophobia without burdening him with my own.

I do know that I would have confronted him anyway. The content and affect of his outburst demanded exploration. Confrontation had long been an accepted character of our work together. But only after offering genuine empathy and acceptance would I have invited him to consider the deeper meanings of his complaints. Did the parade stir up envy of those who were freer to enjoy their sexuality? Did the parade crowds suggest that he need not be so isolated and alienated? Might the intensity of his objections spring from anxieties that he himself was homophobic? Had I not been so vulnerable to criticism, I might have been able to speak more directly to my experience of the parade. I could have spoken of the range of feelings I had from near panic to pride. Presenting Greg with my own conflicts in this way might have provided a way for both of us to voice our needs and have them supported.

CONSEQUENCES AND RESOLUTION

I continued to work with Greg individually for another year. The group disbanded five sessions later before completing the twelve-week course. The confrontation with Greg played a major role in this premature termination. Group members used the incident as evidence that I could not be an effective instrument of therapy for them, and they withdrew.

During the year that followed, Greg and I mended fences. He took the position that he had never lost trust in me as an individual therapist. For my part, I acknowledged my error and apologized. I also consulted with peer supervisors and did some important soul-searching with my therapist.

As months passed, Greg's depression lifted. He became more active in his pursuit of AIDS treatment and negotiated his way into a national pilot study for the treatment of his Kaposi's sarcoma. On the homefront, he volunteered to develop a social center for people with AIDS. He retired from his job with disability leave rather than endure the toxicity of the antigay, anti-AIDS bureaucracy at the hospital. With his new involvements he found more supportive and nurturant people. Even his dependency on alcohol was somewhat reduced.

In June 1987, we had to conclude therapy when Greg decided to move to the city where the pilot study was being conducted. The following October we met for a moment when we both took part in the March on Washington. I marched with psychologists; he marched in the vanguard with other people with AIDS.

In obtaining his release for this study, I discussed the incident once more with Greg. He said that though the confrontation was a painful surprise, it did have positive effects. In the long run, it galvanized him into action. It would seem that while the clash had threatened Greg, he trusted his prior sense of my commitment and concern enough to stay in the relationship and work our differences through.

ACTIVISM VS. THERAPEUTIC NEUTRALITY

Political activism can threaten a therapy relationship, because the therapist who is active in the political struggle against homophobia—and, further, whose activism is public—loses the aura of therapeutic neutrality. Indeed, it may be the visibility more than the activism itself that compromises neutrality. There is a limited range of sanctioned activities that preserve the appearance of neutrality such as volunteering professional services to health and social-service agencies within the gay community and debating homophobia in professional corridors. These activities allow both clients and colleagues to view the therapist as behaving well within the bounds of acceptable professional norms. In this regard, I am reminded of the 1960s when teachers were unionizing. As a teacher in a Catholic secondary school system, I found teachers resistant to organizing because they thought it was unprofessional, despite the fact that they had no job contracts or fringe benefits.

Therapeutic neutrality typically refers to the attempt on the part of the therapist to guarantee the client an environment in which the client can expect acceptance and positive regard from the therapist regardless of the therapist's feelings, values, beliefs, or pathologies (Seligson, 1977). To the extent that the therapist can successfully do this, the therapist also creates an environment in which the client can then explore his or her feelings, values, and behavior with all their strengths and maladaptions (Tripp, 1975). While it is critical to the climate of trust, without which therapy cannot proceed, such neutrality is humanly impossible and, hence, can only be approximated. Consequently, it is incumbent on the therapist to engage in a constant examination of his or her motives and values.

The literature calling for therapist neutrality on homosexuality abounds (Coleman, 1978; Davison, 1982; Malyon, 1985). In this culture homosexuality is stigmatized (Herek, 1988), and the therapist who is not sensitized to the effects of this on lesbians and gays is more likely to compromise the progress of the client in therapy (Isay, 1989). But further, homosexuality is stigmatized not only because of ignorance about it, but also because the understanding of human sexuality itself is extremely limited. In the absence of scientifically proven data, beliefs and politics are more likely to determine policy and practice (Schur, 1980). Indeed, this has been true of recent history with regard to homosexuality. Acknowledging this reality, gays and lesbians lobbied their professional organizations and succeeded in declassifying homosexuality as a disease (Bayer, 1981). The strategic application of political pressure, more than the persuasion of scientific evidence, effected the desired change in classification. The effects of declassification undeniably improved the lives of gays and lesbians who might seek therapy and improved the conditions under which that therapy could be offered.

Lesbian and gay psychologists learned an important lesson from this. Paradoxically, by taking more visible and patently political action in their fight against homophobia, therapists could provide more of the conditions for effective therapy, i.e., a safe environment in which the client can explore feelings and behavior with acceptance and positive regard from the therapist. To the extent that mental health is reflected in a person's having one or more socially sanctioned ways to meet his or needs, then extending those options to lesbians and gays becomes critical. But given society's injunctions against homosexuality, the therapist's work is severely hampered and undermined. Society opens few, if any, avenues to mental health for lesbians and gays (Isay, 1989). Treating the client only, especially the client who has internalized the society's homophobia, will never eliminate this damaging stressor nor successfully resolve the client's conflicts. The situation compels the therapist to press the culture to change its antihomosexual attitudes and injunctions. Consequently, psychologists have appealed to therapists to recognize the political implications in treating gays and lesbians (Hencken, 1982; Paul, 1985; Stein, 1988). Some have gone so far as to exhort therapists to social action (Moses & Hawkins, 1982; Woodman & Lenna, 1980).

Certainly in a homophobic culture, training and practice that emphasizes therapeutic neutrality becomes suspect. Such training encourages professional conduct and clinical practice that is apt to reinforce prevailing moral and political values. Further, traditional training programs have emphasized the importance of intrapsychic processes, i.e., those of the patient and those of the therapist. The social context of those relationships was largely ignored. This has led to therapist insensitivity and blindness to the impact of cultural bias on a client's behavior.

Therapeutic neutrality is an ideal to which a therapist can only aspire. For the activist therapist it is impossible. What is available to the client via the public arena cannot reasonably be excluded from the private arena of the therapy relationship. Consequently, the therapeutic neutrality an activist therapist offers cannot aim to exclude or shield his or her values or activism from the client. It may even mean that there will be considerable disclosure of the therapist's activities, conflicts, and motives. But this relaxation of orthodoxy neither disqualifies the activist as therapist nor necessarily compromises the therapy.

Instead, the activist therapist adheres to a code of strict professional boundaries. These boundaries are those psychological demarcations between the interests and welfare of the client and those of the therapist. This code implies and demands acknowledgment of the primacy of the client's needs in the therapy relationship.

This shift of emphasis from neutrality to boundaries relieves none of the therapist's responsibilities to examine his or her attitudes, feelings, and behaviors. It can, as we have seen, compound and complicate the therapy relationship. But with such a code as a guide the therapist can safely examine the meanings of his or her activism for the client without denying the importance of the activism for the therapist.

REFERENCES

1. Anthony, B. (1985). Lesbian client-lesbian therapist opportunities and challenges in working together. In J. Gonsiorek (Eds.), *A guide to psychotherapy with gay and lesbian clients* (pp. 49–57). New York: Harrington Park.
2. Bayer, R. (1981). *Homosexuality and American psychiatry: The politics of diagnosis*. New York: Basic Books.
3. Coleman, E. (1978). Toward a new model of treatment of homosexuality: A review. *Journal of Homosexuality, 3/4*, 345–359.
4. Davison, G. (1982). Politics, ethics, and therapy for homosexuality. In W. Paul, J. Weinrich, J. Gonsiorek, & M. Hotvedt (Eds.), *Homosexuality: Social, psychological and biological issues* (pp. 89–98). Beverly Hills: Sage.
5. de Montflores, C. (1986). Notes on the management of difference. In T. Stein & C. Cohen (Eds.), *Contemporary perspectives on psychotherapy with lesbians and gay men* (pp. 73–101). New York: Plenum.
6. Fein, S., & Neuhring, E. (1981). Intrapsychic effects of stigma: A process of breakdown and reconstruction of social reality. *Journal of Homosexuality, 7*, 3–13.
7. Hencken, J. (1982). Homosexuality and psychoanalysis: Toward a mutual understanding. In W. Paul, J. Weinrich, J. Gonsiorek, & M. Hotvedt (Eds.), *Homosexuality: Social, psychological and biological issues* (pp. 121–147). Beverly Hills: Sage.
8. Herek, G. (1988). An epidemic of stigma: Public reactions to AIDS. *American Psychologist, 43*, 886–891.
9. Isay, R. A. (1989). *Being homosexual: Gay men and their development*. New York: Farrar, Straus & Giroux.
10. Jacob, J., & Tedford, W. (1980). Factors affecting the self-esteem of the homosexual individual. *Journal of Homosexuality, 5*, 373–382.
11. Kus, R. (1988). Alcoholism and non-acceptance of gay self: The critical link. *Journal of Homosexuality, 15*, 25–41.
12. Lee, J. (1977). Going public: A study in the sociology of homosexual liberation. *Journal of Homosexuality, 3*, 49–78.

13. Malyon, A. (1985). Psychotherapeutic implications of internalized homophobia. In J. Gonsiorek (Ed.), A guide to psychotherapy with gay men and lesbian clients (pp. 59–69). New York: Harrington Park.

14. McConnaughy, E. (1987). The person of the therapist in psychotherapeutic practice. *Psychotherapy, 24,* 303–314.

15. McDonald, G. (1982). Individual differences in the coming out process for gay men: Implications for theoretical models. *Journal of Homosexuality, 8,* 47–60.

16. Moses, A., & Hawkins, R. (1982). *Counseling lesbian women and gay men.* St. Louis: C. V. Mosby.

17. Paul, J. (1985). Bisexuality: Reassessing our paradigms of sexuality. *Journal of Homosexuality, 11,* 21–34.

18. Rochlin, M. (1985). Sexual orientation of the therapist and therapeutic effectiveness with gay clients. In J. Gonsiorek (Ed.), *A guide to psychotherapy with gay and lesbian clients* (pp. 21–29). New York: Harrington Park.

19. Schur, E. (1980). *The politics of deviance: Stigma contests and the use of power.* Englewood Cliffs, NJ: Prentice-Hall.

20. Seligson, R. (1977). Internalization of the therapeutic alliance. *Psychotherapy: Theory, Research and Practice, 14,* 242–244.

21. Sophie, J. (1987). Internalized homophobia and lesbian identity. *Journal of Homosexuality, 14,* 53–65.

22. Stein, T. (1988). Theoretical considerations in psychotherapy with gay men and lesbians. *Journal of Homosexuality, 15,* 75–95.

23. Tripp, C. (1975). *The homosexual matrix.* New York: McGraw-Hill.

24. Wingrove, B., & Rodway, M. (1985). *The healthy homosexual.* Roslyn Heights, NY: Libra.

25. Woodman, N., & Lenna, H. (1980). *Counseling with gay men and women: A guide for facilitating positive life-styles.* San Francisco: Jossey-Bass.

5

DIANNE ELISE

When Sexual and Romantic Feelings Permeate the Therapeutic Relationship

SINCE FREUD'S 1915 PAPER on transference love, very little has been written on the subject of erotic transference and countertransference. Papers by Blum (1973), Person (1985), Rappaport (1955), and Searles (1959), comprise the main contributions to the literature on this topic. I have previously reviewed this literature in depth (Elise, 1988) in an effort to underscore how limited our treatment has been of this topic that is so crucial to clinical practice. Freud cautioned clinicians that erotic transference and our responses to it would be a difficult yet centrally important issue. This warning is taken up and elaborated upon by the above mentioned authors. However, while the warning is given, not much help is provided.

In addition to this scarcity of literature, I have found, in my own experience and that of others, that there are also few courses in training institutions that deal with erotic transference, even though it is a frequently acknowledged phenomenon. Even less attention is given to erotic countertransference. This situation seems ironic given that the erotic transference is a cornerstone of psychoanalytic theory and practice, and that psychotherapists seem to feel a number of confusing and distressing feelings in response to this transference.

While therapists easily acknowledge the existence of erotic transference, we are often plagued by questions regarding this phenomenon. Is erotic transference an inevitable part of the therapeutic process? Is it defensive, a resistance to the therapy as a whole? Should it be "all gone" when the therapy ends? What if it was never present? What is much less openly acknowledged is the presence of an erotic countertransference that raises particularly difficult issues in our efforts towards effective treatment. My focus here is on the somewhat taboo realm where sexual and romantic feelings permeate the therapeutic relationship.

Person (1985) writes:

Despite the current ascendency of the belief that transference is the most effective vehicle for psychoanalytic intervention, the erotic transference maintains its problematic connotations. Compared with other types of transference, it has always been tainted by unsavory associations and continues to be thought of as slightly disreputable. It remains both goldmine and minefield. (p. 163)

Person goes on to mention that "in homosexual women erotic transference may be extremely intense and occur with some regularity" (p. 170). In an article about women in therapy and variables associated with the gender of the therapist, Person (1983) makes a similar comment about the intensity of erotic transference in lesbians in therapy with women therapists. She adds that "this is a difficult transference to interpret or manage and often leads to the disruption of treatment" (p. 201). This statement has strong implications for clinicians treating lesbian clients. The fact that this is a most problematic transference manifestation is explicitly stated. What is only alluded to is that countertransference is also quite difficult to manage.

Much progress has been made towards a positive conceptualization of countertransference as a form of empathic identification and a source of important information about the client (Ogden, 1982). In the classic psychoanalytic definition, countertransference—the projection of the therapist's own unconscious or unresolved issues onto the client—was to be avoided or, at least, kept to a minimum. More recently, countertransference has been defined to include the therapist's reciprocal responses to the client's transference—taking on the role or feelings of the object/parents—and the therapist's identification with the client's often unconscious sense of self. In this expanded definition, countertransference is viewed not only as helpful, but essential to the therapeutic process. However, a taboo still seems to hold regarding erotic countertransference.

It is much easier to acknowledge feelings of nurturance, anger, boredom, or even hate, than sexual love towards one's clients, and erotic countertransference elicits high levels of anxiety in therapists. Feelings on the part of both client *and therapist* threaten the participants and the treatment. I have chosen highly selective and condensed aspects of therapeutic work with a lesbian client to illustrate these difficult twin themes of erotic transference and countertransference.

CLIENT AND THERAPIST

My new client stormed down the hall to my office. She was following behind me, yet I had the feeling that I was only just keeping ahead of her. She then strode past me into the office, seated herself, and directed her gaze towards me. It was a very intense look: curious, somewhat suspicious, with just the slightest hint of self-protectiveness. I felt somewhat taken aback.

Her name was Dale; she was in her early thirties, just a few years younger than me. She had dark hair and blue eyes and at 5'10" she towered over me. Her general appearance was that of a physically power-ful, athletic-looking woman. She worked in a large advertising agency at a fast-paced, highly stressful, dynamic job in a male domain requiring her to be energetic and competitive. Her regular routine involved much verbal interaction with people selling her ideas. She was quick witted and articu-late.

Dale's reasons for seeking therapy were somewhat vague but seemed to center on a love relationship that she had been in for several years. She was dissatisfied with the relationship but felt very conflicted about how to get out of it. She had had a number of love relationships with other women over the preceding twelve years. These relationships had been of varying intensity, commitment, and duration and there was a sense of their being threaded together, with one relationship leading to the next. Dale expressed the idea that she might need to be in therapy for reasons beyond leaving her present lover. She then announced that she would "give me" three months!

During the next weeks, I learned that my client's mother had been the wife of a business executive. The father was frequently away from home during Dale's childhood and there was much underlying anxiety on the part of the mother and children regarding his absence. Dale's only sibling, her sister, was four years younger than she. When Dale was twelve, her father was killed in a plane crash while on a business trip.

Dale felt very close to, and somewhat protective of, her mother and younger sister, especially after her father's death. Dale had always been a tomboy. Her mother seemed to accept and even like Dale's active, aggressive nature and commented that Dale "took after" her father. Dale was proud of her father. He had always seemed a powerful and interesting figure. She was also very angry at him for his frequent absences and final "desertion" of the family.

As a child, Dale was aware of having crushes on women teachers and then, during adolescence, on girlfriends. During high school she dated a little and had a boyfriend. She enjoyed the companionship and sex but did not seem to take her relationship with this boy very seriously. In college she developed a sexual relationship with another young woman and has since identified herself as a lesbian.

Dale's sense of self rests upon a fairly prominent masculine identification. Typically, her love relationships are with women who are generally perceived as feminine. Dale is the aggressor, sexually and otherwise, and maintains a sense of being in control. Almost any *close* relationship with another woman is sexualized and her friendship circle is composed almost entirely of ex-lovers.

These aspects of Dale's character bear directly on the psychodynamic issue most central to the therapy and to the present topic of erotic transference and countertransference. There is a difficulty regarding the vulnerability and dependency that is an essential aspect for the client of the psychotherapeutic process. For a woman who is used to the opposite—being powerful and in control—this relational setting challenges her personal sense of identity and safety. A demand is imposed by the therapeutic context to develop an intimate, but nonsexualized relationship with another woman. Intimacy under these conditions posed a threat to Dale's sense of self as an individual, as a woman, and as a lesbian.

COURSE OF TREATMENT

Dale typically started sessions by sitting forward on her chair, leaning towards me with forearms on knees and feet planted firmly apart. She would look me very directly in the eye and make her initial remark in the form of a dramatic pronouncement. I tended to feel as if a ball had been thrown at me which I was not quite prepared to catch. This feeling of being somewhat caught off guard came up repeatedly throughout our sessions. I understood these countertransference feelings as reflecting my client's need to act upon me rather than be acted upon. Her manner served to deny vulnerability, softness, and uncertainty on her part and to induce these feelings in me. I felt "little"—physically and psychologically.

After a few months (she had lifted the time-limit for therapy), I began to feel that something about Dale's demeanor towards me was sexualized. No obvious flirtation was present nor was any direct reference made to anything sexual or romantic in relation to me. There was just a subtle feeling in the room—a certain subliminal quality in the interaction. It seemed to me objectionably narcissistic to decide that a client was attracted to me when, as yet, there were so few clues. I felt this objection even as I reminded myself that an attraction would be transference, not a statement about me personally. However, these distinctions are more easily maintained in theory than in actual experience. I found myself thinking that certain similarities did exist in appearance, manner, and personality between myself and the women that Dale found appealing. In determining that, yes, I could be considered "her type," I was then brought face to face with the uncomfortable question of whether or not she was *my* type! While not conscious of feeling attracted to her in a sexual or romantic way, I had to conclude that she was.

As the therapy proceeded I did receive more clues to aid my understanding of the transference. It became clear that Dale was very flirtatious in her interactions with other women and had been told on many occasions that she is quite seductive. Friendships kept progressing to sexualized relationships. I became confident that my perceptions regarding an erotic transference were accurate. However, any attempt to interpret this transference was met with flat denial. My client was emphatic that she did *not* feel sexual towards me. I could not get her to examine why I seemed to hold this rather exceptional position. Dale's platonic feeling toward me seemed a striking contrast to her tendency to sexualize close relationships with women. Resistance to the *awareness* of erotic transference was quite high.

I continued to experience a rather urgent, insistent quality in the transference and an increasing sense of feeling seduced. I also felt that my sense of reality was challenged as my client was denying that she wanted anything from me but "friendship." She started to pursue the idea that we should stop therapy and become friends. She was quite persistent in this idea. We were now in the tenth month of therapy and I was feeling quite anxious about my ability to continue to appear poised and in control in the face of this disavowed seduction.

On one occasion she slowly ran her eyes up and down my body and I thought, "That's it! I can't take this anymore." I had spent weeks feeling vulnerable, sexually aggressed upon, and worried that I was blushing.

These feelings, which can be quite pleasurable in another context, felt very threatening to my identity as a therapist. I was experiencing strong, guilt-inducing condemnation from my superego; I judged my feelings as inappropriate to my role as a therapist. I responded to her next pressing reference that we become "friends" with a very firm, direct statement that that was not possible now or ever.

In response to this intervention, my client felt that she had had her hands slapped in a very harsh manner. As a result of this interaction, any evidence of the erotic transference, or countertransferential experience of it, went underground for the next year. I felt both relieved at the abated assault on the boundaries of the therapy relationship and guilty that I had given my client such a strong sense of being rejected that she could no longer express these erotic feelings in the transference in any way. During this next period in the therapy, Dale finally left her lover of five years by starting an affair with a nurse, which lasted for the next year. Attempts to analyze these events in her external life in relation to recent events in the treatment were largely unsuccessful. She greeted the idea that she had substituted another woman in the helping professions for me as preposterous. In her mind, this constituted yet another example of her therapist's apparent egocentricity.

It was not until the beginning of the third year of therapy that we were able to return to the dynamics of erotic transference and countertransference for a second look. Elements of seductiveness started to reappear in the transference. My belief was that this second attempt was now possible due to the work that had been done in the interim, the subsequent increase in trust on her part, and her own strongly felt sense that I was now more valuable to her as her therapist than as a friend or lover.

The reemergence of the erotic transference appeared with full intensity. At this point I felt much more prepared to handle the high-level erotic tension in the room and the resultant countertransference feeling that I was being pulled out of my role. Dale became more able to directly acknowledge that her feelings had a strong sexual/romantic component, which is reflected in her statement, "I don't *always* want to seduce you." Ambivalence is evident in the way that such a sexually provocative statement is put in the negative. Several sessions later:

CLIENT   You know what I was thinking last night (face alive, eyes sparkling)?

THERAPIST   (I say nothing, but have an inquiring look.)

CLIENT   You are a *beautiful* woman.

THERAPIST   (Inwardly I gulp. I am reasonably attractive, but certainly
not beautiful. Even though my intellect tells me that this view of me is
transference-based, my personal narcissism makes it difficult for me
to remain unmoved by this declaration and now—two seconds have
elapsed—I am worried about the fact that I am sure I am blushing. I
wonder about the lighting, hoping that she cannot detect this coloring
and, finally—three seconds have elapsed—I manage to say with poise,
composure, and a somewhat dulled tone:)
    How do you feel telling me that you find me to be beautiful?

    The tension of these moments and of the next ten minutes was such that I
had amnesia for subsequent dialogue by the end of the session. However, I
do vividly remember the feelings I had of extreme interpersonal tension at
being overtly wooed, feeling seduced, and all the while maintaining (I hoped)
a calm, unruffled, therapeutic demeanor. I do not find it half so difficult
within the therapeutic context to cover feelings of hate or intense boredom
as I do those of sexual vulnerability. Even under great duress, some show of
anger does not seem as inappropriate as any indication of sexual responsive-
ness to a client. I felt psychically undressed by this woman, and worst of all,
on one level this feeling was not entirely unpleasant!
    I want to emphasize the difficulty of managing these countertransference
tensions in the situation of a face-to-face psychotherapy. Unlike psychoanalysis where no burden is placed on the unseen analyst to appear any
particular way, in a vis-àvis treatment a very difficult element is added.
Dealing with erotic transference and countertransference while sitting directly across from one another is much more problematic. An entire range
of body language, facial expression, and eye contact is included in what is
responded to and what needs to be managed.
    I have experienced considerable difficulty in my efforts to control my
expression. I have mentioned the example of blushing. I have worried
about a reciprocal sparkle in *my* eyes or a vulnerable smile on my face. I
believe that my client *must* be able to detect in my face some element of
this tension. Even if, with my considerable abilities at self-concealment,
she cannot *consciously* identify my feelings, psychoanalytic training tells us
that clients *can* on some level identify different emotional tones in us.
Surely my "neutral" expression covering this sexualized tension must look
different from my "neutral" expression covering a range of emotions from
fury to boredom.

However, as difficult as these aspects of face-to-face treatment may be, they can also provide a path towards understanding the underlying psychological meaning of erotic transference for a given client. Generally, I maintain continuous visual contact with a client. When my client decides to look at me we are then engaged in a mutual gaze. Dale tended to direct a gaze towards me that in itself was very seductive and overwhelming. I felt that I could not break eye contact even though I wanted to look away to escape the emotional intensity. Once again I felt as if she could catch and keep me in a vulnerable position. I felt trapped. Finally, I was able to address this situation directly:

THERAPIST   How are you feeling as you look at me?
CLIENT   Umm, I don't know. (long pause as she continues her smoldering gaze)
THERAPIST   I notice that you keep looking at me and you know that I will continue to look at you. What is happening here such that you continue to gaze at me knowing that I won't look away? What do you think is going on in the room between us?
CLIENT   (She makes a few comments to the effect that she merely looks at me while she is thinking or wondering what I am thinking.)
THERAPIST   Does anything about this eye contact feel sexual to you?
CLIENT   Well, yes . . . I have this fantasy of coming over and sitting in your lap and distracting you.
THERAPIST   (Oh, dear.) Distracting me from what?
CLIENT   Well . . . from seeing me—from seeing who I am.

She went on to express that she looks at me when she feels in danger of exposure. Her gaze is a beam that prevents me from seeing her as weak or vulnerable. It was this feeling of being vulnerable and overpowered and of *being seen* that had been engendered in me and so preoccupied my thoughts.

This transference-countertransference interaction constitutes a clear example of projective identification as described by Ogden (1982). Feelings that were experienced by this client as objectionable and unmanageable were projected into me to "hold" and to come to terms with in some manner. My client interacted with me in an actual way—sexual seduction—such as to induce in me these feelings of sexualized vulnerability and dependency, and the subsequent confusion and overstimulation. In this manner, longed-for intimacy could be established, but with my client in the aggressive role that she felt psychologically comfortable with, and with me in the vulnerable position by which she was so threatened. The therapy was now at a point where this process could be articulated. We were then able to address her fear of vulnerability and dependency directly.

This client's sense of self had been based on being strong and protective as she had imagined herself to be as a child in relation to her mother and sister. Acceptance and love from important people in her life did not seem to attend upon being weak and dependent. As she and her mother and sister waited out her father's absences, her intrapsychic task was to take over for her father. Even he encouraged this identification: "You take care of your mother and sister for me." The mother was longing for the father and was unconsciously receptive to a young girl taking on some of the husband's position as an object in her—the mother's—internal world.

My client believed that being needy and vulnerable meant the exposure of a weak and flawed self that certainly would be rejected. In the transference she attempted to connect with me in the manner that had seemed acceptable to her mother. By being aggressively seductive she sent the message that she would be strong and would protect a vulnerable and dependent me (mother). Correspondingly, I experienced actual feelings and fantasies that she could and would take care of me.

This transference message was infused with all the oedipal-level eroticism that had originally been directed primarily towards the mother. In the countertransference, I experienced myself as the oedipal mother who in actuality feels like an oedipal daughter who has lost her father. However, the mother now has a chance to regain this husband (father) through her own daughter. In effect, the mother is "remarried" through her daughter to the absent/lost husband (father). In addition to taking my place countertransferentially in my client's family constellation, I experienced the revival of personal feelings of the loss of and longing for my own father—a powerful combination.

As we were able to articulate and examine these dynamics, my client's fears of dependency could be worked through. Rather than projecting aspects of her own intrapsychic experience into me, the client could acknowledge and talk about these thoughts and feelings. Previously in the treatment, I had had only fleeting maternal feelings due to my client's avoidance of dependency. Her defenses against feelings of vulnerability inhibited any reciprocal countertransference of nurturance and protectiveness. Now, seduction and eroticism ebbed out of both the transference and countertransference as my client got "younger" and more vulnerable, and I experienced, for the first time, sustained maternal feelings in the countertransference.

The working through of these dynamics took us well into the fourth year of treatment. At present we are ending the sixth year and are approaching termination. The resolution of intense fear and conflict regarding dependency has allowed the client to establish a love relationship that is based on a more equal exchange of vulnerability and nurturance and on a deeper level of commitment. The therapeutic relationship, no longer beset by sexualized interpersonal tension, has deepened in trust and intimacy.

DISCUSSION

Searles (1989) states that: "Just as the patient must be able to develop transference, the therapist must be able to develop corresponding countertransference." However, managing countertransference once it does develop can be quite a task. Certainly my own romantic/sexual feelings were an unfailing reminder that this issue was most important in the face of the client's denial. By their intensity, these feelings which were induced in me gave me a vivid sense of what my client was grappling with on an unconscious level. My sense of exposed vulnerability and conflicted longing for dependency was a definite indicator that this was the central dynamic conflict for this client. I do not think that I would have known of my client's internal world as quickly, accurately, and deeply without my countertransference, but the experience itself underscores for me that in our peculiar profession we have a strange way of working!

Further Dilemmas

The relatively clear resolution of erotic elements in the case just presented belies the ongoing plethora of confused questioning regarding erotic transference and countertransference. In addition to the difficulties already made evident, further complexities are encountered. Aspects of the erotic transference, potentially quite threatening to the therapist, are in danger of being viewed as purely defensive. In interpreting the defensive function of erotic transference, therapists are likely to be gratifying their own underlying wish to "analyze it away." We need to consider the nondefensive aspects of even a highly sexualized erotic transference.

In the case just presented, I was very uncomfortable with my client's seduction of me and this seduction *did* mask other dynamics; however, some aspect of my client's ability to present herself as sexually attractive and compelling, as able to go after what she felt she wanted, and as protectively nurturing indicates certain strengths within her character that should not be dismissed. The question arises as to where in a treatment it is appropriate to give recognition to this fact. If I acknowledge her strengths on this level does this acknowledgment then place us more on an equal footing than our roles usually seem to allow? Is such an acknowledgment one expression of my therapeutic task or does it indicate my having been seduced out of my role and, thus, a loss of the therapeutic boundary and space? A client's ability to be *successfully* seductive in terms of feelings engendered in the therapist leads to very subtle, yet highly complex, therapeutic dilemmas.

To further complicate matters, a paradox exists regarding the issue of vulnerability and dependency. As therapists, we try to convey to our clients that they can be vulnerable and dependent with us and still be respected as individuals with personal strengths. Do we "model" this in reverse? If a client sees some hint of seduced vulnerability on our face are we undone in our therapeutic position of power and respect? It is paradoxical that we, as therapists, adopt a position of unflagging power and poise, yet attempt to instill in clients a belief that nothing will be lost in being vulnerable and exposed.

I was attempting to work through these very issues with Dale, yet, I felt terribly concerned, even after months and years of treatment with an unfailing therapeutic demeanor on my part, that a fraction of a second of possibly perceived sexualized vulnerability on my part would undo my role and my power to be helpful to her. What *does* it mean to the therapy if our clients perceive that we are affected, *deeply* affected, by them and by their feelings, whether strength or defense?

Guidelines

We are not totally in the dark. In looking at our clinical work, the central point to remember with regard to an erotic transference is that it *has some meaning*. When present, an erotic transference not only needs to be acknowledged, but should be seen as reflecting some very important, and personally specific information which needs to be explored, understood, and worked through. Merely noting the existence of an erotic transference, taking it for granted as some fact about the client or of the therapy and going on, will lead to trouble. I believe that this transference becomes unmanageably intense and leads to treatment disruption because it is so often ignored or denied in therapy as it is in the literature and in training.

Much of my experience with erotic transference has been with lesbian clients and particularly with women who share certain history and personality factors in common. These women have had a relatively early awareness of sexual/romantic feelings toward other females. Feelings of being in love with the mother, women teachers, and/or other female adults, existed in childhood, and a fairly acute awareness of erotic feelings toward other girls existed during adolescence. This awareness is in contrast to the history of many lesbians who have had a basically heterosexual identity through their teens and early adulthood, with boyfriends and even marriage, before "coming out." I view the former group of lesbians as having a stronger masculine identification in their personality structure. By this I mean that their character is built more along lines that we typically think of as masculine and ascribe to males, one that is usually based on an internalization of the father or of the "masculine" in the mother. I regret that we have no classification terms other than "masculine" and "feminine" because this division seems to imply that only males should have masculine traits and vice versa. I do not view a masculine identification in a woman as pathological but as atypical in our culture, just as lesbianism itself is atypical.

A dominant motif in these women's personalities is an avoidance of dependency or feelings of vulnerability, and a tendency to turn hurt feelings into anger. The most comfortable psychological states consist of being in control, being angry, and being sexually aggressive. The erotic transference develops almost immediately and quite intensively with the aim, usually unconscious, of avoiding the dependency and vulnerability inherent in the role of client. Instead, the intent is to turn things around: to become dominant in the relationship by an aggressive seduction which leaves the therapist feeling vulnerable and out of control.

The therapeutic task involves analyzing the seductiveness (which the client often denies) as reflecting intolerance of dependency needs and discomfort with vulnerability and with feelings other than anger. Due to anxiety over erotic feelings toward girlfriends all through the teen years, this particular subgroup of lesbians often has not had the experience of highly intimate, but clearly platonic, "girlfriend" relationships. Instead, all girlfriends become lovers and eventually most love relationships then develop into friendships. Thus, the therapy relationship is often the first situation where intimacy occurs without sexuality—an uncomfortable experience for women who have been familiar with intimacy mainly in the context of feeling sexually powerful.

Just as *meaning* is the key factor in dealing with erotic transference, *awareness* is crucial to management of countertransference reaction to erotic transference. A myriad of reasons exist for remaining unaware of erotic transference and countertransference, underscoring that erotic transference is a "treatment complication" (Person, 1985) primarily for the therapist. Erotic countertransference is feared to be "bad" as the literature indicates. The sense of taboo surrounding erotic feeling in the therapeutic context results in therapists wanting to ignore these feelings.

Erotic countertransference can also feel embarrassing and can entail a level of vulnerability that is quite at odds with our identities as therapists to be calm, confident, and in control. Most of us have some level of countertransference difficulty with a client's anger, yet it is much easier to inquire about anger in the transference. At the vaguest hint we will go on a "fishing expedition" for angry feelings. A very different situation exists with regard to eroticism in the transference. Often we must be hit over the head with sexuality before we bring it up. It is difficult for a therapist to suggest that her client is feeling sexual towards her and especially so when the client is unaware of, or denies, these feelings.

When one *is* hit over the head with these feelings, it is very hard to discuss them in the midst of feeling seduced. The intensity of erotic transference and erotic countertransference can lead to the therapist feeling out of control. These feelings of vulnerability are out of character with our role. I find it *the* most difficult situation in which to maintain my composure. I can be quite comfortable and confident of my neutral expression with a range of feelings, even feelings of hating my client. Feeling sexually aggressed upon makes me worry about blushing, stuttering, my mouth trembling, or a tense, embarrassed smile appearing completely against my volition. I have spent entire sessions with my hand against my mouth in order to "hold my face together."

Usually therapists are aware of the need to talk about erotic transference feelings with the client. However, the problem exists that just "talking about it" does not necessarily help diminish the intensity of feeling. Direct discussion can even *increase* these feelings. In personal life, talking about an attraction with the person involved is a heady experience; this is true in therapy as well. One has to have a theoretical conceptualization of erotic transference meanings and defensive value and one must interpret these in order to lessen the intensity of this transference (and countertransference).

Person (1985) noted the intensity of this transference for lesbian clients in treatment with female therapists. It is significant, I think, that this is a context involving two women. This intensity of erotic transference and countertransference in a therapy where both client and therapist are women can be understood in light of the recent focus on differences in female and male relational styles. Chodorow (1978) has described female ego boundaries as more permeable and the sense of self as more relationally defined. Work by Rubin (1985) and Berzon (1988) focuses on merger and intensity of feeling between heterosexual women friends. I have developed the thesis that nonpathological merger is more likely to evolve in lesbian couples than in heterosexual or gay male couples due to the fact that two *women* are involved (Elise, 1986a, 1986b). It seems that when two women are in a relationship, emotional bonds of an intense nature can develop. It should not surprise us that this can include the therapeutic relationship as well, nor should we be surprised that sexual/romantic feelings might be experienced and deeply felt.

A related factor, with particular clinical implications, is that, paradoxically, women often tend to remain unconscious of erotic feelings toward anyone and especially toward other women for a longer time than men do in their relationships. Women are used to being intimate friends with one another. Platonic elements are focused on, especially by the therapist, as these elements of nurturance and support are felt to be consonant with her role. As the relationship develops, sexual feelings build unconsciously out of the increasing intimacy. By the time sexual feelings are consciously acknowledged, they may have reached quite a pitch.

With specific reference to lesbian clients in therapy with lesbian therapists, further assaults on boundary exist. I have just mentioned increased empathic identification and merger between any two women and the tendency, even for most lesbians, to focus initially on platonic versus erotic intimacy, thus creating a potential time bomb effect. In addition, identification by lesbians as members of a discriminated against subgroup can lead to "let's stick together" feelings for both client and therapist. The therapist can then overempathize with the client, get lost in the transference, and stop functioning therapeutically. Furthermore, identity as a lesbian includes a sense of being a social outlaw. Since certain codes of behavior are already broken by, and in the service of, sexual love for another woman, the likelihood of recreating this dynamic in therapy seems high. Forbidden, secret, sexual love for another woman is a dominant motif in both the client's and the therapist's life.

With regard to the issue of reality-testing—recognizing that the therapist is just that, a therapist, and unavailable as a future lover—one must also consider that the reality in the feminist therapy and humanistic psychology movements during the 1970s did allow for the therapy relationship to be ended in favor of a personal relationship. Many of our clients know of someone who did end up in a love relationship with a former therapist. Many clients at this particular historical point believe, somewhat realistically, that a therapy relationship could be dissolved in favor of the "natural" attraction that is felt. In combination with the above mentioned factors, this unfortunate historical situation leads to further boundary loss for clients and therapists in coping with erotic transference and countertransference.

CONCLUSION

Loosening of ego boundaries for client and therapist is inherent in any depth-therapy relationship and I believe this is especially so for two women, regardless of sexual orientation. For the woman therapist, the female tendency towards boundary loss in the service of empathy and connection is both a strength and a vulnerability in her therapeutic work. The ability to feel, not just think about, what is occurring with clients allows for another level of awareness of transference dynamics and is the basis for becoming "countertransference experts." However, psychotherapists are vulnerable to becoming lost in feelings and losing the anchor of understanding and meaning. In the situation of erotic transference and countertransference, as elsewhere, the struggle with therapeutic empathy requires both an awareness of feelings and an understanding of meanings. This is true for therapists of either gender. Empathy is not merger: It is the paradoxical ability to *both cross and keep* the boundary between one's self and another person. This has proved a most difficult task in the realm of erotic transference and countertransference.

REFERENCES

1. Berzon, J. (1988, March). *Fusion and women's friendships: Implications for expanding our adult developmental theories.* Paper presented at the annual meeting of Division 39, Psychoanalytic Psychology, APA, San Francisco. Manuscript submitted for publication.
2. Blum, H. (1973). The concept of erotized transference. *Journal of the American Psychoanalytic Association, 21,* 6176.
3. Chodorow, N. (1978). *The reproduction of mothering.* Berkeley: University of California Press.

4. Elise, D. (1986a). Lesbian couples: The implications of sex differences in separation-individuation. *Dissertation Abstracts International, 47*, 1704B. (University Microfilms No. 86-13, 538)

5. Elise, D. (1986b). Lesbian couples: The implications of sex differences in separation-individuation. *Psychotherapy, 23* (2), 30510.

6. Elise, D. (1988, October). *The erotic transference and countertransference*. Paper presented at Saturday Seminars, El Cerrito, CA.

7. Freud, S. (1915 1914). Observations on transference-love In J. Strachey (Ed. and Trans.), *The standard edition of the complete psychological works of Sigmund Freud* (Vol. 12, pp. 159171). New York: Norton.

8. Ogden, T. (1982). *Projective identification and psychotherapeutic technique*. New York: Jason Aronson.

9. Person, E. (1983). Women in therapy: Therapist gender as a variable. *International Review of Psycho-analysis, 10*, 193203.

10. Person, E. (1985). The erotic transference in women and in men: Differences and consequences. *Journal of the American Academy of Psychoanalysis, 13*, (2), 159180.

11. Rappaport, E. (1955). The management of an eroticized transference. *Psychoanalytic Quarterly, 25*, 515529.

12. Rubin, L. (1985). *Just friends: The role of friendship in our lives*. New York: Harper & Row.

13. Searles, H. (1959). Oedipal love in the countertransference. *International Journal of Psycho-analysis, 40*, 180190.

14. Searles, H. (1989, December). *The psychodynamics of borderline patients*. Paper presented at The Psychological Forum: Psychoanalytic psychotherapy with borderline patients, San Francisco, CA.

6

JOHN C. GONSIOREK

Short-Term Treatment of a Multiply Abused Young Man With Confusion About Sexual Identity

T HIS CASE STUDY describes a young man who had been physically and verbally abused by an older brother and, later, emotionally and sexually abused by a psychotherapist. This client also presented longstanding confusion over sexual orientation. This case is also of interest because a short-term directive model was used, in which the client was an active participant and the treatment goals limited and explicit. Finally, in this relatively short treatment, strong countertransference challenges emerged.

THE CASE STUDY

Matthew appeared for an intake interview in March 1989 having been referred from an HIV-antibody screening clinic. He had requested HIV-antibody screening even though his only risk behavior was a single incident of same-sex contact in which his risk was very low. The HIV counselor recommended a referral for psychotherapy.

Matthew appeared as a nervous, conservatively dressed young man who, after exchanging some pleasantries and admitting his obvious nervousness, proceeded to outline his concerns in an orderly manner. He noted that because of his nervousness about seeking psychotherapy, he had carefully prepared what he wanted to say. Matthew described his problem areas as confusion about his sexual orientation, a history of physical abuse by his older brother, and problems with his former psychotherapist, who had initiated a sexual relationship after therapy.

Matthew described same-sex interests as far back as he could remember but had effectively repressed them. Early in college he met a woman, Carol, with whom he became close friends. The relationship became romantic and eventually sexual. This was Matthew's first sexual relationship. He described it as characterized by a deep friendship, trust, and open communication. He eventually confided his growing awareness of same-sex desires to Carol; her response was accepting.

Later, Matthew and Carol decided to separate amicably. They both felt they should date others as they had been each other's first relationship. In retrospect, Matthew believed his continuing confusion over sexual orientation also figured unconsciously in the separation. They maintained a strong friendship during this period. Concurrently, Matthew experienced an increase in anxiety symptoms. His second female lover, who knew of his history of physical abuse, suggested that these were related and urged him to seek counseling.

Matthew had never made this connection, but accepted this advice and sought therapy from one of the staff at the college counseling office. This occurred in his junior year. The therapy initially focused on Matthew's relationship with his older brother and related family issues, as well as Matthew's significant problems in managing anxiety. The therapy was weekly and was interrupted during the summer vacation between his junior and senior years when Matthew was away from the campus. In the fall of his senior year, he first informed his therapist about his sexual orientation concerns. Matthew felt that the therapy during his junior year had been helpful, and he had experienced a new confidence over the summer in handling his family and brother. After carefully considering it, he told his therapist about his same-sex feelings.

His therapist was accepting and urged him to explore his same-sex feelings. Matthew's own reaction continued to be cautious and ambivalent. During his senior year their interaction became noticeably warmer and more friendly. This was a relatively small campus where it was typical for students to live on campus, and there was much interaction between the students, faculty, and staff. As his senior year progressed, Matthew continued in weekly therapy, but their relationship also became social and at times physically affectionate, at the therapist's initiation. Matthew stated that the relationship with this therapist was one of complete trust.

Matthew and his therapist began a termination process at the end of his senior year. As the last session drew near, his therapist came out to him and told Matthew about having been married, then coming out, his own struggles with coming to terms with sexuality, and his continuing struggles about being gay and a mental health professional. While the therapist was out to friends and some people in the college community, he was not generally known to be gay, because of job security concerns. During this period there was an increase in physical affection in the form of hugs, initiated by the therapist. Matthew felt these were well-meaning attempts to reassure him, although he did not welcome or like them.

Therapy ended and Matthew was graduated shortly thereafter. He then moved back to his parents' home to begin a job search and resumed his romantic relationship with Carol. Throughout that summer and fall he maintained frequent contact with a number of friends and faculty at the college, his former therapist included. The former therapist became increasingly dependent upon Matthew. He would tell Matthew about his disappointments in trying to form a stable relationship and his fears and concerns about public disclosure. As time went on, he became increasingly demanding of Matthew's time and attention. Matthew's reaction was one of increasing discomfort; however, he felt a strong sense of obligation to his former therapist because of the help he had received from him, and he continued to trust the therapist.

The former therapist became increasingly physically affectionate; eventually, he became clearly sexual in his overtures to Matthew. Initially, Matthew responded by denying that his former therapist was attempting to be sexual, believing instead that he was merely being affectionate. As the former therapist persisted, Matthew became more ambivalent: He felt an obligation to his former therapist, yet he was not attracted sexually to him. After an interaction in which the former therapist was especially insistent, Matthew complied with his sexual demands. He found the sexual experience, which was his first with a man, profoundly upsetting and disorienting.

The former therapist responded by becoming even more emotionally dependent and demanding. He described himself as being in love with Matthew. Matthew could no longer bear these demands and told the therapist he was uncomfortable with any physical contact, did not want any further sexual interaction, and simply wanted to be friends. The former therapist was angry and hurt, but backed off. Since that time, however, the therapist had been escalating his emotional and physical demands to the point where, at the time Matthew presented for the initial intake, he was again finding it unbearable. A few months after the sexual contact, Matthew accepted a work assignment in the Midwest and soon after presented for therapy.

Even though the therapy had technically "ended," Matthew reported that many of the conversations with his "former" therapist were about the issues he discussed in therapy: his family, his anxiety, and his confusion over his sexuality. The former therapist continued to play the role of the "objective expert," and implied that Matthew's sexuality was homosexual.

Developmental History

Matthew is the third of six children of a middle-class, religious, Irish Catholic family on the East Coast. His father put himself through a professional education. Matthew described his father as a quiet, passive man who worked very hard and was devoted to his family, but who did not have a great deal of time for them due to career demands. Nevertheless, Matthew felt he could count on love and support from his father.

He described his mother as loving, but passive and unassertive, a homemaker who was devoted to her family but naive and uninformed about the outside world. Communication within the family was indirect.

Matthew described the second oldest brother as having longstanding problems. This brother was physically violent to the point of being brutal and sadistic. Matthew was the most frequent target of his brother's aggressiveness. The parents were ineffectual in handling his brother. Matthew described a childhood filled with verbal taunting and severe physical beatings. Matthew minimized the amount of verbal and physical abuse inflicted by his brother for fear of upsetting his parents. However, in his adolescence, the violence increased to the point where Matthew began to fear for his physical safety and even his life. His complaints to his parents became more urgent. Initially, they minimized the extent of his brother's behavior, but as Matthew obviously became more panicked, they "talked to" the brother. This had the effect of reducing the amount of physical violence, although verbal threats and intimidation continued. As Matthew matured, he became adept at avoiding his brother and spent much of his adolescence away from home whenever his brother was present. He retreated to his studies and a small group of friends.

Matthew reports no history of alcohol or drug abuse in himself or his family with the exception of his brother who appears to have episodic alcohol and drug abuse. Matthew and his family were without legal history except for the brother, who had a history of legal violations related to acting-out problems. Matthew reported no known history of mental problems in the family. From his description, however, his father sounded significantly depressed and his mother somewhat less so, although neither had ever sought any professional assistance. Matthew himself reported significant problems with depression and anxiety throughout most of his life, although he had only sought assistance on two occasions, once while in college and the second time in this therapy.

Specific History Related to Sexual Orientation

With one exception Matthew's sexual experiences had been heterosexual, primarily with Carol. Matthew described his sexual interest in both sexes as strong. He described his masturbation fantasies as equally oriented towards men and women. His ambient sexual attraction was predominantly towards women; however, when he found men attractive, the strength of that attraction was extremely strong, more so than his attraction for women. His sexual relationship with Carol was primarily characterized by tenderness, warmth, and physical affection. Matthew stated he could imagine a purely sexual relationship with a man but not with a woman. Instead, he saw a sexual relationship with a woman only in relational terms. He was not certain if he could envision himself in an intimate, romantic relationship with a man. He described himself as intellectually accepting homosexuality but emotionally uncomfortable with it.

Personality Dynamics

Symptomatically, Matthew met the criteria for generalized anxiety disorder. While he did not meet the criteria for dysthymia during our interactions, at earlier points in his history he would have met those criteria. I conceptualize him as an emotionally constricted individual with moderate distortions in self-esteem, excessively high and perfectionistic standards, and significant longstanding problems with anxiety. Matthew appeared to have developed and maintained a strong capability for close interpersonal relationships with Carol and other close friends, both male and female. In school and later in work, his ability to be effective and successful was strong. The effects of his two abusive situations can be conceptualized as post-traumatic stress disorders.

Treatment and Case Study Focus

The core issue in my therapy with Matthew was the resolution and integration of his sexual orientation in light of the multiple traumas to his sense of self caused by physical abuse from his brother and the sexual and emotional exploitation by his former psychotherapist.

REVIEW OF THE LITERATURE

While there is a body of information about the effects of physical, emotional, and sexual abuse upon women, literature on male victims is scant. There has been an assumption that what is known about female victims can be readily applied to male victims. There is, however, an increasing amount of questioning of the wisdom of this approach.

Recently there have been some tentative efforts to develop a specifically male perspective on the results of victimization (Bera, Gonsiorek, & LeTourneau, in press; Lew, 1988), although this literature is still in the emergent state. There are suggestions that males have a more difficult time both acknowledging that the experiences which occurred were abusive and also acknowledging the sequelae of abuse (Gonsiorek, 1989).

Another relevant area of literature regards sexual orientation, the coming-out process, and internalized homophobia. It is theorized (Gonsiorek & Rudolph, in press; Malyon, 1982) that negative societal condemnation of homosexuality is internalized as part of the sense of self in individuals who have significant same-sex feelings and attractions. This creates a variety of challenges to a positive sense of self-esteem which vary from mild to severe. These events occur somewhat later than the typical challenges involved in basic self-esteem formation and, therefore, are especially apt to be influenced by other personality dynamics and characteristics, and concurrent developmental events.

PROGRESSION OF THE CASE

Despite the wealth of writing about psychotherapy, very little is written about how one actually does therapy. In particular, the briefer therapies are poorly understood and sometimes erroneously conceptualized as being merely traditional therapies "done quickly" or "finished early." In order to elucidate a brief therapy approach, I have presented the case in detail, session by session. This illustrates important features of brief therapy technique: the acceptance of the clients' goals and pacing, the mutuality of the process, the combination of directedness in some strategic areas with "letting sleeping dogs lie" in others, and the mixture of strategized and opportunistic technique.

The psychotherapy with Matthew extended over a period of fifteen sessions from March 1989 to November 1989. There were telephone follow-ups that occurred approximately 30 and 60 days after termination.

The first session and parts of the second and third sessions were devoted to assessment and obtaining background information; however, as with many short-term therapy techniques, interventions began early in the process. During the first interview, when Matthew began talking about the relationship with his former psychotherapist, I interrupted and explained the Minnesota statutes requiring licensed health-care professionals to report unethical behavior on the part of other licensed health-care professionals. As we discussed this, Matthew determined that at this time he did not want to initiate a complaint against his former psychotherapist. I made certain that he understood that should he ever tell me the psychotherapist's name, I would be mandated to initiate a complaint.

This procedure was more than informed consent; it carried two important therapeutic messages. First, that the sexual involvement with his former therapist was a seriously unethical act and, second, that I would fully inform and involve him in important decision-making during the psychotherapy. In other words, the process of the therapy would behaviorally congruent with the therapeutic goal of empowering him.

Matthew's reaction to this was complex. He seemed relieved at my validation that the behavior of his former therapist was improper. He also seemed unnerved at the potential legal risk to his former therapist. My hypothesis was that he left that first session feeling positive about our interaction but avoidant about discussing the relationship with his former therapist, due to his ambivalent loyalty to him.

In the next two sessions Matthew focused on the physical abuse inflicted by his older brother. I suspected he was avoiding the issues of his sexual orientation and exploitation by his former therapist. The physical abuse was one of the main topics discussed in his first psychotherapy and one he felt was successfully resolved. Matthew had a very difficult time experiencing any reaction to his parents' inability to control the older brother. Despite my probing about this, he steadfastly maintained that he did not have any negative feelings towards them and that they did what they could, given their limitations and way of operating. By the end of the third session, he commented that our discussion of family issues was acutely painful to him.

Between the third and fourth sessions, Matthew visited a local gay bar. This was not something that we had discussed. He came to the fourth session eager to describe that experience. He had started talking to an attractive man who invited him to an after-hours party. At the party, he was disquieted when this individual and his friends overtly treated Matthew as "new and interesting sexual material" and found his confusion and lack of experience an erotic challenge. He abruptly left the party.

He was distressed for a number of reasons. He wanted to explore ways to meet gay men but did not want a repeat of this experience and requested information on other ways to meet men. He also felt guilty about his relationship with Carol. While they had previously discussed his same-sex interests, they had not done so recently. Matthew worried that he had passively let her think his same-sex interests were fading by not discussing them. He also experienced conflict between his own values and the values he perceived in the gay men he had met.

By the end of the third session, I had concluded that Matthew was avoiding his sexual orientation concerns and abuse by his former psychotherapist by focusing on the issue he had resolved the most, his family history. My plan was to allow him to pursue this for part of the next session if he persisted and then suggest that he was avoiding these other issues. Matthew's spontaneous pursuit of sexual orientation issues corroborated that my understanding of his defensive style was on target. During that fourth session I presented didactic material about the coming-out process and information about social alternatives in the gay community. I emphasized that his current challenge was not merely to resolve his sexual orientation but to do so in a way that was congruent with his values. I congratulated his ability to note and take seriously his emotional response to the individuals he had met. We also discussed the pros and cons of his informing Carol about the current state of his sexual orientation concerns. He concluded that he wished to do so.

In the fifth session, Matthew reported that he had informed Carol about his exploration of same-sex options. He was more reflective about his sexuality, asking follow-up questions about the coming-out process, and discussing concerns which suggested he was imagining future situations regarding his sexuality. For example, he had been thinking about how his father might handle the knowledge of his same-sex interest. Matthew wanted the approval of his father, felt strongly that his father deeply cared for him, but worried that his father might not understand.

The sixth session was difficult. Matthew was upset by feelings about his former psychotherapist and his older brother. He also was concerned about Carol as she had experienced distress when she thought more about the depth of his same-sex feelings. I noted that this therapist was the first person in whom he had fully confided the damage caused by his older brother as well as his sexual orientation. Because Matthew was in such a trusting and vulnerable position, the former therapist's behavior was exploitative. Matthew spontaneously noted that before the interaction became sexual, the former therapist had become emotionally dependent upon him, and the relationship had shifted in this manner in the later stages of the therapy. Matthew left the session feeling more ambivalent about his former therapist; he was more angry at him but also more aware of how powerful and positive that experience had been.

I ended the session by checking with Matthew about his reaction towards me. He reiterated that he felt comfortable and appreciated my directness, which was in contrast to his former therapist's indirect style. He stated that he also appreciated that we worked together on problems as opposed to the way his former therapist posed as an expert.

In the seventh session, Matthew reported an increase in distress because his former therapist was increasing phone and letter contact with him. The therapist suggested that Matthew "needed to come to terms" with his sexuality. Most of his distress, however, came from a recognition of the depth of his same-sex desires. He was acutely aware that he found some of the men he had met earlier very attractive. He continued to think through the implications of this in various areas of his life. Matthew worked in a conservative corporation and worried about how disclosure of his sexuality might affect his career. I suggested to Matthew that he was in charge of the pacing of his own exploration process, and that issues related to employer and family were premature as he remained unsure about his sexuality.

Matthew came to the eighth session in great distress. He had received letters from his former psychotherapist and a mutual college friend. They both took Matthew to task for not "really coming to terms" with his sexuality. Matthew learned that the former psychotherapist had been in contact with this friend and had discussed how Matthew needed to "come to terms" with his sexuality and encouraged his friend to push him on this. Also, Carol had entered therapy and reported to Matthew that her therapist wondered out loud if Matthew was using her as a way to avoid resolution of his sexual orientation. Matthew was hurt and angered at the intrusiveness of his former therapist and also the suggestion that he was using Carol. He stated that he had been honest with Carol about his sexuality from the beginning. While he was unclear about how he felt about Carol sexually, he was clear that their relationship was the most important and emotionally meaningful one in his life.

In an earlier session I had made a suggestion to Matthew that he might want to start a journal about his feelings towards his brother and his former therapist. He had done this dutifully but with meager results. He now came into the eighth session with a great deal of journal material, particularly concerning the former therapist. I suggested to Matthew that he might want to use this material to compose a letter to his former therapist in which he described his perceptions of their interaction. Again I discussed his options in filing a complaint against the former therapist.

In the ninth session, Matthew reported that he had written and sent a letter to his former therapist. It was an articulate letter describing what their interaction had been like for Matthew and requesting that the therapist have no contact with Matthew nor discuss Matthew with their mutual friends. What was noteworthy was Matthew's clarity about both the positive and negative aspects of their relationship and the firmness with which he wanted no contact. He had also talked with Carol and received reassurances from her that she perceived he had been honest with her, that their lapses in communication had been partially her doing, that she did not feel their relationship was exploitative, and that, regardless of its outcome, it was an important relationship for her also.

In the tenth session, Matthew reported he had received a letter from his former therapist in which he acknowledged receipt of Matthew's letter and had agreed to his request about no contact and no interference with Matthew's friends. Matthew was aware that his former therapist had not altered his controlling style, and there was no admission on the therapist's part of inappropriate behavior towards Matthew. Matthew felt both triumphant that he had successfully managed to set boundaries and more angry as he felt the former therapist was manipulating him even as he acquiesced to his requests. We spent the rest of that session discussing Matthew's sexuality. I suggested that it was a good time to explore various organizations within the gay community in order to further observe his own reactions.

In both the eleventh and twelfth sessions, Matthew reported that he was "stalled out" about exploring social options. It is noteworthy that he was fully aware of his avoidance. We used this time to discuss his unrealistic fears, stereotypes, and homophobic feelings. He was ashamed that he had not followed through on what we had discussed. I responded that while I thought it would be beneficial for him to do the behavioral tasks we had outlined, I was not disappointed that he hadn't done them but was confident that he would do so in his own time. I commented that having behavioral tasks as a goal was important not only for their intrinsic value but also in eliciting exactly the kind of homophobic and other reactions we were processing. These were as important as meeting any behavioral objectives.

There was a longer period than usual between the twelfth and thirteenth sessions because of Matthew's vacation on the East Coast. During the thirteenth session, he observed what while his sexual interaction with Carol was satisfactory, his main bond with her was emotional, and that his erotic interest in men was strong, clear, and predominant. He stated that his fear of pursuing same-sex interests was primarily his love for Carol, but also internal discomfort about being different and fears of social ostracism. This session ended with Matthew sounding clear in the understanding of his sexuality and the barriers to self-acceptance.

The fourteenth session was about a month and a half after the thirteenth. We had determined that pursuing social interactions within the gay community was now truly essential for more productive discussion; hence, the longer interval. Matthew came to this fourteenth session reporting that he had gone to a number of gay organizations and particularly liked one of the local campus gay groups. I had suggested this to him some months before as a good way to meet peers in age and intellectual ability. He had begun socializing with individuals he met and had a more differentiated view of gay men. He could articulate the diversity that he had seen, as well as his own fears and stereotypes. A minor theme in a number of the earlier sessions was Matthew's dissatisfaction with his current work. While he was on the East Coast, he had explored some job options. In the fourteenth session he reported that he had been following up on these and was seriously considering a move back. We discussed possible termination and its implications.

The fifteenth and last session occurred a month after the fourteenth session, again in order to allow time for Matthew to follow through on his behavioral goals of interacting with the gay community. He also had decided to move back to the East Coast. Further, he had casually dated a man whom he met at the campus gay group. Their relationship had been sexual—he felt assertive and comfortable in their sexual interaction and had enjoyed it. He stated that his primary erotic interest was for men but he was still in a dilemma because the most important emotional relationship in his life was with Carol. While he had not determined a resolution of this dilemma, he understood that productive relationships which suited his values were possible with men. We reviewed his progress in treatment and made plans for follow-up phone contacts.

The first follow-up phone contact occurred a month later. Plans for the move east had progressed. Job options had been explored further, and he had determined to move in approximately another month. His comfort level with his sexuality appeared stable with no increase in anxiety. We agreed that Matthew would contact me a few days before his move so we could do a second follow-up phone interview. This was done about a month later. Matthew reported that he had been pleased with the assertive and thoughtful way with which he had considered his options and planned his move. The comfort level with his sexuality was the same as before. He was appreciative of our interactions and thanked me for them.

Matthew and I also negotiated his willingness to participate in this case study during these phone calls. Initially, his approach was acquiescent. His response in the second call, while continuing to be positive, was more thoughtful about the nature of the release, who would have access to it, and what sort of information might be in the case history. He questioned me in an assertive manner, and we reworked the release to his satisfaction.

COUNTERTRANSFERENCE ISSUES

This case elicited a number of countertransference reactions in me, the management of which was important to the case, particularly as in a short-term therapy situation the available time for correcting errors is attenuated.

My immediate countertransference response was well known to me in working with individuals who have been sexually exploited by their psychotherapists. My personal struggle in these cases is to not foist my eagerness for accountability of the mental health professions onto the client but to be responsive to their ambivalence and allow them to set the pace of any complaint process, and indeed allow them to reject the possibility of a complaint.

By the second or third session it was clear that something more was going on. While my behavioral control in handling the case was adequate in that I was following Matthew's pace, doing so was more of a struggle for me than was typical. Indeed, I had strong impulses to push him to make a complaint against the therapist and to be unproductively disruptive of his avoidance of that area. I realized that my reaction to Matthew was influenced by my response to a former lover, an individual to whom I had been and remained strongly attached. This person had features which paralleled Matthew's history—specifically, he had been abused as a child and sexually exploited by a former psychotherapist. While my "ex" had (in my estimation) done a good job of resolving his early history of abuse, he had taken no action against his former psychotherapist.

There were further parallels between the situations. In both, while it appeared that the therapy had ended, the interaction had become social and perhaps sexualized prior to the therapy ending. Perhaps most importantly, both individuals had prolonged confusion about sexual identity and significant heterosexual interest. In fact, the strength of heterosexual interest in my former partner was a major factor in the termination of our romantic relationship. My ambivalence, then, not only involved Matthew's decision-making about his former therapist, but also his decision-making about his sexual orientation.

I discussed this situation with a trusted colleague both to check my management of the case and to have an opportunity to explore my residual feelings about my former partner. I was surprised to learn that I had strong feelings about my ex's exploitation by his former therapist and that my grieving about "losing" him to his heterosexual side remained in process. The latter was intensified by my ex's heterosexual marriage, which was concurrent with this case.

I did not discuss these countertransference reactions with Matthew. My rationale is that for all clients, but particularly for individuals who have been abused, exploration of the therapist's countertransference is not especially productive and may well precipitate a boundary problem in itself. While many aspects of the therapy were mutual and transparent, this aspect was not.

CONCLUSIONS ABOUT THE CASE

As is often the case with shorter term goal oriented psychotherapy, specific accomplishments are clear, but resolution of more general problems is uncertain. Matthew had increased his ability to act in an empowered fashion; examples of this include his response to the harrassment by his former psychotherapist, his taking risks in meeting gay men, his directness in talking with Carol, his job hunting, and his interaction with me around permission to do this case history. The confusion over his sexual orientation was clarified but not resolved. The meaning of his relationship with Carol was clearer to him. He understood that theirs was an emotionally significant relationship with some sexual component. He could see the strength of his sexual desire for men and could appreciate the possibility of a productive relationship with a man that was congruent with his value system. Yet, he remained unresolved about the choices before him.

Some additional resolution appeared to occur with regard to the physical abuse he received from his older brother, although it appeared that that issue was well resolved by the work with his former psychotherapist. As commentators in the area have noted (Schoener, Milgrom, & Gonsiorek, 1989), it is not accurate to view all exploitative psychotherapists as entirely destructive in their effects. In some situations the therapist is helpful during the period he or she functioned in an appropriate therapeutic role. It is when the boundaries begin to dissolve and inappropriate behavior occurs that the exploitative therapist becomes damaging.

This appeared to be the case with Matthew. It was as if he needed to double-check with me that he really had made some resolution of the situation with his brother during his earlier therapy before he could believe that this was not undone by his former therapist's eventual betrayal of him. There was evidence that there had been significant resolution. During the course of the therapy, Matthew made a number of family visits and reported that he could interact with his family, including his brother, in a way that was far less fearful and resentful. This change began during his earlier therapy.

Matthew's resolution with his former psychotherapist is not what I would have chosen, but I suspect it is truest for him. My preference would have been for him to file a formal complaint against the therapist. His choice of setting a clear boundary and dropping contact with the former therapist seemed most congruent for him. Some might argue that he has not sufficiently resolved his victimization. I would counterargue that pushing clients to "resolve victimization" in a way that they are not ready for, or do not agree with, is a kind of secondary victimization in which a "helper" again violates the wishes and feelings of the client.

My own countertransference response was useful in handling the case in that it warned me about potential errors I might make in substituting my agenda for Matthew's. It also reminded me that even though I have worked for many years doing therapy with individuals experiencing sexual identity concerns, male victims of abuse, and victims of exploitation by psychotherapists, this work is often powerfully charged and continues to elicit strong countertransference responses. I have observed that as I acquire experience in these areas, my countertransference responses are not diminished but rather more quickly elicited and recognized. Another way of saying this is that my patterns of countertransference become more understandable and predictable, and, therefore, more useful as information.

SOME BROADER CONCLUSIONS

This case exemplifies my view that short-term goal oriented treatments are as efficacious as longer, traditional psychotherapies. However, for certain groups, e.g., individuals whose personal problems may be significantly compounded by or primarily caused by external oppression, I believe that short-term goal oriented therapies are the treatment of choice. Longer term therapies either implicitly or explicitly carry the message that the problem is within the individual. I would argue that this is not only untrue but reactionary and serves to further oppress the individual.

Individuals whose sexual orientation is not exclusively heterosexual fall into this category. I would maintain that in the treatment of individuals who are nonexclusively heterosexual, when the goal of the treatment is resolution of sexual identity concerns, the treatment should be short-term and goal oriented. Longer term, more exploratory therapies are appropriate if and only if there are demonstrable ongoing problems that are characterological over and above sexual identity concerns. Further, this treatment should be empowering for the client. Treatment of individuals of any sexual orientation who have been victimized should be sensitive to similar concerns.

The rapid development in recent years of long-term treatments for sexual and physical abuse victims runs the risk of further victimizing clients by suggesting implicitly or explicitly that the primary problem is their personality, not their traumatic experiences. Again, if there is evidence that there are ongoing problems over and above the victimization, more traditional therapies may be appropriate. The structure of therapy is a political choice. I urge therapists to consider the implications and to accept responsibility for the choices they make.

While the literature on treatment of victims of sexual exploitation by psychotherapists is relatively new, it has already begun to show signs of the premature decisiveness and dogmatic rigidity that has characterized the literature on treatment of sexual abuse victims in general. This case description illustrates a more thoughtful and individually tailored approach. While such clients have patterns and similarities in the sequelae of their victimization (Schoener, Milgrom, & Gonsiorek, 1989), such sequelae are general, not specific, and only serve as a guide for an individual assessment of the client, not as a diagnosis or "syndrome."

In a similar light, this case illustrates how an affirmative gay perspective can be individually tailored to a client who is confused about sexual orientation. To prematurely push Matthew to resolve his sexual orientation would have been counterproductive. Although his resolution was incomplete, what he learned about himself, he learned primarily by himself. The therapy ended with the client appropriately grappling with not only psychological but also existential dilemmas about the meaning of love, intimacy, and sex. Too often, it is the therapist's need for resolution of the client's sexual orientation that takes precedence. An unknown, unidentified sexuality in flux can be intimidating. The goal of therapy with such individuals is to move towards a resolution which is theirs, not one which relieves the therapist of his or her anxiety.

Finally, the case illustrates that a short-term goal oriented treatment model can be directive, yet respectful; that goals can be clear without violence to the client's psychological process; and that even in relatively brief psychotherapies, powerful countertransference responses can be elicited.

REFERENCES

1. Bera, W., Gonsiorek, J., & LeTourneau, D. (in press). *Sexual abuse: The male adolescent experience.* Newbury Park, CA: Sage.
2. Gonsiorek, J. (1989). Sexual exploitation by psychotherapists: Some observations on male victims and sexual orientation issues. In G. Schoener, J. Milgrom, J. Gonsiorek, E. Leupker, & R. Conroe (Ed.), *Psychotherapists' sexual involvement with clients: Intervention and prevention* (pp. 113–119). Minneapolis: Walk-In Counseling Center.
3. Gonsiorek, J., & Rudolph, J. (1991). Sexual identity formation: Coming out and other developmental events in gay men and lesbians. In J. Gonsiorek & J. Weinrich (Eds.), *Homosexuality: Research findings for public policy.* Newbury Park, CA: Sage.
4. Lew, M. (1988). *Victims no longer.* New York: Nevraumont Publishing.
5. Malyon, A. (1982). Psychotherapeutic implications of internalized homophobia in gay men. In J. Gonsiorek (Ed.), *Homosexuality and psychotherapy: A practitioner's handbook of affirmative models* (pp. 59–69). New York: Haworth.
6. Schoener, G., Milgrom, J., & Gonsiorek, J. (1989). Therapeutic responses to clients who have been sexually abused by psychotherapists. In G. Schoener, J. Milgrom, J. Gonsiorek, E. Leupker, & R. Conroe (Eds.), *Psychotherapists' sexual involvement with clients: Intervention and prevention* (pp. 95–112). Minneapolis: Walk-In Counseling Center.

7

MARNY HALL

Ex-Therapy to Sex-Therapy: Notes from the Margins

IT IS CURIOUS THAT therapists, whose work often depends on mysterious hunches and intuitive leaps, place so much confidence in the precision of traditional science—in particular, in the subject/object split that characterizes empiricism. This faith is most obvious in the persistent image of ourselves as fixed points outside the influence of our clients. In the standard version of the therapy process, clients' effects on us are shortlived, typically limited to the empathy we feel during the hour or so that we spend in session. Reactions that exceed these bounds must be monitored closely. Dubbed "countertransference," such feelings signal potential trouble.

This belief in our imperturbability is easier to sustain if, when clients exit from the office, they depart from our lives. In this freeze-framed reality, our missions are accomplished, our roles vis-à-vis one another remain intact. If, however, our paths and those of our clients intersect regularly after therapy is over, as is the case in the lesbian community, such crisp role divisions and confidence in the "results" of therapy may erode quickly. Because we run into our clients at meetings or parties or because our social networks touch at many points, we are constantly

I would like to thank Jeanne Adleman, Candi Ellis, Nanette Gartrell, Richard Hall, Susan Kennedy, Kat Podgornoff, Diana Russell, Susan Summerfield, and Celeste West for their assistance in the preparation of this chapter.

engaged in inadvertent follow-up evaluations. When we bump into ex-clients who report that the benefits of therapy have continued, we can feel assured that our mission has indeed been successful. As often as not, however, I encounter different realities: X, who I thought I had success-fully escorted through the quicksands of an extramarital affair, tells me during intermission at the Women's Philharmonic that she has broken up with her original lover. Y, sitting alone in the back row of the gay Al-Anon meeting, mumbles ruefully that after she stopped therapy she started "iso-lating like before." I remember when I see Z riding her motorcycle in the gay parade that she never did pay her bill—a particularly eloquent state-ment about the value of therapy. Through the grapevine, I hear that Sally and Sue, who I believed had concluded things comfortably with me, are seeing another therapist, and that the rekindled eroticism of Janelle and Paige fizzled a month after they stopped seeing me.

Some lesbian therapists are undaunted by this immediate feedback loop. Those of us with thinner skins venture out into the community less, recite the Serenity Prayer in our spare moments, or engage in endless rounds of our own therapy in an attempt to get to the bottom of our grandiose rescue fantasies. Thus, for lesbian therapists embedded in kindred commu-nities, change is hardly a one-way street. Even if we manage to avoid serious countertransference problems, we are bound to be affected by the multiple, informal encounters we have with our clients and ex-clients in the community.

Though twelve-step programs and my own therapy helped me maintain my composure when I encountered disconsolate, decidedly "uncured" ex-clients, these palliatives became less useful as the disturbing evidence mounted. I was finally forced to conclude that my treatment, particularly of lesbians' sexual complaints, wasn't very effective and that, in fact, it needed major revamping. What follows is my reconsideration of the sex-therapy techniques I had been using and my construction and application of a new, more appropriate framework for lesbians' sexual problems.

BACKGROUND FOR ANTI-SEX THERAPY

My initial training as a once undaunted sex therapist came from the University of California Medical School's Human Sexuality Department in the mid-seventies. At that time the tenets of Masters and Johnson held sway, i.e., sex was a natural function; sexual dysfunction was the result of performance anxiety which could be allayed by a regimen of goal-less mutual sensuality. Masters and Johnson posited pleasure, particularly female pleasure—not old-fashioned penis-in-vagina, thrusting-to-orgasm—as the guiding principle of sexuality (Masters & Johnson, 1970).

If women were slower to apprehend this capacity, it was largely an accident of anatomy. Men, after all, had daily contact with their genitals when they urinated, insuring familiarity. We women had some catching up to do.

This theme was thrust home by color coded slides depicting penises and vulvas. Matching colors denoted homologous structures. Thus the scrotum and labia majora were the identical deep purple, the glans penis and glans clitoris were both yellow, etc. The message was explicit—the differences between men and women were largely a matter of sex role stereotyping and quirks, not innate capacity. Clitorises, we were told, had to be educated and penises reeducated.

Thoroughly convinced, I began to pass on this information to my clients. The effect of this new gospel of desire was not as dramatic as I had hoped. Unlike their heterosexual counterparts, lesbians seeking treatment for sexual problems already knew exactly where their clitorises were, had long since given themselves permission to touch their genitals, and, with great gusto and mixed results, had been rubbing themselves raw for years. Couples in treatment often replaced battles about whether or not to have sex with battles about whether or not to do the sensuality exercises I prescribed.

Standard sex therapy clearly did not work very well with lesbians and long before devising the approach discussed here, I had begun to use a modified approach (Hall, 1987). Though I could claim some "successes" with it, I would often find out from couples who had stopped therapy that one of the partners had subsequently started a new liaison. In other cases, lovers would reconcile themselves to a different sort of partnership, perhaps focusing on "recovery" from alcohol or incest, or simply breaking up.

In time, I concluded that the new pleasure principles defined by Masters and Johnson were *cavoli riscaldati* (reheated cabbage). The first clue that their emphasis on pleasure, rather than on intercourse, was misleading emerged when I reconsidered the pre-orgasmic—actually masturbation training—groups for women offered at the University of California. If a more general sensuality had really been the goal, then it would seem that the U. C. training staff would have considered their task accomplished when women were comfortably conversant with their genitals. The program architects, however, decreed the masturbation groups inadequate. Secondary pre-orgasmic groups were formed. In contrast to the original primary groups, these secondary groups were designed for women who were by now regularly or fitfully orgasmic. Through a series of "bridge maneuvers," these women were trained to train their partners to "pleasure" them. This impetus back to the couple was also implicitly, and sometimes explicitly, an impetus back toward intercourse.

There were other signs that the new sensuality had not really replaced the old penis-in-vagina sexuality. If the tyrannical intercourse model had truly been banished, the frequently invoked diagnosis of Inhibited Sexual Desire should apply to an inhibition of all erotic manifestations. A close reading of journals suggests, however, that Inhibited Sexual Desire was the label applied to women who did not want heterosexual intercourse. Typical of descriptions of ISD women is one which appears in a sex-therapy journal article: "The ISD group had less fantasies but no less masturbation or orgasms" (Nutter & Condron, 1983, p. 277). Orgasms achieved by means other than intercourse, we can infer, are not evidence of sexual desire. In addition, pharmaceutical companies and medical suppliers have continued to develop and refine erection aids. Drugs, penile implants, devices which measure penile blood-flow, and microsurgical techniques are routinely recommended by physicians to men complaining of erection problems. No aids to assist women to arousal have been similarly marketed since, for women, arousal is clearly incidental to intercourse.

But the most startling inconsistencies came from Masters and Johnson themselves. These champions of nonintercourse-based sexual pleasuring wrote: "The vaginal barrel performs a dual role, providing the primary physical means of heterosexual expression for the human female and serving simultaneously as an integral part of her conceptive mechanism. . . . To appreciate vaginal anatomy and physiology is to comprehend the fundamentals of the human female's primary means [sic] of sexual expression" (Miller & Fowlkes, 1980, p. 261). Why, it seems logical to ask, promote one set of standards while embracing another, quite opposite set?

If we accept the fact that we live in a patriarchal culture, we must assume that male sovereignty depends on the continuing pliancy, sexual and otherwise, of women. In "enlightened" societies in which some women, under some circumstances, feel entitled to control access to their bodies and where sanctions against rape are sometimes invoked, it is important to ensure sexual availability of women by strategic, rather than forceful means. Scrutiny of the hidden versus the stated goals of the liberated sexual agenda of the '70s suggests that the new Pleasure Imperative is the latest patriarchal strategy. If women could be convinced that they were lusty pleasure-seekers who had been blighted in the past by ignorance and Victorian prudery, they would acquiesce without coercion. If a woman feels ashamed of her "sexual unresponsiveness," she will force herself— more effectively than any man ever could—to have sex. And when we examine certain written and social texts closely, we see that sex has not diverged from the old coital model.

At some level believing that sex is erection and insertion, thrusting and ejaculation, lesbians have four sexual options:

1. By frequent partner changes, we can maintain a limerent state in which all forms of contact are so highly charged that sex, itself, is almost incidental.
2. We can encapsulate sex/intercourse by role-playing, i.e., butch-femme, S-and-M, by fantasies that incorporate aspects of intercourse, and/or by channeling all sensuality toward orgasm.
3. We can feel apathetic toward or repelled by partners' overtures, thereby avoiding sex altogether.
4. We can insist on our ability to do "it" at any time or place. This relentless phantom phallus-brandishing almost guarantees that some circumstance, typically an unwilling partner, will prevent any sexual expression.

The last two positions are the most painful and defensive solutions to the dilemma of sex-as-intercourse. I realized I could be most helpful to the women who chose these positions if, instead of doing traditional sex therapy, i.e., reinforcing the pleasure imperative which I came to perceive as simply another patriarchal strategy, I illuminated and deconstructed the sex-qua-intercourse model.

GINA AND MELANIE

Gina and Melanie, lovers for about a year, came to couples therapy feeling desperate. After five months of living together they had begun to fight chronically and were increasingly polarized over sex. Gina described herself as "completely shut down" while Melanie complained that an essential part of herself, her sexuality, had no outlet.

Gina and Melanie were both white women in their mid-thirties who had grown up in turbulent, disrupted families. Melanie, along with two older siblings, was shuttled back and forth between her divorced parents from the age of six. Though she felt loved, her relationship with each parent was discontinuous, punctuated by alcoholism and violence. Gina is the middle child in a family of six children. Following her parents' divorce when she was four, she rarely saw her father. Her mother, anxious about the family's economic survival and embroiled in a series of abusive marriages, was emotionally inaccessible.

Gina, fair and slight, bore no physical resemblance to huskier, darker Melanie, but they shared an ironic sense of humor, dedication to their own recoveries in twelve-step programs and, as might be expected from their histories, an engaging waif-like quality. Both were extremely likable.

Melanie worked full-time to put herself through training in computer programming. Gina also worked full-time in a semiskilled job that depleted and frustrated her. Shortages of time, money, and the absence of work-related satisfactions added to their domestic friction. Both reported that the little time they had together was spent arguing. Nevertheless, whenever they disagreed, as they did regularly in therapy, they seemed to listen to each other's point of view and to respond in nonblaming ways. Thus, the sort of communication tinkering that sometimes relieves distressed couples seemed unnecessary. They had clearly, in the *patois* of therapy, done a great deal of "work" on themselves.

THERAPY

The nine sessions I had with Gina and Melanie were spread over three months. From the beginning, I was active—questioning, interpreting, explaining, reframing, suggesting assignments. After listening to their histories, I suggested that their fighting might be an ingenious way to avoid depression about grim past and present circumstances. Because they were deprived of nurturing while they were growing up and now endured so much stress in their lives, neither had much in the way of reserves. Instead of giving support to each other, they both needed to be adopted by a Lady Bountiful who could make up for past neglect. Since neither could be such a benefactor, they had fights in which Gina assumed the role of the long-suffering mother and Melanie, in her words, became the "brat." Gina could, by distancing and punishing Melanie, keep her own crying,

lost child at bay. Melanie, in turn, could keep alive the hope of repara-
tion—a hope which, because of the intermittent reappearance of each
parent, had never died—by continuing to demand that Gina respond lov-
ingly to her. And, of course, at times, Gina did. Since the fighting, considered in this light, was serviceable, I could suggest only one improvement:
that Gina call Melanie "Gina" when she was distancing and that Melanie,
when she was inveighing against Gina's cold treatment, call Gina by one
of her own parents' names. With this slight adjustment, they could extract
the highest possible emotional octane from their fights. They accepted this
assignment in a jocular spirit and reported the following week that it had
diffused the intensity of their fighting.

In the first session, also in response to their histories, I said that any
description of themselves as being simply a lesbian couple did not express
the uniqueness of their partnership. They were, in fact, "waifs together."
When they seemed dubious about this assertion, I explained that I was
fond of that particular configuration because it has a certain Huck and Jim
appeal and is certainly as valid as the couple constellations of mother/
child, dominant/submissive, egalitarian, etc. With that in mind, I asked
them to look at each other, to notice that they were looking at another
waif, and to recommit to each other on that basis. Their ongoing assignment, then, was to be "waifs together." This meant sitting in the same
room, feeling quite abandoned and forlorn without trying to rescue the
other from a perfectly reasonable state of being. Both Melanie and Gina
speculated that this assignment, which I continued to ask about and renew,
was perhaps the most useful aspect of therapy. They said they were increasingly able to tolerate their own and their partner's depressions.

Entwined with these assignments was an ongoing discussion of the
precepts of what I call anti-sex. I outlined for Melanie and Gina the
rather tortuous path I had followed to anti-sex, including my Masters and
Johnson training and my own previous hit-and-miss treatment record with
"lesbian bed-death." Though the description of anti-sex therapy that follows
addresses what I discussed with Melanie and Gina, it doesn't capture the
interactive quality of the exchanges we had about the topic.

DECONSTRUCTING PHALLOCENTRIC SEX

Phallocentric sex depends on particular divisions of both time and space.
The periods of time, for example, considered appropriate for sex are distinct from the time we spend working, eating, or sleeping. Sexual time is

further subdivided into a period of "foreplay," followed by intercourse, and then by resolution. These phases, which become the universal model for lovemaking, reflect the sequence characteristic of male arousal: erection, ejaculation, and withdrawal. As well as partitioning time, patriarchal sex also divides space into zones. Various bodies, body parts, and physical spaces are also cordoned off as appropriate or inappropriate for phallocentric sex.

The purpose of anti-sex therapy is to diffuse these phallocentric designations of correct erotic attitudes and of proper places and times to have sex. It would be wonderful if we could bypass this deconstructing process and simply start elaborating the replacement of sex/intercourse, i.e., if we could simply describe an alternative set of activities that might afford pleasure, closeness, and excitement. The very demolition, however, of old categories sets the stage for the new ones. Anti-sex, despite its oppositional designation, is apposite, rather than opposite, patriarchal sex. Consequently, at the same time that anti-sex challenges old constructions, it contains elements of the old which may be teased and twisted into new pleasure scripts that are tailored to the histories, fantasies, and neurophysiologies of intimates. In this scrambling process, old phallocentric practices, instead of serving as the invisible template of lovemaking, can be impelled into consciousness, rearranged, refurbished, and combined with elements from other dimensions of experience.

Though exercises provide some structures with which to devise one's own version of anti-sex, there are no standardized "homework assignments" that one must "complete" — another patriarchal legacy — but rather, improvisations which not only scramble phallocentric givens, but suffuse the whole proceeding with a multifocused rather than a one-pointed quality. Can we have encounters that are neither sexual nor nonsexual? Can we imagine, for example, massages that blur erotic/nonerotic boundaries or ritualized/stylized fucks which playfully bracket sex/intercourse?

We might imagine a few other examples of anti-sex: A notices B's elbow, endows it with sacred and profane meaning. She gives B a glimpse of her own elbow. B modestly covers hers. Both beg the other to allow her access to the divine spot. Each plays at acceding and demurring. Before they go to bed, as a special treat, A lets B lightly gnaw her elbow.

Following perfunctory orgasms, C and D discuss the prospects of the 1000 Komodo dragons just spawned. They find their philosophies of child rearing and education surprisingly in accord, but disagree about how much the "babies" will be allowed to watch TV.

L pushes back V's cuticles gently with unguent, gives her a tender breast exam, and then holds her as she cries.

Growling, roaring, hissing, and butting, L, straddling K, menaces her. K cringes, squirms, emits high-pitched squeaks of dismay.

These encounters dramatize the new territory without actually defining it. Experiments that undermine the misfitting metaphor of heterosexual intercourse can also erode our defensive stances, leaving us free to play, have sex outside the definitions of patriarchal structures, or respond in whatever fashion the moment suggests.

IMPROVISING

By asking each partner questions about early play/physicality/eroticism, I broadened sexual history-taking to include memories of aggression, silliness, fun, trauma, frustration, disappointment, sensuality, affection, and fantasy. The exercises we devised drew on these recollections. Gina, for example, remembered the pleasure of hiding, of feeling confined and, at the same time, sheltered in a field of weeds, and again in the crevice of a half-folded couch. Another memory, hovering between neutral and somewhat exciting, was one of erotic "zone" exploration with boys. I asked if they would experiment with a massage that incorporated some elements of restraint or containment and that scrambled standard erotic/nonerotic zones. Perhaps they could avoid the standard sequences of working up to the erotic zones by interspersing touches of noses, nipples, toes, vaginas, knees, etc., or by designating a new sacred zone: If they used the elbow, for example, they could work up gradually to it through a subordination of all the other, now less important, zones.

They came back to report that they had wedged the massage into their already jammed schedules and had felt dissatisfied with the exercise because both had been tired. Their fatigue was, I told them, a particularly useful and unexpected sort of scramble. If patriarchal sex defines correct space and time, it simultaneously designates correct attitudes toward intimacy. Intimacy is for people who are not tired, since it requires single-minded focus and ultimate satisfaction. Having an intimate experience that was not satisfying, I suggested, was another means of scrambling patriarchal attitudes toward intimacy.

At another point, Gina reported having had humping experiences with boys in car backseats that had been pleasurable. So I suggested Gina and Melanie might disrobe under a blanket, perhaps in the backseat of their car. Instead of Gina's old scenario, they simply could be "waifs together," i.e., be simultaneously naked and woebegone. They did some variation of this exercise and both reported intimacy, touching, sadness, and feelings of closeness.

Exercises, which became more improvisational toward the end of therapy, sometimes incorporated genital contact and sometimes did not. Gina became more aware of the ebb and flow of erotic feelings, particularly in inappropriate places. She said, for example, that she often felt turned-on during the therapy sessions. I suggested exercises which might increase this range of "inappropriate" eroticism. On a day before they planned to go to the park and play catch, I suggested that along with a ball which they could throw underhanded, from their crotches, they could also toss dirty words at each other. In addition, I suggested that Gina could combine fatigue and genital sensation by tying a scarf around herself in such a way that it brushed against her genitals when she was going to sleep.

The anti-sex approach to therapy was a relief to Gina because it released her from the Identified Patient role. Melanie, though receptive, was less enthusiastic. Even if sex was patriarchal, she said she couldn't imagine any comparably gratifying substitutes. This split between Gina and Melanie that reflected their initial polarization about sex, varied during the course of therapy and never completely disappeared. When any of the exercises seemed to create new forms of intimacy, the division between them would close. However, when exercises seemed too ambiguous to them or contrived, or when they didn't have the energy for another sortie into uncharted territory, Melanie would feel baffled and cheated, and Gina would feel guilty that my therapeutic approach seemed weighted in her favor.

Although they no longer complained about fighting and said they were able to be complacent while depressed together, at the end of three months both were tired of struggling with the ambiguity of anti-sex and wanted a break from what seemed like a taxing and difficult process. At the end of our last session, I had no idea whether their earlier polarization would resurface or if the work we had done would make a difference.

FOLLOW-UP

When I requested a follow-up interview five months later, explaining that I wanted to write an article about anti-sex therapy, both were eager to talk about therapy and posttherapy experiences. I paid for their time at the same rate they had paid me, and I tape-recorded the session.

They told me that they had broken up after therapy. However, they still lived together as "family," and Melanie had started a relationship with another woman. She said she had been very dissatisfied, even mistrustful, after couples therapy. She claimed her needs "weren't being addressed. . . ."

I felt pretty good about the tools I'd gotten but felt totally untrained in how to use them . . . but every exercise held some hope and I really wanted them to work and after each therapy session I felt more and more boxed into having to give up everything I want . . . I mean I wanted a sex life of abandon and I was told over and over again, 'it's OK to abandon your sex life.' I would have liked to have had some structure that says, 'this is the path, this is the format to follow to dismantle the old relationship and these are the tools that you'll have in order to balance the relationship in your new way.' The exercises were just beginning to twist on me in a way that wasn't comfortable. I feel like that was the intention but it didn't seem to add anything to my life. . . . For me it was a bomb, and I was really mad at you for awhile. I still haven't been able to get used to the idea of pulling sex apart . . . I think you're on to something, but you haven't nailed it for my needs. It doesn't fly, Orville. It needs work.

In contrast, Gina said she was disappointed when they decided to stop therapy:

I felt we were on the right track for me . . . I felt I had moved so much while I was in therapy . . . not being able to pigeonhole sex . . . and I knew it wasn't going to improve if we weren't in therapy . . . I feel like maybe it could have worked if we were in therapy every day . . . I feel like I wanted more structure but it was more structure to just hold me while I went through my stuff . . . I remember when we moved the mattress into the living room and it was pretty late and we were going to be sexual . . . I think we had been kissing and I was stimulated and then at some point I started crying and it just hurt. I started out hating Melanie and then it shifted and I just hated myself . . . I think for me that means the exercises were working . . . to be able to get to that place and Melanie was amazingly present. She was able to talk to me and say, 'you know we're not going to do anything. I just want to hold your hand,' and then I didn't even want her to hold my hand and we were talking about something and Melanie was giving me the image of flowers, just inside my hand and there was this total hatred that came back and said, 'I'm not going to do it. I know that will work and I'm not going to do it' and for me that was progress . . . but without the support of reporting that right away or something it must have made me shut down more.

After they stopped seeing me, their fighting had increased to pretherapy levels. Their polarization had reemerged strongly and reached an intolerable pitch for both. When they agreed to stop being lovers, the crisis ended.

Melanie said, "There was some kind of permission to just be with her as a person, to really love her and accept the relationship the way it was without sex. We started to get along much better."

During the follow-up interview, Gina described their situation as

feeling so easy now . . . I have family, I have intimacy, I have someone to touch me when I want it. I have someone trained not to touch me when I don't want it and Melanie is getting her needs met so I don't have to feel guilty like I'm the poor lover or the bad mother.

For Melanie, the situation was less ideal:

I'm beginning to feel frustrated that I have to go to two places when I want one relationship . . . and I still feel so wrapped up with Gina that I don't feel room to feel a whole lot of abandon in this other relationship.

Gina and Melanie's feedback, as might be imagined, was disappointing. Even though I might claim some effectiveness while working with them, the residual impact of therapy seemed ambiguous. While I may have accelerated a process already underway and provided Gina with validation for her sexual misgivings, the result of these efforts was not at all what I'd hoped for.

POSTSCRIPT AND POST-POSTSCRIPT

I received two follow-up letters that confirmed how incidental couples therapy had actually been in Gina and Melanie's unfolding story. Gina wrote that the follow-up session had served as additional therapy and that perhaps it had even sparked the sexual renascence she and Melanie were currently experiencing. There were other possible catalysts. Gina wrote,

I know the fact that Melanie was having sex with some other woman was an aphrodisiac for me. And I know that we had some really good fights as I worked through my jealousy, which also is very stimulating. I personally see your scrambling influence as a good one which I am only beginning to grasp in actions as well as thoughts . . . Melanie and I are "acting like lovers." She has broken off with The Other Woman, which set me into a panic.

In the next letter, over a month later, Gina wrote,

As I predicted, my sexual desire has now returned to now not quite zero . . . I often find myself wishing that Melanie was a boy so that we could just fuck for a few minutes and she would have an orgasm then we would be done with that Chore (big sigh). Then we could have a little bit of the close physical contact and intimacy that I would like, without the overbearing Push for Something More that seems to arise with that Chore . . . This flavor of light witticism is not so great a cover for a larger feeling of despair. Will I ever be Normal? In the corners of my heart still lurks a little hope for that brand of sexuality that is outside the patriarchal model, but it is still cowering from the light you were able to shed on it. Will I have the patience and the faith to let it grow? Will Melanie leave me for a Sexual Woman? Will I continue to grin and Be Willing and bear it? Will we go to therapy for help, or will we struggle alone? Can any of this happen without further footwork on my part? These are the questions that this lesbian consumer (of therapy) is asking.

CONCLUSIONS

After this contact, I shared the feelings Gina expressed in her letter. My painstaking attempt to fuse lesbian feminist theory and practice, my rapport with Melanie and Gina, and my heartfelt desire to help them had yielded what? Gradually, it occurred to me that I faced the same challenge, in a slightly different register, that I had presented to them. I had expected them to find intimate/erotic meaning beyond sex/intercourse. Correspondingly, it was up to me to find meaning in our work that didn't hinge upon the achievement of "results" that notions of "successful" therapy require.

With this in mind, I considered what had happened in therapy. I had not achieved my "goals." However, what would happen if I demoted myself from conquistadore of sexual problems and imagined myself, instead, as a purveyor of a delicate wash which subtly tinges old perspectives, charting the space between change and no change? After all, I can see from Gina's letters that therapy has affected lives teeming with other events and influences.

It sounds good, but I realize this new version of my role leaves me flying false colors. I see myself reflected through clients' eyes as "expert." What, then, about the claims which suffuse such a role—claims which remain unfilled when I do not deliver promised remedies? I cannot resolve this paradox, but, as I contemplate it, I see I have neglected other crucial steps, interventions I must make in my own interventions. Most significantly, I see that I began deconstructing sex without deconstructing either "expert" or "achievement." As a result, anti-sex as I, the Feminist Expert, presented it to my clients became a mountain peak to scale in the same way that having sex had been previously.

Keeping the focus small, remarking again and again that I am as much a stranger in this uncharted land as my clients, might have framed our floundering as understandable disorientation instead of failure. Equally important to keep in focus was the impossibility of a quick fix. We couldn't expect to reverse the cumulative effects of the millennia of Western civilization or the intense reinforcement of orgasmic responses with a few exercises. But we could start.

There is another area of deconstruction that, in hindsight, I can see I neglected. In the phallocentric universe, the couple itself is designated as the appropriate zone for eroticism. Perhaps too eager to validate lesbians whose intimate relationships are rendered invisible by a homophobic culture, or beguiled by Melanie and Gina's insistence on "working it out," I never questioned their primary intimacy. Is it really possible to deconstruct phallocentric sex, while continuing to respect its fundamental conjugal premise? Should I perhaps have tried to help Melanie and Gina dismantle their relationship or invent another framework for it? At the very least, I think I might have made their continuing couplehood an issue to consider.

In retrospect I see that the process of change which has enveloped both myself and my clients has turned both the notions of professional detachment and therapeutic "outcome" topsy-turvy. Certainly, my blindspots have abounded. If they are contemplated long and hard enough, however, these "mistakes" turn into illuminations which, I believe, will help me in the future. Gina and Melanie's irresolution and my own tentativeness are, I see, not signs of success or failure but of the disorientation inevitable in a new territory. My fledgling optimism is fragile. Will it, I wonder, survive a chance encounter with Melanie and Gina, disconsolate and decidedly "uncured?"

REFERENCES

1. Hall, M. (1987). Sex therapy with lesbian couples: A four stage approach. *Journal of Homosexuality, 14*, 137–156.
2. Masters, W. H., & Johnson, V. E. (1970). *Human sexual inadequacy*. Boston: Little Brown.
3. Miller, P. Y., & Fowlkes, M. R. (1980). Social and behavioral constructions of female sexuality. In C. R. Stimpson & E. S. Person (Eds.), *Women: Sex and sexuality*. Chicago: The University of Chicago Press.
4. Nutter, D. E., & Condron, M. K. (1983). Sexual fantasy and activity patterns of females with inhibited sexual desire versus normal controls. *Journal of Sex & Marital Therapy, 9*, 276–282.

8

PATRICIA I. ZIBUNG HUFFMAN

Recovery as a Necessary Precursor to Effective Therapy

ICKEY, A 25-YEAR-OLD woman who has been in therapy for over four years, first came to me with her partner of eight months, Jane. Their presenting problems, as individuals and as a couple, reflected the abusive/codependent behaviors of most adult children of alcoholics (ACOAs) and child abuse survivors.

Mickey was self-critical, she relied on approval from Jane to help her feel good about herself, she was dissatisfied with her low paying and boring job but did not want to find another one that might have been more challenging, and she described herself as playing a role because she did not know who she was and did not know what was considered "normal" behavior. In addition, Mickey drank heavily and smoked large quantities of marijuana. Her behavior, especially her sexual relationship with Jane, reflected the effects of having been sexually abused by her mother, though she was unaware of the abuse for the first two years of therapy. She experienced flashbacks of feelings—especially shame, guilt, and dread—when she and Jane made love. Woititz (1983) deals with the effects of living with one or more alcoholic parents and Briere and Runtz (1988) cover the aftereffects of being sexually abused. Her already low self-esteem was additionally undermined by her internalized homophobia, which had been strongly conveyed by her parents.

Many thanks to Randi Campbell, Candice Fulton, Roger Wolfe, Karen Mattocks, and the other members of my consultation group.

Jane grew up as the oldest child in a family with a schizophrenic mother and an absent father. She presented as being in charge of her own life and ready to help fix Mickey. She wanted to dominate the relationship and to be the more important of the two of them in the eyes of their friends. Their apartment was furnished with her things. She rewarded Mickey with presents for compliant, submissive behaviors. She also punished Mickey by withdrawing her attention or responding to her with hostile, belittling, or threatening statements. Later, Mickey disclosed that they had had a number of fights in which Jane had hit her. Jane also drank and smoked marijuana.

In addition to the issues of sex, money, and control of the relationship, Mickey and Jane, as a couple, were ineffectual communicators. The only time they experienced any peace in their relationship was when they were drinking or smoking. Jane stated that Mickey seemed to be in more pain in the relationship (i.e., Mickey was angry and less willing to be controlled than when they started the relationship).

HISTORY OF THE PRESENTING PROBLEM

The main focus of this chapter is the effect of Mickey's substance abuse on her life and her therapy. However, since the issues of growing up with alcoholic parents and being sexually abused are intertwined with the substance abuse, they will be discussed as appropriate.

Substance Abuse

Mickey started drinking when she was a toddler: Her parents would give her sips of their beer. Drinking was a regular part of her parents' social activities, and they drank a lot. Mickey started drinking heavily at age 14. The first time she drank with her peers, she intentionally got drunk. The same day, she also smoked marijuana and was sexually abused by a horse trainer at a show in which she and her friends were participating. Thus, drinking, drugs, and sex were all associated for her.

In high school, Mickey and her friends would drink on weekends. Mickey almost always drank to get drunk; her tolerance was high and sometimes she would not feel drunk. Her friends were interested in sex as well. Because Mickey was afraid of boys and hadn't yet come out to herself, she avoided situations where sex would be a part of the night's activities. She did have several male friends with whom she occasionally smoked marijuana. By the time she was a high school senior, Mickey was drinking and smoking every weekend. Her desire to conform to the social norms of her peers, her fear of getting caught, and her desire to do well in sports kept her from drinking and smoking more frequently. After high school graduation, Mickey spent a year as a student in Australia. In a culture where people enjoyed drinking but did not get drunk, Mickey curbed her drinking. She wanted to normalize her alcohol consumption and she did not want to embarrass her family. Halfway through the year, she contracted hepatitis and mononucleosis and stopped drinking altogether.

When Mickey returned from Australia, she enrolled in college. At first, she played soccer and continued to refrain from all drinking and drug use; she was feeling healthy and strong. Mickey was excited about being away from home and being around people her own age. She soon made friends on the soccer team. As these friendships lengthened, she was invited to her first college party where drugs were used. Within two weeks, she was smoking marijuana every day. Her life deteriorated rapidly. During one quarter at school, she spent her tuition money on drugs. The next quarter she did almost no academic work. At the end of the year, she left school and thought consciously about suicide for the first time. She was 19.

Even though Mickey was very depressed that summer, she realized that she had to quit using drugs. She tried keeping her thoughts in a journal. The process of writing gave her the opportunity to express her thoughts and feelings about the deterioration of her life and about her desire to make changes, but this had no effect on her substance abuse. Within two years, she had quit school and started working as a stock clerk at a local department store. She met Jane, whose drug of choice was alcohol. Mickey was also using drugs on the street, where she was putting herself in serious danger every day. By the time Mickey started therapy with me, she was alternately frantic and depressed and was abusing drugs daily (though she managed to work part-time to pay bills and buy drugs), and her emotionally abusive, codependent relationship with Jane was failing. Mickey and Jane started therapy together, but after three sessions, Jane dropped out. Within three months she and Mickey ended their relationship.

History of Incest

In her third year of therapy, Mickey became aware of the possibility that she had been sexually abused. At the time, she was involved in her first healthy relationship with Sarah, her current partner. She was experiencing repeated feelings of fear and rage in even the simplest, most gentle sexual experiences with Sarah. Mickey is uncertain about many of the aspects of her incest—when it started, what happened, how long it continued. A critical moment in Mickey's self-discovery came one day when she spent several hours obsessing about cutting her wrists with a razor blade, but she stopped herself from doing actual harm. Later, as she acknowledged the possibility of incest, the self-injurious thoughts stopped altogether. After a year of intensive therapy, Mickey started to have dreams and flashbacks about experiences with her mother. She remembered being awakened at night. She remembered feeling "horrible and crazy," her body convulsing with fear and dread. She remembered being unable to stop any of this from happening. Last year, she had a urinary tract infection, the pain of which "felt familiar." Recently, she had a very brief flashback of her mother's hand touching her vagina. These dreams and flashbacks were conclusive evidence to her that her mother did abuse her sexually and that she had reason to feel angry and scared about being sexual.

FAMILY HISTORY

Mickey is the middle child of three; her younger brother was adopted as an infant. Mickey's father, John, is the middle child of seven children and was raised in a rigidly fundamentalist family. His mother was a fragile woman who had periods of depression that would last as long as five years at a time. While depressed, she would spend long periods in bed during which John's oldest sister would take care of the youngest children. Mickey believes that John, his younger sister and her husband, and his other sister's husband are all alcoholic, as judged by their drinking behavior in social situations.

Mickey's mother, Fran, had four siblings, two of whom died before the age of two. Fran's father was an alcoholic who stopped drinking in 1969 (after his children were grown). Fran's mother, Margaret, had a "nervous breakdown" at one point; Mickey doesn't know who took care of the children while she was recovering. Fran, her sister Jolene, both of their husbands, and Fran's father and mother were all alcoholics. In addition, all of Margaret's siblings, their spouses, and their parents were alcoholics.

DEVELOPMENTAL HISTORY

John and Fran created a rigid, harsh, and cold emotional environment for their children. Denial of parental responsibility and fear of sexual feelings were two major dynamics in this family, which provided an ideal environment for the fostering of incest, alcoholism, and child abuse. In addition, a strong double bind message to each child was "You are the best child/ you are not enough." John and Fran used this message to randomly reinforce behavior and to squelch individuality and appropriate separation.

Mickey was born several weeks prematurely. Stories from Mickey's favorite aunt indicate that her mother gave her reasonable care, keeping Mickey fed, clothed, and warm. Mickey has no memories of inappropriate touching before the age of four. She had enough mirroring from birth to six months to experience an adequate attachment to her mother and to begin the developmental process of separation. It is hypothesized that grooming for incest started at this time (Wolfe, 1990; Zaphiris, 1980). Because of inadequate, inconsistent parenting and her mother's emotional unavailability, Mickey did not separate in a healthy manner. She was punished physically and emotionally (hitting, withdrawing of affection, name-calling, being blamed for parents' drinking) when she expressed independence, anger, or resistance to parental authority. Mickey was enraged at feeling that she could not be separate and terrified that she would be abandoned.

Mickey's clearest childhood memories are of her parents' drunken parties, of being expected to sit quietly in church, and of feeling confused and frustrated when she was punished for stating her own mind. Mickey's mother was verbally abusive and humiliated Mickey frequently. Mickey's father was physically abusive. All of the children were hit; Steven, the youngest son, was sometimes beaten with a strap.

Mickey felt pressure to uphold the honor of the family by getting good grades in school. She was nearsighted, but her parents didn't discover this until she had been in school for several years. She also had to sit at the front of the classroom because she wouldn't pay attention. The emotional reasons why she was not doing well in school were not addressed, but Mickey did have several teachers during her school career who took extra time with her when she couldn't concentrate or calmed her down when she was distressed. They inspired her to learn and, for brief periods, to feel good about herself.

By the time she reached puberty, Mickey's home environment was extremely dysfunctional. Fran and John's drinking had increased consistently over the years and John had lost a number of jobs because of it.

PERSONALITY CHARACTERISTICS

In addition to being an ACOA, Mickey displayed typical behaviors of an incest survivor: She had low self-esteem, fear of intimacy, and sexual problems (including flashback memories of the incest). She forgot and then denied details of the incest, she blamed herself for the incest, she was self-destructive, and she was chronically depressed.

Mickey came into therapy using drugs and alcohol to cover her fear of abandonment. She used splitting (seeing people as good or bad and changing from one to the other without warning; seeing parts of herself and others as bad and therefore splitting them off and not acknowledging them), polarized thinking (things are either good or bad), and denial as defenses.

THERAPEUTIC ISSUES

To date, Mickey has worked on the following issues:

1. Starting a recovery program. This initial step was necessary so that she could stay in contact with her own thoughts and feelings long enough to perceive and react to them.
2. The development of trust in the therapeutic relationship. This task is challenging for an incest survivor, even more so for an incest survivor recovering from drug and alcohol abuse.
3. Challenging old beliefs about the incest (i.e., it was her fault, it didn't really happen, she must be a really bad person).
4. Examining what happened when her mother abused her and how the abuse influences her sexual feelings and behavior today.
5. Challenging her internalized homophobia which was reinforced by the stigma of alcohol/drug abuse and incest.
6. Examining and challenging the lessons she learned in her family about trust and intimacy in relationships (i.e., there is no room for her as a separate person, it is better for her to leave a relationship first than to be abandoned).
7. Risking increased intimacy with Sarah and learning ways to express feelings, especially anger, in order to develop a healthy relationship.
8. Challenging herself to pursue a career that truly interests her.

If Mickey were starting therapy today with these goals, the framework of her treatment plan would be straightforward and simple. That Mickey's first six months of therapy were conducted differently may speak more of my lack of experience and countertransference issues than to a specific strategy. However, the purpose of this section is to lay out a viable treatment plan.

The treatment plan for an individual who is in recovery from drugs or alcohol (or who needs to be) and who is working on emotional issues, has three components. The first component is an assessment by a substance abuse specialist. The purpose of the assessment is to:

1. Gauge the person's level of denial of the facts about her or his substance use/abuse;
2. determine the level of dysfunction and stress created by substance use/abuse; and
3. create a recovery program tailored to the individual.

The program may start with homework assignments designed to break through denial. The success an individual has with these assignments is usually correlated with success in recovery and therapy. My substance abuse colleague advises me of how the individual's recovery goals fit into her or his therapy goals and forewarns me of potential rough spots (i.e., the factors that would contribute to a relapse). Three or four checkups are scheduled over the next six months.

Sometimes, an individual's level of abuse or denial is so strong that outpatient therapy is not an appropriate place to start working. Two other alternatives are intensive inpatient treatment and intensive outpatient treatment. An individual who participates in intensive inpatient treatment stays for twenty days or longer, is separated from friends and family (except for family therapy sessions), learns about nutrition and the physiology of addiction, and participates in many group therapy meetings. In addition, the individual attends an extensive aftercare program in which the lessons learned on the inpatient unit are reinforced and progress is followed. An individual who participates in an intensive outpatient program goes to weekly group meetings (once or more than once per week) in addition to Alcoholics Anonymous (AA) or Narcotics Anonymous (NA) meetings; progress is followed closely and group members receive information, support, and confrontation as necessary.

The second component of the treatment plan is incorporating the development of a support network into the individual's life. Most people opt to attend AA or NA meetings. Many people are drawn to the sense of structure and ritual they experience when they attend such meetings regularly; they can find a "home group" (a meeting where they become known and can make friends) and choose a sponsor (a person who has been in recovery for a long time, is running a successful program, and is available to answer questions and to provide support).

After working extensively with individuals with eating disorders and substance abuse problems, Root (in preparation) has discovered that rituals for connection and transformation are important for the recovery of "wounded spirits" (survivors of trauma). There is often a strong connection between success in therapy and success in recovery. Success in recovery consists of recognizing oneself in the stories of others, acknowledging to others the reality of one's substance abuse/use, and focusing on other issues of recovery such as other addictions, problems with relationships, and asking for and taking reinforcement for successes. Many people discover the same messages about self-esteem, boundaries, expressing feelings, and relationships with family members in both therapy and recovery. In fact, one of the milestones that marks success in therapy and in recovery is when an individual becomes familiar enough with her or his themes to perceive them as themes and to face the world with equanimity. Such individuals are often asked to be sponsors.

The final component of the treatment plan is traditional psychotherapy with the themes described above. The work of therapy and recovery always run along parallel tracks.

Recovery As a Necessary Precursor to Effective Therapy

Two key issues have been identified in the discussion of Mickey's work: her drug and alcohol use and incest by her mother. It is not uncommon to see these two characteristics occurring together (Sullivan, 1988). Even so, the characteristic which is primary to the success of therapy is a successful recovery program (Kus, 1988).

Literature Review

There is general agreement that drinking and drug use is higher for gay men and lesbians than for heterosexuals (Retner, 1988). Schaefer et al. (1987) estimated that alcoholism among the homosexual and bisexual population is three times that of the general public. Alcoholism in the general population is estimated at about 10%. Similarly, Anderson and Henderson (1985) estimate that approximately one-third of lesbian women are alcoholics. Thus, the therapist is obliged to ask about drug/alcohol history with all clients. The therapist must be sensitive to ignorance (preconscious information) and to denial and withholding information, especially regarding the minimizing of substance use.

Not only is it important to inquire about drug and alcohol abuse, but it is crucial to have clients begin therapy by starting a recovery program. After interviewing twenty homosexual men, each of whom who had at least one year of sobriety, Kus (1988) discovered that these men accepted being homosexual as a positive aspect of self only after recovery. For lesbians and gay men who are also facing recovery from incest and for whom issues of low self-esteem and self-concept are primary, drinking and/or taking drugs impedes recovery in both areas.

The body of literature about child sexual abuse is large and that of adults sexually abused as children is growing. Earliest research indicated that sexual abuse did not occur very often (Weinberg, 1955; Weiner, 1982), that the effects were limited (Landis, 1956; Yorukoglu & Kemph, 1966), or that the child victim was a cooperating participant in her own sexual abuse (Bender & Blau, 1937; Kaufman, Peck & Tagiuri, 1954; Landis, 1956). Beginning in the late 1970s, however, research in the area of child sexual abuse took a radically different tone and several themes were emphasized:

1. The rate of sexual abuse is much higher than originally thought. The most often quoted rate is 25% for girls and 14% for boys. (Thanks to the Sexual Assault Center in Seattle for verifying these statistics.)
2. Children are not in any way responsible for their own sexual victimization. The adult offender is an adult and is therefore responsible for maintaining his or her personal boundaries.
3. The definition of sexual abuse has been expanded. King County Rape Relief (1979) offers this definition: Sexual assault means the forcing of sexual contact. When children are victimized, the sexual contact may involve handling of the child's genitals or requests for sexual handling by an older child or adult. Sometimes the contact is oral sex. Sexual contact includes attempts at penetration of the vagina or anus and, rarely, actual penetration. Some kinds of assaults involve

no physical contact. A child may be forced to look at the genitals of an older child or adult, or the child may be requested to undress or otherwise expose her/himself. (p. 5)

4. Incest is almost always a devastating experience for the victim (Forward & Buck, 1978). There are serious short- and long-term consequences to being sexually abused. Short-term effects in children include significant damage to self-esteem, feelings of guilt and shame, self-destructive behaviors, sleep problems, physical complaints, school problems, problems paying attention, irritable or withdrawn behaviors, overly compliant or overly aggressive behaviors, phobias, night terrors, and/or fear of strange men or strange situations (Finkelhor, 1988; Justice & Justice, 1979; Sanford, 1980). Long-term consequences for adult women include sexual dysfunction, low self-esteem, sleeping and eating disorders, depression that can lead to suicide attempts, self-destructive behaviors (e.g., substance abuse, prostitution, or battering in a relationship), greater use of psychological symptomology and psychoactive medication, and relationship problems (Briere & Runtz, 1988; Butler, 1978; Courtois & Watts, 1982; Forward & Buck, 1978; Herman & Hirshman, 1981).

The issue of women sexually abused as children became an area of interest shortly after the reality of childhood sexual abuse came to light. In addition to the research mentioned above, Bass and Davis's book (1988), *The Courage to Heal*, has been a significant source of support and information to many women recovering from sexual abuse. Wyatt and Powell (1988) have also edited a collection of research articles exploring theory, research, treatment, and social policy.

Discussion

An aspect of effective therapy that all therapists experience is countertransference. Lal Sharma (1986) defines countertransference as "any conscious or unconscious feelings, attitudes or reactions of the therapist toward the client which hinders the therapist's understanding of the client's conflicts and troubles and/or generates anxiety in him" (or her). As a therapist, I am more aware of some of my emotional vulnerabilities and less aware of others. When I continue to be confused by a client's work or if I am not sure whose work is being done—the client's or mine—I know I am probably experiencing countertransference. The solution may be as simple as reviewing my vulnerability and how it is being tapped. On the other hand, it may be that I have encountered a new issue that will become part of my own work in therapy.

For me, substance abuse was a new issue and I handled my vulnerability by seeing only clients who were successfully completing a recovery program. Mickey was the exception. I was unaware of how serious her substance abuse problem was because I colluded in minimizing her drinking and drug use. I didn't understand the degree to which drinking and drug use altered Mickey's perceptions of her daily experiences. Mickey was not cooperative. She couldn't remember. Her moods fluctuated from week to week, and neither of us understood why.

I liked therapy to proceed in an orderly fashion. I liked my clients to be in control of their lives so that there would be no surprises from week to week. I was scared of Mickey's inconsistencies; neither of us was in charge because the alcohol was in control. I didn't want to set limits and because I tried to work around her substance abuse, I condoned and enabled (made it easier for her to continue) her habit.

At last, a crisis occurred. Mickey went on a 12-hour binge. By nightfall, she was suicidal. Because the city was engulfed in a record snowstorm, I couldn't see her. Several friends eventually walked her to a hospital where she stayed for nine days.

Even though I experienced a significant amount of stress during this crisis, I still tried to work around Mickey's substance abuse by focusing on her depression. When she left the hospital, I hoped that she had recovered, that she was back in control of herself, and that she wouldn't be enraged, feel suicidal, or cut her wrists. But she was still out of control and several weeks later, she was suicidal again.

At this point, I called for a consultation with my substance abuse colleague. She gave me some good information and support about how to acknowledge Mickey's substance abuse to myself and to her, how to set a no-substance-abuse limit with her if she were going to be in therapy, and how to direct her in creating a substance-free support network for herself. Mickey went to her first NA meeting shortly thereafter. My colleague also suggested that I attend some AA or NA meetings so that I would know firsthand what the meetings are like and how they would enhance Mickey's therapy and recovery.

These suggestions took care of the immediate problems of what to do with Mickey's lack of control over her anger and behavior. Three events in the next six months helped me to start the process of understanding my countertransference about this issue. I read Janet Woititz's book *Adult Children of Alcoholics* (1983). In this short book, Woititz lists thirteen characteristics she has repeatedly observed in people who grew up in families with one or more alcoholic parents. I believed that I myself had 12 of the 13 characteristics, even though neither of my parents drank at all when I was growing up. I sent a letter to my mother and asked her if any of my grandparents had problems with alcohol. She stated that they did not. Perplexed, I decided that either she didn't have enough information about my grandparents or that she was in denial. Two months later, I attended an ACOA conference and discovered that the characteristics Woititz mentioned in her book are more or less applicable to people who have grown up in many types of dysfunctional families. I decided that I was an ACOW (Adult Child of a Workaholic), and I started to explore the implications of my family's style as well as my sadness and anger about how it could have been different. Finally, three months after the conference, I started participating in a new consultation group and was able to explore the issues that were raised by attending the conference. I discovered that when Mickey presented me with her cry for attention, I felt scared; I ignored the cry and tried to divert her attention. Because Mickey's behavior was self-destructive and out of control, I was even more scared and felt powerless. As soon as I took my power back (by setting limits on Mickey's substance abuse and suicidal behaviors) and stopped feeling so scared that something awful was going to happen and it would be my fault, Mickey and I both calmed down.

Mickey's therapy and recovery moved ahead more smoothly after this bumpy start. She attended NA meetings on a regular basis, found a sponsor with whom she could talk about the process of recovery, and made a number of friends who were also in the program. As her body detoxified, especially from the marijuana, she noticed that she had more energy and that her memory improved. She experienced strong emotional responses—happiness, sadness, and fear, as well as anger—to events in her life and she learned that those responses were normal. She learned to attach feelings to memories of her childhood. As a result, experiences such as her parents' drinking, the sexual abuse by the horse trainer when she was 14, the expectations placed on her to perform well in school, and her feelings of depression, rage, and low self-esteem took on a greater sense of reality. Mickey learned to say "no," to ask for what she wanted, and to see herself as a separate person who was responsible for the running of her life. As her self-esteem increased, she made changes in her life: a healthy relationship, a challenging job where her work was respected and appreciated, and a boundaried relationship with her family where *she* was in charge of contact with family members without feeling guilty, ashamed, or scared.

For my part, I learned more about my denial and about setting appropriate limits for Mickey and other clients around other recovery issues. Thus, a person who has had a relapse (usually a brief period of drinking) immediately goes back to my consultant to evaluate what happened and to build up her or his recovery program (by going to more meetings, sharing more in meetings, making better use of her or his sponsor, setting clear limits around distractions such as friends who won't honor the recovery program). A person who is more entrenched in denial will work more extensively with the consultant. She or he might keep a journal of thoughts and feelings that come up with the urge to drink or may be instructed to drink two drinks if she or he is going to drink. It is easier in the early to middle stages of the development of alcoholism to abstain from drinking than to stop after two drinks. This ability to abstain maintains the myth that she or he has no problems with alcohol (Campbell, 1988). Finally, if a client does not start a recovery program immediately after the drug/ alcohol evaluation, I will work with that person specifically on denial for a very brief period of time, one week to six months, depending upon the individual. Any longer period of time would signal my collusion and denial. Campbell (1990) maintains that the power a primary therapist has in the intervention of alcohol abuse/alcoholism is one of the most powerful tools available. The relationship between primary therapist and client allows the client to enter quickly into a trusting relationship with a substance abuse counselor. In addition, the primary therapist's willingness to set boundaries in the relationship with their drinking client is often the first intervention a client has had and can be dramatic in breaking through denial.

In this past year of Mickey's recovery/therapy, she has continued to deal with the ramifications of her incest. She started school and has placed a no-contact limit on her parents. Mickey has just celebrated her fourth year of recovery. Specific problems with recovery—denial about the seriousness of her addiction, forming a relationship with a sponsor, seeking support from friends in the program when she is scared—rarely came up. Mickey has also had occasion to challenge my denial when I minimize the fact that she is still in active recovery.

According to the AA model, the process of recovery is a lifetime commitment. I agree. It is an angry, fearful, confusing, exhausting, joyous process (Aldrich, 1983). Sometimes it is like a dream, full of metaphor (Swallow, 1983), especially when the person in recovery is reviewing old memories that can hardly be believed. Lesbians and gay men in recovery cope with two issues: the recovery process itself and homophobia (Gosselin & Nice, 1987). Thus, the struggles encountered in recovery—experiencing and incorporating grief, shame and low self-esteem, handling stress, creating healthy relationships, and setting limits with dysfunctional families—are all exacerbated by rage, grief, and shame responses from self and others that may surface when coming to grips with the reality of sexual orientation. In addition, in the lesbian and gay community, drinking and bars have historically played an important part in the development of identity for people just coming out (Nardi, 1982). As a result, giving up that aspect of one's lifestyle means finding other sources of support in the community. Fortunately for lesbians and gay men in Seattle, there are alternatives including gay AA meetings and drug- and alcohol-free social events. The latter especially have become increasingly supported in the last five years.

CONCLUSIONS

The premise of chemically dependent clients participating in a recovery program in conjunction with therapy is obvious. Unfortunately, most therapists learn this lesson through experience rather than in graduate school. Minimization and denial are the therapist's major symptoms. Treatment alternatives include consultation with or evaluation by a substance abuse specialist. This issue, though complex, can be easily addressed. As Mickey stated, "If I as a therapist could see the effect of alcohol and drugs on your life, I wouldn't be able to ignore it. I would have to set a limit on what I would accept."

REFERENCES

1. Aldrich, A. (1983). Sobering thoughts. In J. Swallow (Ed.), *Out from under: sober dykes and our friends* (pp. 152–160). San Francisco: Spinsters, Ink.
2. Anderson, S. C., & Henderson, D. C. (1985). Working with lesbian alcoholics. *Social Work, 30*, 518–525.
3. Bass, E. & Davis, L. (1988). *The courage to heal: A guide for survivors of child sexual abuse*. New York: Harper & Row.
4. Bender, L., & Blau, A. (1937). The reaction of children to sexual relations with adults. *American Journal of Orthopsychiatry, 7*, 500–518.
5. Briere, J., & Runtz, M. (1988). Post sexual abuse trauma. In G. Wyatt & G. J.

Powell (Eds.), *Lasting effects of child sexual abuse* (pp. 85–99). Newbury Park, CA: Sage Publications.

6. Butler, S. (1978). *Conspiracy of silence: The trauma of incest.* San Francisco: New Glide Publications.

7. Campbell, R. (1988). Personal communication.

8. Campbell, R. (1990). Personal communication.

9. Courtois, C. A. & Watts, D. L. (1982). Counseling adult women who experienced incest in childhood or adolescence. *The Personnel and Guidance Journal, 60,* 275–279.

10. Finkelhor, D. (1988). The trauma of child sexual abuse. In G. Wyatt & G. J. Powell (Eds.), *Lasting effects of child sexual abuse* (pp. 61–82). Newbury Park, CA: Sage Publications.

11. Forward, S., & Buck, C. (1978). *Betrayal of innocence: Incest and its devastation.* Los Angeles: J. P. Tarcher.

12. Gosselin, R., & Nice, S. (1987). *Lesbian and gay issues in early recovery.* Center City, MN: Hazelden.

13. Herman, J. L., & Hirshman, L. (1981). *Father-daughter incest.* Cambridge, MA: Harvard University Press.

14. Justice, B., & Justice, R. (1979). *The broken taboo: Sex in the family.* New York: Human Sciences Press.

15. Kaufman, I., Peck, A. L., & Tagiuri, C. K. (1954). The family constellation and overt incestuous relations between father and daughter. *American Journal of Orthopsychiatry, 24,* 266–279.

16. King County Rape Relief. (1979). *He told me not to tell.* Seattle, WA: Washington State Department of Social and Health Services.

17. Kus, R. J. (1988). Alcoholism and non-acceptance of gay self: The critical link. *Journal of Homosexuality, 15,* 25–41.

18. Lal Sharma, S. (1986). *The therapeutic dialogue: A theoretical and practical guide to psychotherapy* (p. 227). Albuquerque, NM: University of New Mexico Press.

19. Landis, J. T. (1956). Experiences of 500 children with adult sexual deviation. *Psychiatric Quarterly Supplement, 30,* 91–109.

20. Nardi, P. M. (1982). Alcoholism treatment and the non-traditional "family" structures of gays and lesbians. *Journal of Alcohol and Drug Education, 27,* 83–89.

21. Retner, E. (1988). A model for the treatment of lesbian and gay alcohol abusers. *Alcoholism Treatment Quarterly, 5,* 25–46.

22. Root, M. P. P. *Wounded spirits and poison potions.* Manuscript in progress.

23. Sanford, L. T. (1980). *The silent children: A parent's guide to the prevention of child sexual abuse.* Garden City, NY: Anchor Press/Doubleday.

24. Schaefer, S., Evans, S., & Coleman, E. (1987). Sexual orientation concerns among chemically dependent individuals. *Journal of Chemical Dependency Treatment, 1,* 121–140.

25. Sullivan, E. J. (1988). Associations between chemical dependency and sexual problems in nurses. *Journal of Interpersonal Violence, 3,* 326–330.

26. Swallow, J. (1983). Recovery: The story of an ACA. In J. Swallow (Ed.), *Out from under: sober dykes and our friends* (pp. 187–198). San Francisco: Spinsters, Ink.

27. Weinberg, S. K. (1955). *Incest Behavior.* New York: Citadel.

28. Weiner, I. B. (1962). Father-daughter incest: A clinical report. *Psychiatric Quarterly, 36,* 607–632.

29. Woititz, J. G. (1983). Adult children of alcoholics. Hollywood, FL: Health Communications.

30. Wolfe, R. (1990). Personal communication.

31. Wyatt, G. E., & Powell, G. J. (Eds.). (1988). *Lasting effects of child sexual abuse*. Newbury Park, CA: Sage Publications.
32. Yorukoglu, A., & Kemph, J. P. (1966). Children not severely damaged by incest with a parent. *Journal of the American Academy of Child Psychiatry, 5*, 111–124.
33. Zaphiris, A. (1980). The etiology, diagnosis and treatment of childhood sexual abuse. Paper presented at the meeting of the Mental Health Services for Clark County, Springfield, OH.

9

PATRICIA A. HUNTER

Psychotherapy With a Patient With Borderline Features

EBRA IS A 41-YEAR-OLD woman whom I have been seeing in individual psychotherapy for over two years. She presented with a variety of problems: feelings of depression and an inability to concentrate on daily life tasks (e.g., work, parenting), intense fears of divorcing a violent and drug-addicted husband of ten years who threatened to kill her if she left him, and anger and frustration surrounding a two-year romantic, yet nonsexual, relationship with a female artist.

At the time therapy began, Debra was living with her husband and eight-year-old son in an affluent suburb of New York City. The common theme running through all of Debra's problems appeared to be her deficient sense of personal identity. Who she was or what she wanted were questions Debra had never had the emotional capacity to answer for herself. For most of her life, Debra had had difficulties acting on personally defined goals, interests, or values. In her kind and gentle way she had allowed herself to be abused in most of the important relationships in her life, and she had reached her most difficult crisis thus far with a drug-abusing, violent husband who had threatened to kill her a number of times. Debra was severely depressed and looked to her girlfriend of two years for emotional support. Unfortunately, here too, Debra's passive interpersonal pattern repeated itself. She deffered to her friend in almost all matters, never expressing what she wanted from the relationship, only to berate herself later for being equally ineffectual and unhappy in this relationship.

Debra first became aware of her problem with identity/assertiveness issues in early adolescence when her eighth-grade teacher accused her of being empty. Evidently, Debra's blank stare and lack of emotional reaction when criticized rubbed him the wrong way. She still recalls this incident with horror and shame. Soon after, Debra began withdrawing from people and became socially phobic. She found the prospect of speaking up in class, presenting book reports, or even socializing with peers overwhelming. This was surprising to her because she recalled being outgoing in elementary school and having lots of friends. She didn't understand what was happening to her. Her teacher's comment consolidated her own fears that there was something drastically wrong with her.

One day during early adolescence, while drinking alcohol with others, Debra discovered, almost by accident, a way to help herself diminish her fears. She began medicating herself with alcohol on a regular basis. Debra drank before organization meetings, public speaking tasks, or school dances. Despite her drinking, she continued to do well academically and was admitted her senior year to a first-rate university. Unfortunately, Debra could not maintain her performance. She left college her sophomore year with poor grades and drifted into a pattern of part-time jobs and frequent parties. Her love life consisted of temporary sexual encounters with men and romantic fantasies about women. She was undirected personally and professionally. In an effort to soothe herself, she allowed her alcohol use to escalate to a dangerous point. At age 29, Debra was admitted to an inpatient hospital unit for alcohol detoxification. Her health at that point had been severely compromised.

By the time I saw Debra in individual therapy, ten years later, she had been sober for over nine years with only one major slip-up. She had been actively involved with Alcoholics Anonymous during that time and, despite her poor marriage and depression, she was functioning fairly well on a practical level. She worked regularly as a house painter and took reasonable care of her eight-year-old son. In her free time she read widely and took an interest in current events. She seemed to be very well liked by others. When she wasn't being threatened by her husband, she related as well as she could to him. In short, Debra was doing the best she could with a very difficult situation.

The details of Debra's early childhood are sketchy. Debra thinks her alcohol use has damaged her memory, which may be true. She remembers feeling extremely close to her mother and being favored by her mother over her four other siblings. Debra's father died when she was six months old and that may have contributed to her extremely close bond to her mother. As a child, Debra was frequently sick and required special attention. It seems Debra was considered both fragile and extremely intelligent (she excelled academically) by her sisters and brother. She remembers ignoring her siblings most of the time, preferring to relate to and identify with children in the neighborhood who were better off financially than her family was. Debra fought often with her stepfather. She thought he didn't like her, and she hated his occasional violence towards her mother. As far back as she could remember, it had seemed like she and her mother were pitted against her stepfather and the other members of the family.

At no time does Debra recall being related to by either parent as an individual in her own right or receiving any realistic guidance about school or interpersonal matters. Her mother, although approving, supported anything Debra did in an indiscriminate way. As adolescence approached, Debra had no real idea how to relate emotionally to peers. Her models at home included clinging (with mother), hostility (with stepfather), or avoidance (with siblings). Despite her favored status with her mother and her academic and athletic achievements in school until that point, the transition from childhood to adolescence was terrifying to Debra. She had no one to turn to with her frightened feelings for her mother admired her and looked to her for strength, and her stepfather seemed to take pleasure in her having problems. Debra's high intelligence became a burden to her as she catalogued her inadequacies and punished herself for each limitation.

By the time Debra left for college, she had only a dim awareness, through crushes on teachers or movie stars (unavailable older women), of her romantic feelings for women. Since sex was the one social activity she enjoyed with men, she had no doubts about her sexuality per se. Debra began college in 1967 as the women's movement was beginning, and the gay and lesbian social scene was still peripheral to campus life. As Debra struggled with academic and personal demands, she rarely gave any thought to her sexual/emotional preferences. She does remember enjoying a close relationship with her roommate that occasionally became sexual when she was drunk but doesn't remember thinking about or discussing the emotional or sexual aspects of the relationship when sober.

As the media began covering the evolving gay and lesbian political scene (e.g., in 1969 with the Stonewall riots), Debra remembers beginning to take notice of and identifying with gays and lesbians. She made attempts to define herself outside the mainstream by telling friends she was bisexual and taking pride in that revelation. She identified with the lesbian characters in the newly emerging feminist literature. Once hospitalized for alcoholism, however, Debra's social and political awareness became restricted as she struggled to take fewer risks in her life in order to support her sobriety. Her close relationship with her roommate had ended when she returned to her hometown to try and stabilize her compromised physical health. As she was attempting to forge a new path, becoming increasingly involved in Alcoholics Anonymous, Debra began dating Jim, a man she had known as an acquaintance in high school. Despite her ambivalence about marrying somebody like Jim (she knew he had anger problems), Debra went ahead and married anyway. She attempted to stabilize herself by making a commitment to a more traditional marriage and the possibility of children.

Debra did appear more emotionally stable once married, in a defensive effort to balance her husband's instability. As his rages began increasing, Debra reacted by focusing on her own physical survival and protection of her young son. Her daily life consisted of defending herself (by remaining extremely calm) during the difficult times and enjoying feelings of relief that accompanied occasional recreational outings with her husband and child during the less violent periods. Her life routine was circumscribed by her husband's more obvious emotional problems, and this afforded Debra an opportunity to operate as the more realistic, responsible member of the marital dyad.

The personality dynamics and consequent life problems that Debra presented dictated the therapeutic issues I initially addressed. Debra's childhood, adolescent, and adult history indicated an unstable pattern: a borderline personality disorder. Her alcohol use over the years had soothed her abandonment fears and leveled out her feelings of anger, irritability, and rage, but overall, Debra had struggled with problems all persons with borderline personality struggle with: intense interpersonal relationships, impulsiveness (e.g., alcoholism, sex), suicidal thoughts, threats, impulses, and an inability to experience a consistent identity or sense of direction in the world.

Although Debra had maintained a ten-year marriage, she had attempted to flee many times, only to change her mind at the last minute. Upon leaving Jim, Debra would feel overwhelmed with the prospect of creating an independent life style, frightened of her husband's threats of violence if she left him (he said he would kill them all if she left), and sadness at the loss of her familiar role as somebody's wife. Debra also felt intimidated at the thought of raising her son alone, as she felt her husband was the more adequate and interested parent. Although popular, Debra's friendships tended to be structured around AA activities rather than the sharing of personal thoughts or feelings. True intimacy, which is contingent on one's having a fairly solid sense of identity, was not possible for Debra.

Debra was extremely depressed and negative about her abilities and her life. She felt defeated by her husband's irrational violence. (He had recently burned down the Christmas tree and all of Debra and her son's presents.) Although she appeared clearheaded in our sessions, Debra continually complained about feeling foggy and unable to concentrate. She obviously took pride in her intellectual abilities and seemed more oriented toward a cognitive interpretation of reality, telling me she did not want to discuss her past. I decided I could help Debra most by teaching her to change her thoughts (Beck et al., 1979; Ellis & Harper, 1975), which would help her to change her feelings and become more calm, rational, and less critical of herself and lead to more productive behavior (e.g., assertiveness, improved social skills and relationships with others). Debra was in a dangerous situation, one that was potentially suicidal or homicidal, and in retrospect, this was one reason why my treatment goals were so straightforward and task-oriented. Had the circumstances been less urgent, I might have spent more time getting to know Debra, building a trusting relationship, and slowly identifying underlying issues which had put her at risk in the first place. But most research in crisis treatment indicates the necessity for immediate, practical, short-term strategies, and that's how I proceeded.

THE BORDERLINE PERSONALITY DISORDER

Borderline personality disorder as an official diagnostic category didn't appear until DSM-III in 1980 (Linehan & Wagner, 1990). Its history in the psychoanalytic community is extensive, however, with major theories proposed by Adler (1985), Gunderson (1984), Kernberg (1984), and Masterson (1976). Behavior therapists, who historically have resisted diagnostic categorization on principle, have also shown a slow but steady interest in the behavioral problems associated with borderline personality disorder. Most recently, Linehan (1987) proposed a feminist behavioral approach for treating clients with borderline personality disorder called dialectical behavior therapy, which considers the theoretical construct of dialectics in treating people suffering from emotional instability in major life areas. Family systems therapists (Bowen, 1978; Haley, 1976; Minuchin & Fishman, 1981) have treated people with borderline personality problems for years, though they have tended toward a more problem-defined and group focus. Family therapists treat dysfunctional families with alcoholism, delinquency, and eating disorders, to name a few, all of which indicate some version of underlying borderline pathology.

To date, almost all published treatments for individuals meeting criteria for borderline personality disorder have been pharmacological (Brinkley, Beitman, & Friedal, 1979; Goldberg et al., 1986; Leone, 1982; Serban & Siegal, 1984) or have been based on psychoanalytic theory (Adler, 1985; Chatham, 1985; Kernberg, 1984; Masterson, 1976; Meissner, 1984), or a combination of the two. Although behaviorists have developed treatment strategies for many individual behavior patterns associated with the diagnosis of borderline personality disorder, with few exceptions (Turner, 1984), they have not integrated these strategies into a comprehensive treatment approach.

According to Linehan (1987), the behavior pattern most associated with the borderline diagnosis—parasuicide—has been comparatively ignored by behaviorists and psychoanalysts alike. Parasuicide (intentional, acute, self-injurious behavior sometimes referred to as suicide attempts or suicide gestures, but also including head banging and self-mutilation) is particularly prevalent among individuals meeting criteria for borderline personality disorder. Gunderson (1984) suggests that this behavior may come closest to representing the "behavioral specialty" of this personality disorder. The empirical data bear him out (Clarkin, Widiger, Frances, Hurt, & Gilmore, 1983: Conte, Plutchik, Karasu, & Jerrett, 1980; Graff & Mallin, 1967; Grunebaum & Klerman, 1967).

In short, the literature on borderline personality disorder is long on theory and short on application. Silverstein (1988) addressed the potential prevalence of borderline personality disorder within the gay and lesbian population, hypothesizing a relationship between confusing and stressful social conditions and internalized personality structure. But, for the most part, the gap between personality theory and empirical documentation of treatment results remains unbridged.

THERAPEUTIC INTERVENTIONS

The issue which has inspired my work with Debra for the past two years revolved around how to help Debra develop a more stable sense of identity, emotionally, behaviorally, and interpersonally. When Debra began therapy, I set specific cognitive-behavioral goals to alleviate her depression and help manage her marital crisis. These goals involved teaching her to recognize automatic thought patterns and how these could be altered, to understand assertiveness principles and techniques for relating better with her girlfriend and her husband, and to break down her impending goal of divorce into smaller, more manageable tasks that she could accomplish during specific time periods. Initially, I saw Debra twice a week to provide needed emotional support and guidance. She attended sessions regularly and within two months had left her husband and found a new apartment in the community for herself and her son.

During the third month of therapy, I was surprised when I heard that Debra had gotten drunk, fallen on a radiator and sustained third-degree burns, and slashed an artery in her wrist. This occurred a month after she moved into her new home. I was shocked because she had been doing so well and seemed to be benefiting from treatment. I had been under the impression that we had achieved fairly good rapport.

Linehan (1987) describes the tendency for borderline clients to feel emotionally invalidated when their therapists do not recognize the degree of their emotional distress:

Recognition of the discrepancy between one's own capacities for emotional and behavioral control, and excessive demands and criticism by the environment, can lead to both anger and attempts to prove to significant individuals the error of their ways. How better to do that than by suicidal behavior? (p.266)

Clearly, Debra had gotten her point across. I felt both distressed for her and guilty, and I also felt like a fool for pushing her so fast. Linehan (1987) also suggests that borderline clients often look more competent than they really are:

In addition to much competency, they [borderline clients] often have many areas of intertwined incompetency, which they find extraordinarily difficult to communicate directly to others. . . . When therapists go along with the competency expectancies, they may not only be too demanding in terms of performance expectations, but they may also be unresponsive to low-level communications of distress and difficulty. (p.268)

Obviously, Debra had been distressed and I had not recognized it. Her behavior in my office had seemed relaxed to me. She was bright, verbal, and able to laugh at herself. But, clearly, her capacity to modulate her affect in my office did not generalize to her own living space. She had become extremely depressed after she left my office the Friday before the suicide attempt. She got drunk for the first time in several years, fell on a radiator and burned herself, and then slashed her wrist. Debra admitted to having felt misunderstood by me in therapy and anxious that she couldn't live up to my expectations. Although charming and controlled when I visited her in the intensive care unit of the hospital, Debra eventually expressed her feelings of shame and humiliation when she saw me there. She felt she had failed in her role as patient. From my standpoint, I was the one who had failed, for I had expected to help Debra improve her life, not frustrate her and miss signs of acute emotional distress. She and I both struggled during that difficult time to maintain feelings of self-esteem.

Debra decided that she would move back into her new apartment when she left the hospital and that she would continue in therapy with me twice a week, with phone calls to me if she felt depressed. I set what I thought were more manageable, less demanding goals for therapy. The specter of her husband's drug addiction, which was worsening as the divorce proceeded, and his potential for violence loomed in the background, but Debra proceeded with her life despite her anxiety, and I admired her for that. During therapy sessions, I tried to be more empathic and what I thought Debra would construe as less demanding. I felt sensitized to Debra's fears of change and of disappointing me, and I took more time to discuss how certain cognitive habits develop, how difficult it is to become assertive after a lifetime of feeling pushed around, and the loss issues surrounding divorce, even when a person chooses it. I paid particular attention to the way Debra interpreted some of the behavioral tasks I assigned (e.g., planning a recreational activity with a friend) and tried to be alert to signs that she didn't understand them or didn't want to complete them.

One day, after things had been going well for some time, Debra's husband, whom Debra only saw when their son was visiting him, held her at gunpoint with an M-16 rifle and threatened her life. Debra escaped and, at my insistence, retreated to a battered women's shelter until things calmed down. When the situation improved, and her husband's behavior seemed to have stabilized (Debra had filed a police report against him), we discussed the incident in therapy. In her evasive, by now routine way of discussing things, Debra explained that she had had sex with her husband the night before the incident. Evidently, she had been struggling with fears of loss, of being single, and of being a lesbian and had relieved her fears through inadvertently creating a crisis by sleeping with her extremely temperamental husband. The crisis, of course, not only put her at great risk but masked the original issue: how to help her deal better with her fears of changing.

Throughout our work together that first year, predicting and preventing major life crises became a major goal of therapy. Learning to identify and resolve her emotional problems more directly, rather than indirectly acting upon them, was a major accomplishment for her.

The girlfriend Debra had discussed when therapy began occupied much of our conversation during that time as well. Mary was consistently unreliable and frustrated Debra (i.e., playing hard to get and then pursuing Debra when ignored), and I encouraged Debra to get out of the relationship and make new lesbian friends who might be more available for romance. Within a few months, she had a new girlfriend, less interesting to her than Mary had been, but attractive nonetheless. Within six months, Debra settled into a routine of love, parenting, and work that was more stable than anything she had experienced until that point. Her girlfriend was kind to her and her son, her husband was no longer threatening her, and her house painting business was stable. Debra was rarely depressed and almost never had thoughts of suicide.

That's when we came to our second therapeutic impasse, as Debra began to feel empty and bored with her life on a day-to-day basis. I felt that many of our therapeutic goals had been achieved, and Debra seemed more upbeat and funny than she had ever been in therapy, so I wasn't sure how to proceed. I felt uncomfortable with the amount of nonverbal attention I was receiving from Debra (she seemed almost adoring), and the more active I became in response to Debra's complaints of emptiness and boredom, the more passive about her life she seemed to become, although she remained entertaining during therapy. In an effort to encourage her to take more initiative in therapy, I provided less advice and encouragement, which Debra then interpreted as a form of rejection. I realized that the attention I felt I was receiving from her had something to do with my less active attitude as well, but I felt too uncomfortable and unskilled to do anything about it (I had little real experience interpreting transference issues). After we had both discussed her boredom for several weeks, and I had explained my behavior in terms of wanting her to take more of the lead in our sessions and her not really knowing how to, Debra suggested she take a break from therapy. I felt ambivalent about this and somehow disappointed, but I would be lying if I didn't admit to feeling relieved at escaping a situation (my own countertransference) I wasn't sure how to handle.

THE COUNTERTRANSFERENCE

What to do about Debra? Despite a termination that was reasonably friendly on the surface, that question was frequently on my mind. I was worried about Debra and felt at a loss to help her. She had refused to see another therapist when I had offered a referral. At the same time, through both a personal experience and while doing some personal reading about intimacy issues (Lerner, 1989), I was becoming more aware of my tendency to focus on the problems of others when I became anxious, rather than on my own. I was spending some emotional energy grieving about that realization and learning to take more risks in my own personal relationships. In addition, while reading about Bowen's work with families for a family I was treating, I began to realize how overly responsible I felt as a therapist. Both experiences were illuminating for me on both a personal and professional level, and I began to think about what had happened between Debra and me. I questioned whether I had been more active and caretaking with her than I needed to be, and whether I had conveniently avoided having to confront my own feelings of anxiety in our sessions by doing so. I admitted to myself that I had become threatened by feelings of both closeness and frustration in our sessions and had withdrawn and encouraged Debra to take the lead as a result. I imagined that Debra had sensed this withdrawal, although she had never mentioned it, and quit in response. After a lot of personal reflections, I decided to call her and try to discuss what might have happened.

Debra seemed pleased to hear from me and expressed a desire to continue therapy. She had been thinking of calling me because she had felt depressed, despite her having continued to avoid crises and function well. When she came back, I was both excited and anxious. I began to deal with my own anxiety by making clearer statements about what I thought I was feeling and what I thought might be happening for Debra in the sessions. I shared some of what I had read about family systems concepts of overfunctioning, underfunctioning, and triangles in order to give us both a language for describing interpersonal behavior. I occasionally admitted to feeling uncomfortable or confused by Debra's behavior and would ask her to clarify what she meant during a particular session. I invited her to discuss feelings and thoughts she had about me either during or outside of our sessions in order to encourage a more immediate relationship between us.

Although Debra rarely discussed anything bordering on transferential feelings, I felt relief at a door having been opened for the future, and I sensed a change in her attitude toward me. I hoped that the interactions between us would take on a more egalitarian flavor. Therapy since that time has had its illuminating days and its boring days, but essentially the relationship between Debra and me has become more genuine and more defined. Although Debra isn't always optimistic about herself, her life, or her therapy sessions, she continues to lead a more life affirming, rather than life threatening, existence with a partner she cares about and work that she enjoys. Her son has worked through the trauma he experienced when his parents were together and is getting along better in all ways, which is a great relief to Debra. At my prompting, Debra has begun reaching out to the siblings she rejected so long ago and to redefine her role in her original family. She and her mother have remained close, although less so than before. However, her stepfather's death four years ago prevents her from renegotiating that relationship. Despite periodic setbacks with bouts of emotional withdrawal, Debra reports that her friends find her more open and easier to talk to, and she says she now is more open about herself with her friends. She still has a tendency to look to others to fill the empty places in herself, but as she discusses feelings involving losses and is able to grieve those losses in therapy, her feelings of boredom and emptiness seem to be diminishing.

In presenting this case history of how Debra and I came to work together in a way that helped her begin to resolve her serious emotional problems, I was struck by the flexibility needed in order for my work with her to be effective. For me, conducting therapy has never been as smooth and predictable as I expected it to be when I was a student of behavior therapy in graduate school, and my work with Debra taught me much more than any textbook ever could about being sensitive to a client's unique patterns of behavior. I didn't always feel comfortable or competent working with Debra, but I always felt interested in the process of our work together and willing to experiment. I began my work with Debra with one set of expectations (i.e., short-term, cognitive-behavioral crisis therapy) and over the course of two years modified my expectations in a way I hadn't foreseen in the beginning (i.e., dealing with deeper-seated personality issues). I hope the benefits of therapy will be lasting for Debra. The benefits for me, the development of a greater sense of flexibility and identity as a therapist, have been immeasurable.

REFERENCES

1. Adler, G. (1985). *Borderline psychopathology and its treatment*. New York: Aronson.
2. Beck, A., Rush, A., Shaw, B., & Emery, G. (1979). *Cognitive therapy of depression*. New York: Guilford.
3. Bowen, M. (1978). *Family therapy in clinical practice*. New York: Aronson.

4. Brinkley, J., Beitman, B., & Friedel, R. (1979). Low-dose neuroleptic regimens in the treatment of borderline patients. *Archives of General Psychiatry, 36,* 319–326.
5. Chatham, P. (1985). *Treatment of the borderline personality.* New York: Aronson.
6. Clarkin, J., Widiger, T., Frances, A., Hurt, S., & Gilmore, M. (1983). Prototypic topology and the borderline personality disorder. *Journal of Abnormal Psychology, 92,* 263–275.
7. Conte, H., Plutchik, R., Karasu, T., & Jerrett, I. (1980). A self-report borderline scale: Discrimination validity and preliminary norms. *Journal of Nervous and Mental Diseases, 168,* 428–435.
8. Ellis, A., & Harper, R. (1975). *A new guide to rational living.* Englewood Cliffs, NJ: Prentice-Hall.
9. Goldberg, S., Schulz, S., Schulz, P., Resnick, R., Hamer, R., & Friedel, R. (1986). Borderline and schizotypal personality disorders treated with low-dose thiothixene vs. placebo. *Archives of General Psychiatry, 43,* 680–686.
10. Graff, H., & Mallin, R. (1967). The syndrome of the wrist cutter. *American Journal of Psychiatry, 124,* 36–42.
11. Grunebaum, H., & Klerman, G. (1967). Wrist slashing. *American Journal of Psychiatry, 124,* 527–534.
12. Gunderson, J. (1984). *Borderline personality disorder.* Washington, DC: American Psychiatric Press.
13. Haley, J. (1976). *Problem-solving therapy.* New York: Harper & Row.
14. Kernberg, O. (1984). *Severe personality disorders: Psychotherapeutic strategies.* New Haven, CT: Yale University Press.
15. Leone, N. (1982). Response of borderline patients to loxapine and chlorpromazine. *Journal of Clinical Psychiatry, 43,* 148–150.
16. Lerner, H. (1989). *The dance of intimacy: A woman's guide to courageous acts of change in key relationships.* New York: Harper & Row.
17. Linehan, M. (1987). Dialectical behavior therapy for borderline personality disorder. *Bulletin of the Menninger Clinic, 51(3),* 261–276.
18. Linehan, M., & Wagner, A. (1990). Dialectical behavior therapy: A feminist-behavioral treatment of borderline personality disorder. *The Behavior Therapist, 13(1),* 9–14.
19. Masterson, J. (1976). *Psychotherapy of the borderline adult: A developmental approach.* New York: Brunner/Mazel.
20. Meissner, W. (1984). *The borderline spectrum: Differential diagnosis and development issues.* New York: Aronson.
21. Minuchin, S., & Fishman, H. (1981). *Family therapy techniques.* Cambridge, MA: Harvard University Press.
22. Serban, G., & Siegal, S. (1984). Response of borderline and schizotypal patients to small doses of thiothixene and haloperidol. *American Journal of Psychiatry, 141,* 1455–1458.
23. Silverstein, C. (1988). The borderline personality disorder and gay people. *Journal of Homosexuality, 13,* 185–212.
24. Turner, R. (1984, November). *Assessment and treatment of borderline personality disorders.* Paper presented at the meeting of the Association for the Advancement of Behavior Therapy, Philadelphia, PA.

10

ROCHELLE L. KLINGER

Treatment of a Lesbian Batterer

THIS CHAPTER WILL present a case of treatment of a lesbian whose major conflict was her battering of lovers in successive relationships. I will review the case study, literature on the issue, and summarize how the treatment was formulated, designed, and carried out.

CASE STUDY: PRESENTING PROBLEM

Pat was a lesbian in her late thirties who presented to a colleague for couples therapy with her lover, Marcia. The couple asked for help in resolving frequent arguments and physical abuse of Marcia by Pat. After two conjoint sessions, the couples therapist felt that couples work was increasing the episodes of domestic violence and was contraindicated. She referred Pat to me for individual psychotherapy and evaluation for antidepressant medication.

Pat was 10 years older than Marcia and had been Marcia's work supervisor before they became lovers five years before presentation. They had quickly moved in together and combined their financial resources. After nine months of living together, they had a minister preside over a commitment ceremony. They considered themselves married and monogamous for life.

Pat initially described the first four years of their relationship as idyllic, emphasizing that they had the same interests and friends and, particularly, that they had never spent a night apart in their five years together. Pat described herself as the primary decision-maker in the relationship and was occasionally psychologically and physically threatening to Marcia when she would not agree with her, but she did not initially see this as a problem. Later in therapy, Pat saw some of the negative points of their early relationship.

Six months before presentation, Pat became infatuated with a straight woman with whom she worked, who was divorcing. Pat asked Marcia to agree to their relationship becoming nonmonogamous. Marcia was opposed to this, but Pat insisted. Soon after that, Pat and the other woman went away for a weekend together. Afterwards, Pat decided that she did not wish to have an affair and told Marcia she wanted to be monogamous again. However, Marcia decided that she would now have an affair (with Pat's ex-lover, Sandy) and refused. This affair was still going on at the time of presentation.

This conflict escalated into severe arguments with increasing psychological and physical abuse by Pat. Among the abuses Pat inflicted on Marcia were threats, keeping Marcia isolated, pushing, restraining, slapping, throwing objects, kicking, hitting with fists, and threatening to hurt her with a knife. At times, Pat's abusive behavior was preceded by her drinking alcohol, but at other times she was sober. The week of presentation Pat had actually pulled a knife on Marcia for the first time, threatening to kill Marcia and herself. This culminated in Marcia calling Pat's mother to come get her, which Pat found humiliating.

On presentation, Pat complained of feeling out of control of her actions, frequent worrying, dysphoria, constant preoccupation with the conflict, and crying almost continuously. She also noted poor appetite and sleep, a twelve-pound weight loss, feelings of panic, suicidal ideation, homicidal ideation towards Sandy, and poor concentration. Fortunately, she was on vacation from her job, because her occupational functioning would certainly have been impaired. An additional stressor was that one month before her father had died after a long illness. Pat had no independent friends—all of her friends were "couple friends," who had originally been friends of and loyal to Marcia. Pat's only source of support was her mother, who was caring but very compulsive and hypercritical. Her fundamentalist religion made her uncomfortable with Pat's lesbianism and knowledge of Pat's abusive behavior made this worse.

Pat's initial goals for therapy were magical wishes to have Marcia back and everything the same as before the conflict. At this point, Marcia had moved out and was hiding for safety. Pat described focusing all of her efforts on what she could do to get Marcia back. She seemed to have no independent goals and believed that her actions could somehow influence Marcia to come back. She desired instruction from me on what she could do to fix the relationship. This was her first experience with psychotherapy, and she felt ashamed and weak for needing help. She was very deferential and self-effacing in therapy, often asking if it was OK to feel certain things, or saying how crazy I must think she was.

Developmental History

Pat was the second of four daughters born to a working-class, fundamentalist family in the South. Her father was a factory worker, and her mother was a clerical worker. She described her father as pleasant but undemonstrative and her mother as controlling and hypercritical, with numerous rigid rules about how things should be done. Neither parent was alcoholic or physically abusive, but her mother was often emotionally abusive when Pat did not perform tasks in the way she desired. She also had a difficult time at school, where she was teased for being masculine and a tomboy. This verbal abuse escalated when she reached high school. She had few friends, performed adequately in academic subjects, and excelled at sports. She had little interest in boys in junior high and high school, but did not become aware of her attraction to women until her senior year of high school.

Gay and Lesbian History

Pat did not act on her lesbianism until college, when she became involved with her first lover in her freshman year. Despite efforts to be discreet, they were suspected of being lovers by their roommates. Their college was a small, conservative southern one, and Pat was called into the Dean's office and asked if she was a lesbian. She denied everything and barely avoided getting expelled. However, after that, she and her lover began dating men, and the relationship broke up. Her lover got married three weeks after graduation. Pat said that she was not that upset by this, which I suspected was denial and/or repression. There was no abuse in this relationship.

She began to date her second lover as a senior in college. They moved to her lover's hometown where she took a job. They moved two more times, once precipitated by their landlord figuring out that they were lesbians and evicting them. In relating these events, Pat expressed little anger. Of note, however, is that Pat first became abusive to another woman at this point. Frequent arguments, often culminating in verbal and physical abuse began at this time. During one argument about where they should spend Christmas, Pat threatened her lover with a gun, and shot it at the floor. (Gun ownership for hunting or protection is fairly common in the South, even among women.) They were together for seven years. In this relationship, as in all others until Marcia, Pat had no contact with the lesbian community. She met her third lover, Sandy, while she was still with her second lover.

Sandy was also an employee of Pat's. Pat had originally hoped that they could continue as a threesome, but this did not work due to frequent arguments and fights among the three women. She described the first year with Sandy as passionate, but after that they also had frequent incidents of fighting and abuse. As in her previous relationship, the content of the fights varied, but they all centered around power and control. Pat described becoming enraged whenever her lovers expressed strong opinions which differed from hers, or whenever things were not done her way. Despite this, she and Sandy stayed together for six years, until Pat left her for Marcia.

Pat was very closeted and isolated from the lesbian community until she met Marcia, who introduced her to a small circle of lesbian friends. Pat was very uncomfortable with her lesbianism, as one would expect from the combined effects of her religious and cultural upbringing and her life experiences. In addition, she and Marcia were both in fields where disclosure of their sexual orientation carried a real risk of being fired from their jobs. As part of her abusive behavior, when they argued, Pat sometimes capitalized on this by threatening to disclose Marcia's sexual orientation to her employer.

Personality Dynamics

Pat's personality dynamics became manifest early in the course of therapy. She had a rigid set of rules and expectations about how things should be done and divided the world into black and white, right and wrong. In therapy, this caused her to be extremely deferential to me; she considered me her moral superior because I was the therapist, and she considered herself as weak and inferior because she needed help.

Believing that her rules were the one right way, she tried to control everyone, including Marcia and her coworkers. When people disregarded her rules, she became very angry and punitive. She expected her "superiors" to have a rigid set of rules for her, and she was equally hard on herself when she felt she had been less than perfect. She had no real insight into the irrationality of her rigidity. Her primary defenses were obsessive-compulsive, with some dependent and passive aggressive traits.

Two additional factors are prominent in a discussion of Pat's personality dynamics—sexism and homophobia. Pat's developmental history is striking in regards to the number of times she was persecuted for her lesbianism and, as a woman in the South, she endured much sexism as well. Homophobia, the irrational fear and hatred of gays and lesbians, can be internalized and cause great damage, particularly when it is unconscious. Pat clearly internalized the external negative attitudes against gays and lesbians and acted them out upon herself and, particularly, upon her lovers. She also appeared to internalize the rigid male/female power differential so prominent in her cultural surroundings and to act this out in her relationships.

Therapeutic Issues

Initially, therapy focused upon contracting for the safety of Pat, Sandy, and Marcia and stabilizing Pat's depressive symptoms. Her suicidal ideation remitted fairly quickly. Pat wished to focus the therapy on how she could control Marcia in order to win her back. I confronted this goal, and pointed out that she only had control over her own behavior, not Marcia's, and that she could not force Marcia to come back. Other initial issues to be focused on were her belief that there were rigid rules about life and the legitimacy of her feelings. I repeatedly urged her to be less judgmental and self-deprecatory.

As the therapy progressed, we turned to the goal of helping her to develop independent goals and interests, which she had never had in any of her relationships. This was initially very difficult, both because she wasn't sure she wanted to work on anything but the relationship, and because she felt so bad about herself that she doubted anyone would want to be her friend. Like many lesbian couples, Pat and Marcia's relationship suffered from an excessive degree of merger or fusion. This fusion, in combination with Pat's personality dynamics, contributed to Pat's intolerance of any difference between Marcia and herself. (This issue will be discussed at greater length in the literature review.) Pat's motivation to seek independent interests gradually improved after many months of work.

Throughout the first year and a half of therapy, the couple had meetings and near reconciliations and even moved back in together once, briefly. With each near reconciliation, Pat lost track of her independent goals and tried to fuse again. However, Marcia was very ambivalent, stating that she was unwilling to trust Pat, yet frequently telling her she loved her and did not want to give up on the relationship. Each honeymoon period culminated in Pat becoming controlling and Marcia becoming angry and distancing. Pat's mood and motivation varied greatly with these events. She tended to cancel sessions when things were good and to appear in crisis every few weeks when Marcia rejected her. This was actively confronted.

In the first year of therapy, Pat frequently wanted me to tell her what to do to make things OK and wished for a structured setting such as a lesbian abuser group which was not available in our area. I interpreted this as her desire for a parent to tell her the correct rules again. She attended AA because the original couples therapist had suggested that it might be helpful, although I did not see her alcohol use as problematic. Her motivation to attend was her hope that it would help to convince Marcia that she was trying to change. It turned out that Pat found the structure and steps of AA fairly helpful but didn't talk about her abusive behavior in the meetings for fear of censure.

During the middle of the therapy, Pat pushed down a coworker, who complained to her supervisor. Pat almost lost her job and was placed on probation. The dynamics of her abuse at work appeared to be identical to those at home, i.e., based on control issues.

A turning point occurred after one and a half years of therapy when Pat began to consider the idea of getting out of the relationship to protect herself from Marcia's alternate pursuing and distancing. After Pat had indecisively considered this for several months, Marcia became involved with a new lover. Pat was grief stricken over this but was at last able to mourn the loss of the relationship and move on. She was able to stand back and consider what she wanted for herself as an independent person for the first time. Pat pushed the couple to sell their house and divide up their possessions in order to get on with her life. Marcia actively resisted this, but Pat was able to negotiate and compromise for the first time with Marcia. Pat's work performance also improved greatly.

After two years and four months of therapy, Pat had much improvement in her self-esteem and independence. She was much more aware and accepting of her feelings and often noticed herself becoming self-deprecatory and changed her phrasing. She had developed a good network of friends in the lesbian community, many through the gay church she had joined in seeking independent activities. She was less closeted and more accepting of her lesbianism.

REVIEW OF LITERATURE: DEFINITION/PHENOMENOLOGY

Domestic violence is defined as any pattern of behavior designed to coerce, dominate, or isolate within a relationship or the exercise of any form of power to maintain control. Abuse is always based on unequal power. In heterosexual relationships, this is usually the result of sexism but, of course, power differences also occur in lesbian relationships (Walber, 1988). In fact, lesbians appear to have great difficulty negotiating power differences (Burch, 1987). Lesbians appear to batter for the same reasons as males—to get what they want (Hart, 1986). Battering appears to be a learned pattern of behavior; when the individual gets what she wants by being violent, this behavior is reinforced. While there is a high incidence of substance abuse and childhood history of abuse in batterers, certainly all individuals with these histories do not batter (Leeder, 1988).

Phenomenologically, abuse takes similar forms in lesbian couples as in heterosexual couples. Forms of abuse include physical abuse, isolation, threats, psychological and emotional abuse, property destruction, sexual abuse and rape, economic controls, and threats or actions to expose a victim's sexual orientation. Walker's (1979) cycle theory of violence frames domestic violence as encompassing three stages. The couple first experiences the tension building stage. This is followed by the stage of acute battering incident, and finally, the stage of loving, contrite behavior. During this third stage, the couple makes up and magically hopes that the abuse will not recur. Unfortunately, in most cases the cycle recurs again and again.

There is virtually no literature discussing possible etiologies of battering in lesbian relationships. This can be traced, in part, to denial in the lesbian community about the existence of battering at all. While some of this denial may be based on fear of losing hard-won ground in the political arena, there is also a tendency to romanticize relationships between women as being always harmonious. In order to better understand this trend, we need to review recent literature on women's development and psychology and its effect on relationships.

In the last decade there has been an explosion of literature on theories of women's development that take women's socialization into account (Chodorow, 1978; Dinnerstein, 1976; Flax, 1978; Gilligan, 1982; Miller, 1976). These differ from established theories that equate psychological health with the achievement of separation and autonomy manifested by culturally successful males. In contrast, relatedness is seen as paramount for women, without implying that this is pathological as traditional paradigms do.

If women are socialized to value relational harmony and relatedness as primary, it is not surprising that fusion or excess relatedness is common in lesbian couples. In comparison to heterosexual and gay male couples, lesbians generally have the most intense and romantic relationships with the least distance (Blumstein & Schwartz, 1983; Vargo, 1987). This, in and of itself, is not pathological, in fact, it may be seen as enviable. However, there is also a tendency towards fear of any difference or individuality in partners. External homophobia can also push lesbian couples towards merger.

When partners give up their differences, enmeshment replaces the ebb and flow of connection and separation that is the mark of true intimacy in relationships. Potential consequences are diminishment of excitement and sexual attraction, repression of competitive and individual feelings, and active discouragement of difference by one or both partners (Krestan & Bepko, 1980). In the extreme, this could be a component of the etiology of abuse in a relationship.

Incidence

Until very recently, the occurrence of battering in gay and lesbian relationships was not even mentioned in the literature. In the past five years, there has been some interest in this. Brand and Kidd (1986) studied 75 heterosexual and 55 lesbian women between the ages of 19 and 58 who were given a 24-item anonymous questionnaire to determine how many had been physically or sexually abused. As expected, the overall frequency of violence in heterosexual couples was significantly higher than in lesbian couples. However, 25% of the lesbian women in a committed relationship had experienced physical abuse. In dating relationships with other women, 7% of the lesbians had been raped, 5% had dates attempt rapes, and 7% had pain inflicted beyond consent when practicing S-and-M. (This study was limited to Caucasian, middle-class subjects.)

Bradford and Ryan (1988) surveyed health and mental health issues in a group of 1,917 lesbians in the National Lesbian Health Care Survey. These women represented a cross section of age, racial, and ethnic backgrounds, and rural and urban locations. They found that 22% of the women had been victims of physical abuse as adults and, of this group, half had experienced it at the hands of lesbian lovers. The incidence of abuse was higher in older women and in Latina and black women. They did not survey the incidence of lesbians who admitted to being perpetrators of domestic violence—it would be interesting to see if the reported incidence would be the same. Large, diverse retrospective studies like this are a valuable contribution to the literature and need to be continued and expanded. In addition, prospective studies of domestic violence in lesbian relationships should be pursued.

Treatment of Abusers

Brennan (1985) reviewed models for treating male spouse abusers, primarily based on the prototype organization Emerge in Boston (Adams & McCormick, 1982). The literature reviewed here rejects a unitary theory of battering as a clinical syndrome but, rather, sees it as a behavior which can be reached by many paths. Males are predisposed to domestic violence by sexism, which teaches them to suppress feelings other than anger, to be aggressive, and also legitimizes violence as a way of dominating women. Sexism can also be operative in lesbian relationships, particularly when one or both partners adopt male/female roles. Just as homophobia can be internalized by gays and lesbians, a lesbian can batter her partner, partly because she has internalized negative attitudes toward women.

This model suggests that males who do not live up to their own expectations of maleness are prone to battering; men who are less confident and assertive or who feel impotent and powerless are more likely to abuse. Thus, treatment must deal with social stereotypes, individual personality deficits, and patterns of relational interaction. In their long-term psychoeducational/psychotherapeutic groups Brennan (1985) focused on attribution of responsibility for violence, intensive reconstruction of violence and cues; and skills training including stress management, anger control, assertiveness training, and communication skills. They found this to be effective in decreasing and eliminating physical violence, but emotional abuse often continued until relational and couples issues were addressed in more advanced treatment.

Leeder (1988) discusses individual and couples treatment of lesbian batterers and victims. She divides abuse into three types: situational, chronic, and emotional. This particular case would fall under chronic abuse according to Leeder's classification. Based on her clinical experience, Leeder characterizes the typical chronically abusive couple as emotionally and financially enmeshed. She describes the abusers as suffering from poor self-esteem, as fearing abandonment and loss, and as having poor communication skills. She recommends working individually with the batterer for an extended period of time. Initially, she recommends building trust and rapport with the batterer during the history gathering. Later, the therapist should work with the batterer to help her recognize when she is getting angry and define alternatives to violence such as time-out, while also working on communication and assertiveness skills. As the batterer learns to trust the therapist's support and caring, confrontation of the abuse and limit-setting is more successful. Leeder, like most authors on this subject, recommends bringing the couple together for conjoint work only in the final stages of treatment, when domestic violence has ceased.

Gilbert and Zemsky (1988) outlined a model of a fifteen-week voluntary group program for lesbian abusers who wish to change this behavior. Each two-hour group session consisted of one hour of structured skills work and one hour of support and therapy. Women were encouraged to take the group sequence more than once if they wished to.

They framed battering as learned behavior about which abusers have a choice. Abuse behavior is based on a desire to control another individual, which is a response to internal pain felt by the abuser. They noted that all of their clients to date were themselves formerly victimized. Clients must be willing to look at themselves and focus on the pain which fuels the abuse. Their goal is empowerment of these women so they don't need to abuse in order to feel powerful.

The group work included assertiveness, empathy, and self-determination training; treatment of codependency; and cognitive restructuring of black/white, catastrophic, and perfectionistic thinking. Skills which were taught included relaxation training to deal with anger and anxiety, time-out, giving and receiving feedback, cues to abuse, management plans for abuse, forgiveness, social awareness, and empowerment techniques. Because this was presented in a workshop format and not data-based, there is no way to assess the efficacy of this approach.

None of the literature directly addressed how one would treat the couple conjointly after the abuser was treated individually. If fusion were a primary component, there is clinical literature suggesting treatment methods. Treatment consists of educating and encouraging the couple towards some differentiation as a positive attribute or "distancing for intimacy." Referring each woman to an individual therapist is often a prominent suggestion. Other issues usually include power, dependency, and roles in nurturance (Kaufman, Harrison, & Hyde, 1984).

TREATING A LESBIAN BATTERER IN PSYCHOTHERAPY: EMERGENT ISSUES

With Pat, as with all clients, the first issue to be assessed and dealt with was safety. Her possible homicidal and suicidal ideation necessitated immediate attention. Although she voiced fantasies about hurting Marcia and Sandy, she denied that she would act on these. Of course, if I felt that either person was at significant risk, I would be obligated to warn them as per the Tarasoff ruling. In fact, both Marcia and Sandy were quite aware of Pat's feelings and were hiding from her.

In terms of suicidal ideation, Pat voiced a strong desire to be reunited with Marcia, and thus she was motivated to stay alive as long as she thought there was hope for reunion. Therefore, she was able to contract for safety in a way that I felt reasonably sure of. I did worry about potential suicide attempts if Marcia broke up with her outright. Inpatient treatment was raised as one option, but Pat was against this and was able to convince me that she would be safe as an outpatient with close follow-up.

Differential diagnosis in service of designing a treatment plan was the second order of business. Pat's depressive and anxiety symptoms were sufficient to qualify her for a *DSM-III-R* diagnosis of major depressive episode. Because of this, I elected to use pharmacotherapy in addition to psychotherapy. I started her on a gradually increasing dose of imipramine, a tricyclic antidepressant, raising the dose to 200 mg per day over three weeks. I gave her very small prescriptions at any one time because of the risk of lethal overdose with tricyclics. Interestingly, Pat's depressive symptoms improved markedly after only one week of imipramine treatment, which would be unusually early for a pharmacological improvement, suggesting a placebo effect may have been prominent. Pat was maintained on imipramine for eight months, then successfully tapered with no recurrence of major depressive syndrome.

Psychotherapy in the first few weeks was crisis oriented and centered around supporting Pat's return to the day-to-day activities that were necessary to caring for herself and getting support from others. Initially, very basic issues were dealt with, e.g., sleep, nutrition, and daily living skills.

Power/Control Issues

As mentioned earlier, Pat's goal for at least the first year or more of therapy was to get Marcia to come back to her. Therefore, a major thrust of the first half of therapy was to delineate what Pat did and didn't have control over. Pat battered Marcia when she was unable to be in control of Marcia's actions, thoughts, or affects, which she equated with being right, OK, good, and loved. When Marcia would not allow Pat to control her, Pat felt rejected, unloved, and ashamed, as if she'd done something wrong. She had never recognized or questioned this belief before but took it as a universal given.

I spent much time in the first half of therapy repeatedly pointing out to Pat when she spoke for Marcia or for the couple, e.g., when she expressed a desire to work on changing Marcia's behavior and the impossibility of this. This work was often frustrating because Pat had a great deal of difficulty understanding this. In reviewing our therapeutic work for this chapter, I was heartened to hear Pat say that this was one of the major ways in which therapy was helpful.

I also repeatedly confronted Pat about the arbitrary nature of her rigid rules. In a session during her third month of therapy, she described in detail how she required Marcia to put food on the refrigerator shelves in a particular order. I expressed the opinion that there was not one right way to order the refrigerator's contents and told her that I found her rule about it amusing. I disclosed to her that the first fight my lover and I had was about whether or not it was OK to put catnip on top of the bed and that I had had a similarly rigid rule. It took Pat a while to try out this new perspective of looking at her rules as humorous. However, this opened the door for her to start reality-testing some of her rules outside of the therapy.

The other major focus in the power/control arena was Pat's increasing awareness and pursuit of independent feelings and interests. Pat had rigid rules and expectations about what were "worthwhile" activities. For the first year of therapy, her major independent interests that fulfilled these criteria were training for a marathon in a compulsive, extremely disciplined manner and working two part-time jobs in addition to her primary job. Later, she was able to find some activities which she enjoyed just for fun, like playing softball.

Transference Issues

Pat's behavior in therapy was consistent with her developmental and relational history of rigidity and placing everything on a continuum of power and rightness. Pat felt inferior to me because she was coming to me with a problem. She idealized me as being perfect and morally superior to her. One day, about midway through the therapy, we were discussing an appointment time change. She had signed up for classes and a part-time job without first consulting me and had left herself with only one free afternoon, expecting that I would offer her an appointment then. She was very surprised when I told her that I saw my own therapist on Thursday afternoons and couldn't see her. She couldn't imagine a therapist needing or wanting psychotherapy herself.

Pat was well aware of social attitudes towards battering and was deeply ashamed of her behavior. She expected me to be judgmental and hypercritical of her, and she often started statements in sessions with "I know this is really crazy or terrible to feel this, but. . . . " She was also extremely deferential to me, calling me "ma'am" so often that I asked her several different times if she'd been in the military. This rigid transferential view of the therapist was consistent with the way she had viewed her mother when she was a child and felt weak and inferior, and in the opposite role of wishing to be powerful and in control of Marcia. Of course, these dynamics can be seen in anyone with rigid, compulsive defenses and are not unique to a client who batters.

In therapy, I offered her continual feedback that despite what she thought, I wasn't judging or censuring her. I frequently legitimized her affects and urged her to be less judgmental of them. Nonetheless, it took over two years of work before she stopped apologizing before every statement of affect. I also encouraged her to be flexible about seeing the plurality of views in the world rather than her black/white thinking. This, too, took almost two years for her to accept and apply in her therapeutic and extratherapeutic relationships. Towards the end of therapy, she became much more comfortable in challenging my opinion and assertively offering hers in our discussions.

Countertransference Issues

Most therapists would have strong countertransference issues in treating a lesbian batterer. I would expect a client like Pat to be particularly affect-provoking to a beginning therapist. Reactions can be related to political and social beliefs, personal history (particularly if the therapist was abused as a child or adult), fear, and defensive revulsion and judgement.

Heterosexual and lesbian therapists may not believe that lesbians can batter, as most women equate battering with the male/female power differential. Lesbian therapists, in particular, might idealize lesbian relationships as free of the conflicts that men and women have. A gay or heterosexual male therapist may also react with disbelief and anger, or may unconsciously identify with the abuser due to internalized homophobia and sexism. Gay male or lesbian therapists may wish to deny that abuse is a potential in their own relationships and feel overly angry and judgmental toward the abuser, as if to say "this won't happen to me because my lover is not a bad person like this patient is."

If the therapist had been abused him or herself, as a child or in a relationship, powerful conscious and unconscious affects could be stimulated by the batterer. In my case, my father and a former lover had been physically abusive to me. Pat was not the first lesbian batterer that I'd treated, but she was the first with whom this was the primary issue—the others were much more disturbed clients whose abuse was less prominent than other, more serious problems.

I had a mixture of feelings in working with Pat. Initially, I felt angry at her and even wondered if I could work effectively with her. I also would start thinking about my abusive ex-lover whenever Pat described battering. When I'd think about that, I started to feel guilty for "prompting" my lover to batter me, even though I knew this was irrational. I also think I sometimes felt like a bad kid who caused her parent to abuse her (so that I wouldn't have to blame my father, which was too frightening as a child). Because of this, I also felt some anger at Marcia for being passive-aggressive toward Pat and precipitating the abuse. As I got to know Pat better, I became more aware of the reasons for the battering and of the pain she bore, and I felt more compassionate. As this occurred, I was able to tolerate Pat's talking about the abuse in detail with less overwhelming feelings. It also helped that, through my own therapeutic work, I had forgiven my ex-lover and my father by the time we got into the intense parts of Pat's treatment. I would recommend supervision and/or personal psychotherapy to other therapists with a personal history of abuse.

Lesbian Issues

We focused specifically on Pat's homophobia, both external and internal. It is worth noting that Pat entered therapy with me, an openly lesbian clinician, which suggests that she was ready to deal with these issues at this time. Pat benefited from my modeling of being an open lesbian who was comfortable with her sexual orientation and was later able to actively seek lesbian friends in the community. She was still circumspect about revealing her sexual orientation at work but did come out to several long time heterosexual friends and acquaintances. Overall, she was much more comfortable with her lesbianism as the therapy progressed.

Specific Work on Battering

As I outlined the components of Pat's therapy, it became clear that all of it related to her battering. In this section, I will discuss *specific* work on battering behavior. Much of this work was based on the extremely detailed and helpful handouts from Gilbert and Zemsky's presentation (1988).

We initially focused on recognizing the situations involving power and control which predisposed Pat to batter. We outlined Pat's physical and emotional cues that abuse was brewing—she would feel angry, become physically hot an flushed, move closer to Marcia, feel frustrated at an inability to control Marcia, and then grab Marcia in a way that was initially meant to be loving but became violent. This final sequence in which the embrace became violent was always blacked out by Pat, whether or not she was consuming alcohol at the time.

We also worked on specific skills that Pat could utilize when she became aware of the potential for abuse, including standing back, breathing slower, and sitting down. Mentally, she worked on saying to herself, "OK, I can't *make* her do it." She also regularly practiced relaxation techniques and tried to utilize them at this time. The most difficult therapeutic task was Pat's forgiving herself for her abusive behavior. When she was able to do this, I felt she truly had the skills she needed to deal with her potential to batter.

Spiritual Issues

Two extratherapeutic activities had a major positive effect on Pat's recovery from battering—her involvement in AA and in a gay/lesbian Christian church. Having been raised in a fundamentalist church, Pat was deeply confused about the place of God and religion in her life as a lesbian and a batterer, both of which she felt made her a bad person. After four years of practice in the South, I am convinced that almost no one who is raised in this manner can then neatly leave religion behind him or herself when reaching adulthood without underlying conflicts. The combination of positive spirituality, fellowship, and forgiveness which Pat received in these two organizations was extremely helpful in allowing her to forgive herself and be with others in a more meaningful way than she ever had before. The AA concept of turning things over to a higher power was particularly helpful to Pat.

When reviewing the treatment with me for this case study, Pat cited the twelve steps of AA as being very helpful. She particularly mentioned the twelfth step, in which one helps someone else to recover from the same problem. Being the subject of this chapter was one way Pat worked on that twelfth step, by showing other lesbian batterers and their therapists that they are not alone and that there is hope.

CONCLUSIONS

It is important to note that much of the beneficial effects of Pat's therapy did not deal directly with her battering. As with many clients, attention to basic issues of self esteem, flexibility, choice, independence, support, and attention to affect comprised the majority of the work, with only a small percentage of therapeutic time spent directly on the battering.

A turning point in the treatment occurred when Pat considered the option of not continuing to reconcile with Marcia and ultimately when Marcia became involved with a new lover. This opportunity to fully and voluntarily mourn the relationship helped Pat to invest in herself and move away from the relationship. There is no question that Pat will always have personality traits which predispose her to rigidity, compulsivity, and conflicts with power and control. However, at the end of the therapy she had the skills and flexibility to cope with these in a healthier manner.

It is hoped that reviewing Pat's history and treatment in this chapter will help contribute to more literature being written on treatment of lesbian batterers. Many more research and case studies are needed concerning this important, common clinical issue.

REFERENCES

1. Adams, D., & McCormick, A. (1982). Men unlearning violence: A group approach based on the collective model. In M. Roy (Ed.), *The abusive partner: An analysis of domestic battering*. New York: Van Nostrand Reinhold.

2. Blumstein, P., & Schwartz, P. (1983). *American couples*. New York: William Morrow.
3. Bradford, J., & Ryan, C. (1988). *The national lesbian health care survey*. Washington DC: National Lesbian & Gay Health Foundation.
4. Brand, P., & Kidd, A. (1986). Frequency of physical aggression in heterosexual and female homosexual dyads. *Psychological Reports, 59*, 1307–1313.
5. Brennan, A. (1985). Political and psychosocial issues in psychotherapy for spouse abusers: Implications for treatment. *Psychotherapy, 22(3)*, 643–654.
6. Burch, B. (1987). Barriers to intimacy: Conflicts over power, dependency, and nurturing in lesbian relationships. In Boston Lesbian Psychologies Collective (Ed.), *Lesbian psychologies: Explorations & challenges*. Urbana, IL: University of Illinois Press.
7. Chodorow, N. (1978). *The reproduction of mothering: Psychoanalysis and the sociology of gender*. Berkeley: University of California Press.
8. Dinnerstein, D. (1976). *The mermaid and the minotaur: Sexual arrangements and human malaise*. New York: Harper & Row.
9. Flax, J. (1978). The conflict between nurturance and autonomy in mother/daughter relationships within feminism. *Feminist Studies, 4*: 171–89.
10. Gilbert, L., & Zemsky, B. (1988). Abuse prevention groups for lesbians who batter. Presented at the annual meeting of the National Lesbian and Gay Foundation, Boston, MA.
11. Gilligan, C. (1982). *In a different voice*. Cambridge, MA: Harvard University Press.
12. Hart, B. (1986). In K. Lobel (Ed.), *Naming the violence: Speaking out against lesbian battering*. Washington: Seal Press.
13. Kaufman, P., Harrison, E., & Hyde, M. (1984). Distancing for intimacy in lesbian relationships. *American Journal of Psychiatry, 141*:4.
14. Krestan, J., & Bepko, C. (1980). The problem of fusion in the lesbian relationship. *Family Process, 19*:272–89.
15. Leeder, E. (1988). Enmeshed in pain: Counseling lesbian battering couples. *Women and Therapy, 7*, 1:81–89.
16. Miller, J. B. (1976). *Toward a new psychology of women*. Boston: Beacon.
17. Vargo, S. (1987). The effects of women's socialization on lesbian couples. In Boston Lesbian Psychologies Collective (Ed.), *Lesbian psychologies: Explorations & challenges*. Urbana, IL: University of Illinois Press.
18. Walber, E. (1988). Behind closed doors: Battering and abuse in the lesbian and gay community. In M. Shernoff, & W. Scott (Eds.), *The sourcebook on lesbian & gay health foundation*. Washington, DC: National Lesbian & Gay Health Foundation.
19. Walker, L. (1979). *The battered woman*. New York: Harper & Row.

11

HAROLD KOODEN

Self-Disclosure: The Gay Male Therapist as Agent of Social Change

IN OUR SOCIETY, THE gay male has lacked the proper anticipatory social-ization for entrance into full adulthood. Psychotherapy is a corrective socialization process where the gay male therapist works to eradicate inter-nalized homophobia and effect the transition into adulthood. For the therapist to be an effective agent of social change, he must understand the clinical relevance of self-disclosure and role-modeling.

As a therapist, looking at my participation in the therapeutic process is as important as recognizing my own level of development. As a middle-aged gay man, I have accomplished much but still have additional steps to take. The many maturational and life-threatening issues surrounding AIDS have broadened the scope of clients that I work with as well as made the depths to which we can go more profound.

I believe that I cannot fully take a client to a psychological place to which I have not gone myself, nor can I help resolve an issue that I myself have not dealt with. This means that I must constantly work to develop my full potential if I want to be more than a problem-solving therapist (Jourard, 1961). I have to understand the stages of my own life cycle and incorporate them into therapy, so as to facilitate the client's maximum development.

It is from this perspective that I discuss the following two concepts: therapist self-disclosure and the therapist as role model. In the process of developing my psychotherapeutic techniques, these concepts have become of paramount importance.

THERAPIST SELF-DISCLOSURE

Traditional psychoanalytic therapy does not distinguish between counter-transference and self-disclosure. There is a danger in describing all the therapist's disclosures as countertransference, even though this is a valid psychotherapeutic concept (Winnicott, 1965). I refer to "countertransfer-ence disclosure" as disclosures about the therapist's specific reactions to the client that appear as irrational and inappropriate. But this is only one type of self-disclosure. Five additional categories of self-disclosure are relevant to psychotherapy: historical, emotional, relational, philosophical, and fantasy.

Historical disclosure refers to statements revealing information about the therapist's past and current life, e.g., age, background, education, sexual orientation, relationship status, community involvement, and relevant per-sonal experiences.

Emotional disclosure refers to the emotions, feelings, or sensations being experienced at the moment in the therapy session.

Relational disclosures denotes the therapist's interactions with and thoughts/feelings about the client, both during and outside the session.

Philosophical disclosure refers to discursive statements about psychotherapy, spirituality, homophobia, morality, nutrition, safer sex. Although some of the examples in the last category could be seen as "factual," I consider them philosophical, because I believe that "facts" are embedded in a philosophical context. One's belief system determines the set of facts one chooses and how one interprets them. I also believe that the therapist's belief system determines which theory of therapy to follow. The choice is based on what is emotion-ally, intellectually, and spiritually consistent with who the therapist is and evolves as the therapist evolves. It has become evident to me that the primary factors in successful therapy are the personality of the therapist and the thera-peutic relationship rather than the specific therapeutic techniques being used.

The last category, *fantasy disclosure*, has proven most helpful to me when therapy is at an impasse, when both my client and I are stuck, or when I do not understand what my client is trying to say. At such times I may intervene using the fantasies that have been stimulated in me during our interaction. Based upon early Whitaker and Malone (1953) ideas about the use of the therapist's fantasies and dreams about clients, I may explore the possible relationship between some of my fantasies or recollected expe-riences during therapy and what is happening to my client at that moment in therapy. This includes remembered movies, books, stories, dreams, songs, or plays.

Given the vast range of fantasies available to me and the millions of past experiences that I could choose to recollect at any moment, I assume that what comes to me is specific to that moment. I then try to abstract a theme from that image or experience, a lesson that I have learned, or a dominant feeling. I reframe that theme, lesson, or feeling as my suggestion about what the client is experiencing or trying to say. This has been useful for working through these "stuck" moments. It invariably leads us to take a next step and brings us closer together. In order to stay with this process, I have to be open to what is happening inside me and to see our relationship as an interactive one. My fantasies or memories are connected to something the client is communicating to me, even in silence. By not immediately dismissing seemingly intrusive fantasies as being strictly countertransferential material, I am open to another productive level of therapeutic work.

The therapist must be self-aware, flexible, and have a sense of what's appropriate. In this framework, countertransference is a valuable source of information for therapy (De Angelis, 1990). After recognizing the emergence of a countertransferential feeling or thought, the therapist can then look to what it was within the therapeutic interaction that stimulated this internal reaction in himself (Winnicott, 1965). It is equally relevant to note what behavior is being prompted within the therapist.

A clear communication to the client about the therapist's internal reaction can have many effects. It shows, first, that these transference reactions can be talked about without being acted out, and second, that reactions can be successfully analyzed and altered; it also vividly demonstrates both the difference between transference and the reality of the ongoing relationship and the fact that transference is usually the result of a present interactive process between two persons.

As always, all self-disclosures must be clinically appropriate, i.e., they must enhance the goals toward which we are working in therapy. Whether to disclose or not to disclose is a clinical decision for that specific moment; self-disclosure is preferable only insofar as it furthers the therapeutic process (Jourard, 1960; 1964).

ROLE MODEL

In order to develop a positive identity, most people need positive role models with which to identify. The role model should be symbolic of what the person can successfully attain. If there are only a few positive role models, then their visibility becomes all the more important for a person's maturation. The person does not have to become like the role model because, in truth, the role model is just a stimulus for the person. At different times in a person's life, different role models are necessary. For example, a supportive, loving, non-gay therapist can be a positive role model for a gay person who is establishing his identity. This is not a role model with which the gay person identifies, but one who functions more as a significant person giving the client permission to continue in his unique development.

At another stage of ego development, it can be equally important to have a positive gay role model to counter the negative gay role models and homophobic attitudes that have become internalized and limited a gay person's self-expectations. Interaction with positive role models helps to expand the boundaries of self-expectations when these positively regarded people have clearly extended their own limits and are encouraging others to do the same.

For many gay males, psychotherapy with a gay male therapist and/or a group is their first experience toward making the transition to adult manhood. In this socialization process, the gay male psychotherapy group can also function as the first positively regarded group of which the client feels he is a participating member. Participating in the group combats his lifelong feelings of isolation and of being an outsider. I believe that successful therapy is the result of the therapist's presenting himself as a mature and competent adult who is establishing a healing relationship with the client. Explicit in this relationship is the expectation that the client can achieve the same level of development as the therapist.

CASE STUDY

In our first interview, I had difficulty understanding Jack because he spoke quickly and mumbled. He answered every question openly. A friend suggested that Jack explore group therapy with gay men while continuing individual therapy with his non-gay psychiatrist. Jack identified himself as bisexual, which was a function of his heterosexual behavior, although his sexual fantasies were predominantly homosexual. He had a long-term, unhappy sexual relationship with one woman on whom he was dependent, and several other relationships with women that were generally satisfying sexually, but in which he behaved immaturely. His current heterosexual relationship was anxiety-laden because of the conflict between heterosexuality/bisexuality/homosexuality, but he felt it was the most satisfying non-gay relationship he had. Besides taking antidepressants and antianxiety medication, he consumed large quantities of marijuana, caffeine, nicotine, and alcohol. Given his extremely high level of anxiety, bouts of depression, hyperactivity, and negative self-image, I was amazed that he had finished college and medical school.

Although 38 years of age, he was an adolescent emotionally. He was intelligent, articulate, and in touch with his pain. His low self-esteem was maintained by his inability to evaluate accurately his behavior or perceive how others saw him. This latter point is crucial because he did not care that he also presented himself as a warm, caring person who could make emotional contact with others. He wanted to be seen as "hot, butch, athletic, and talented." His inability to incorporate most of his positive behavior led him to feel that he was constantly starting at ground zero in any endeavor.

Jack was an only child of somewhat observant Jewish parents with whom he had a symbiotic relationship. Jack's father was a successful businessman who had extreme temper tantrums with family, business partners, and customers. Jack claimed his verbal and emotional behavior was identical to his father's except that his father never listened to anyone. Jack's mother had only recently begun to stand up to her husband as a result of therapy. Though he was employed and maintained his own apartment, Jack still received $20,000 a year from his parents. Though this sum came regularly, there was a history of unfulfilled financial promises from his father about which Jack was still furious.

Jack regarded his short stature and lithe physique as further proof of his inadequacy (much later, this evolved into discussions about his feelings about the size of his penis). Initially, he had a full, shaggy beard, "wild, fuzzy hair," and was always neatly dressed. His extensive social life was almost completely heterosexual. His homosexual feelings were secret except to two gay friends. His sexual experience with men was confined to one-night stands. He stated initially that he wanted to be able to have mature emotional relationships and sex with both men and women. Other than discomfort with being homosexual, Jack was not consciously aware of any homophobic feelings. His intellect and value system would not allow his being judgmental toward others.

Jack had been in psychotherapy for over fifteen years with three different therapists. Three years of therapy with his first therapist, now deceased, had enabled him to leave New York and finish medical school. Jack was

still not clear what his motivation was to become a physician. He had a
formal relationship with his current therapist, in which, after nine years of
two sessions per week, they still called each other by their full titles. He
had been hospitalized twice, for intense anxiety disorder and because he
was afraid of committing suicide; he had previously attempted suicide
when he was in college.

Jack would readily refer to himself as "a mental patient who needed to
be in therapy for the rest of his life." He thought of himself as crazy,
depressed, weird, and maniacal. He could more easily think of himself
as being schizophrenic and out of touch with reality than as being narcissistic.

His decision to be in a group was a wise one. I sensed that he was
interested in more than a group experience. The group would be a safe
way for him to deal with his homosexuality and to experience his first gay
male therapist without severing ties with his non-gay therapist. In the
group, he could gain a sense of who I was without having to commit
himself to individual therapy with me. That kind of commitment would
have been tantamount to declaring himself gay. Getting into group therapy
was also a courageous step. He was an only child, the constant center of
attention, and therefore never learned how to share his parental figures
with others. Consequently, learning to share in the group would be difficult. He had always felt isolated and not part of a group. He felt that he
was undersocialized and did not know how to act as an adult, and he felt
that he was a child who did not want to grow up.

Because he had a dependent personality, there was the possibility that
he would become dependent upon the group. This would be positive,
because it would mean that he could learn to seek out men for emotional
support. Implicit in this was that he would look to the therapist less and
begin to establish more self-reliance. This would also mean that he would
learn how to receive and give feedback. This process would help him to
be more realistic about himself and about how others perceived him,
and it would strengthen his weak ego. It would also strengthen his poor
boundaries in relationships, as he would be relating to other men con-
cretely and would be open about the distortions in his thinking. I also saw
that the group experience would help "tighten him up." He was used to
years of therapy sessions during which he was flooded by his emotions,
and he had not developed a sense of control so that he could focus and
take steps to resolve his constant pain.

DISCUSSION

Jack could easily relate to me as the rescuer-therapist but not as a positive role model with whom he had an interactive relationship. Since there were sporadic individual sessions as well as continual group sessions before he made the commitment to work individually with me, he had ample opportunity over two years to gain a sense of who I was. My task was to be responsive to him, so that he felt free to ask what I thought or felt. I would answer his questions, as long as we could discuss why he was asking. The freedom to ask questions minimized his sense of isolation.

A large part of his mood swings and panic attacks was directly related to interpersonal issues, though, at first, he was unable to see the connection between the stimulus and his behavior. Using our relationship as a baseline, he began to make sense of his behavior. As he began to see how I was presenting myself, he found it easier to identify the accuracy of his perceptions. At times, he would react as if I were distant and withholding. Through a careful analysis of how he misperceived a situation, he began to develop control over his flood of emotions and resulting immobilization. His being able to see the contradictions between his perception of my behavior and my actual behavior gave him one of the first indications of control in an emotional world over which he felt he had no control. He learned to distinguish between what he fantasized or distorted and what was clearly external to him. As I became more of a real person to him, he became stronger.

Equally important was that by understanding our relationship, my own countertransference became clearer. Recently, this became apparent when he confronted me about my misperceptions. I was seeing him as he had been and not acknowledging a significant change he had made. The shift in our relationship was most obvious to me when I felt punitive towards him. When I felt as if I were facing a pouting, recalcitrant child or a person having a temper tantrum, I used it as an important clue. The person facing me was in pain, was pleading for help, yet I felt like shaking him. At other times, he could be saying exactly the same words, and I would not feel punitive. I discovered that by accepting my punitive reaction as a connection to his feeling like a petulant child and telling him about it, we could through the impasse or simply accept it. When I suddenly felt like the punitive parent, I knew he was not in a place where he wanted to work clinically but just needed reassurance. Given the number of "suicidal" phone calls and emergency sessions, it was critical that I should know the difference.

Jack also learned another important lesson in clarifying the difference between talking about feelings and acting them out. His most difficult moments in group involved his sharing feelings and thoughts he considered "crazy." To avoid being thought "crazy" he would remain silent and/or act in ways that were clearly distancing and inappropriate. He would "act crazy" to avoid being thought "crazy." This distinction finally became apparent to him, and he could act on it after many intense discussions. This important step relates to the previous discussion of relational and countertransference disclosure. Since I could consistently demonstrate the differences among having a feeling, talking about it, and acting it out, it gave him an intellectual and behavioral framework within which to function.

An invaluable process in our therapy together was the fantasy self-disclosure. As he spoke or communicated nonverbally, it evoked many past experiences that were usually connected to other gay men, including lovers. Once I could identify what I felt and thought about those experiences, I could understand Jack's emotional state more clearly. At times, I could translate what I had learned from my own experience to what Jack was currently learning. Initially, I did not disclose the content of my experiences nor their themes. I simply presented them as a hunch about what he was experiencing. In time, my disclosing the source of my "hunches" had another beneficial effect. Jack began to see that he was not the only one who had certain problems and that these were part of the development and progress that people—even his therapist—go through. We had already established the vocabulary around the concept of developmental stages, a concept that he agreed with intellectually. This enabled him to see that many of his problems were not "pathological" but part of a developmental process in which he was behind schedule. With a smile, he began to refer to himself as "socially retarded" rather than crazy. In time, this self-deprecation also diminished.

Jack is an intelligent man who has used his intellect as his principal defense. Since his defense was already so strong, I enlisted it as a constructive tool that he could use to continue his development. For this reason, and to demystify therapy and my role in it, I shared my philosophical position on therapy and therapeutic techniques with him. Whenever appropriate, I would explain exactly the "what and why" of my actions. I found that the more Jack understood, the more progress he made emotionally. Besides giving him a way out of the morass of his emotional confusion, the act of sharing forced him into a less formal and more equal relationship with me.

The power issue was a sensitive area for Jack. He initially felt threatened by any indication that I saw him as a person with power. His self-identity was that of a powerless child who would have to be taken care of for the rest of his life. He experienced any push I gave him towards increased independence and self-reliance as abandonment. Because my treating him as someone other than a dependent child was threatening, the steps that I took to do so were incremental. Given his history of dependency on his therapists and his last nine years in therapy, I firmly believed that unless the therapist-client relationship were altered, he would remain as he was. While respecting his need for dependence from the beginning, I used every opportunity, no matter how subtle or infrequent, to support any indication of his power.

Equally important was that I not use our relationship to maintain a superior position to him or fall into any "doctor-patient" traps. This was difficult since Jack was constantly trying to have me come to his rescue and prove his helplessness. It became clear that my avoiding a superior position was the correct process since the progress was faster than in his previous therapeutic relationship, which had reinforced his sense of powerlessness. He was also ready for these changes, as he chose both the therapist who would provide this opportunity and a therapy that would give him a new model of power that was consistent with his already established ethical system of nonmanipulation and fairness. As he became more comfortable with himself as a gay man, he began to volunteer with gay organizations. By then, he knew about my activism.

Jack was chosen for this chapter because he began group therapy with a child's ego and an adult's intellect. The group and individual therapies have resulted in his continuing emergence as an adult man who feels that he is a sharing member of a group and in his becoming a leader in a community. He has altered his relationship with his parents, so that he has calmly and supportively told them about the lover with whom he now lives. He is able to handle the old behavior patterns that formerly immobilized him. His positive sense of self is reflected in his dramatically changed personal appearance and presentation as an attractive and well-dressed man with highly developed social skills. His humor and buoyancy are additional assets in his interactions and he is more at ease. An important component of these interactions is that he can now see himself as a unique adult and does not react narcissistically in all his social interactions. He no loner interprets others' behavior as always being specifically directed toward or in reaction to himself. He definitely has a positive attitude about himself and his future as a gay man.

SUMMARY

I recognize the psychological necessity for many gay men to relate to another gay man who is successful in his profession, openly gay in all aspects of his life, active in a community, and committed to personal development. The emotional intimacy of this experience encourages many gay men to start confronting their internalized homophobia and the resultant destructive patterns that have impeded their development. This process is accelerated when they can accept me as a member of a group to which they want to belong. I am seen as an authority figure and yet as accessible to them. Since most authority figures have been members of groups from which they felt excluded, this may be their first sense of inclusion. This also permits them to hear and accept what I say more easily. I am one of them, and yet I have something to teach them that corrects what had been absent from their lives. They have not felt part of a tradition that is only now being created. In other words, I am one of the older men teaching one of the younger as part of the developmental process. This is a redefinition of the elder teaching his own kind. Thus, when I talk about self-disclosure being a clinical intervention and about role-modeling as a therapeutic process, it is in this larger context of an elder effecting the passage of a young gay male into his adulthood.

JACK'S STATEMENT AFTER READING
THE CHAPTER

It is of historical (and therapeutic) interest that before entering medical school I underwent psychotherapy for several years with an elderly, straight psychiatrist who, in fact, utilized self-disclosure and shared many stylistic qualities with the author of this chapter, including not propagating his own power (i.e., therapy not utilized for *his* own ends) and a marked lack of rigidity.

This therapist initially decided that I was gay, then towards the end of my first year in therapy changed his mind. Overall, this therapeutic intervention enabled me to attend medical school and to complete two years of residency training without further therapy.

I returned to New York after residency to reenter therapy with the same therapist. Unfortunately, this therapist died three months before my return to New York, and I entered therapy with another non-gay psychiatrist, the one mentioned in the preceding case study.

This therapy was formal, rigid, absolutely nondisclosing, and power-based. It was impossible to win an argument with this therapist, and he never admitted making an error, which at times enhanced my feeling of being "crazy." While he was supportive about my coming-out, other issues, about which I failed to progress in therapy with him, prevented the gay socialization process from progressing.

The fact that the author of this paper—my current gay therapist—presented himself as human and fallible and admitted making errors when I was finally able to confront him was initially upsetting. At the time, I probably could not "handle" an adult, peer-like therapeutic relationship (I initially saw the process of fostering independence as being rejected and not cared for), and I think I also demanded an "infallible" therapist because of the intermittent intensity of my suicidal ideation (one mistake, as it were, and "I'd be dead"). However, as I began to be less therapeutically dependent and realized that this therapist, too, was "always on target" about the issue of suicidal ideation and intent, I became much more comfortable with the therapist, fallibility, and engaging in a more peer-like relationship.

The group milieu enabled me to see myself as a functional gay male, but the individual therapy seemed to me to have more effect on my functioning as a *peer* in that group. Functioning in that group was exceedingly difficult for some time, as was the process of decreasing my dependence on the therapist in the group situation. In a sense, the fostering of independence that occurred during individual therapy eventually carried over into group and greatly facilitated my functioning appropriately there. Likewise, a tremendous amount of transference occurred in both therapeutic situations, which for me was a significant problem because, at first, I thought that the only resolution possible was to end therapy. I have the sense—it may not be correct—that the use of self-disclosure actually exacerbated the problem for me, but ultimately (and paradoxically) it was important in its resolution.

Although I don't think I've made *enough* progress in some areas (i.e., narcissistic thinking, remnants of feeling inadequate), I have made significant changes: I'm a different person from who I was when I started group four years ago. I'm in a relationship with a mature, caring, loving, and politically active gay man, and the significant stresses that have occurred over the last twelve months, which might have precipitated hospitalization in the past, are now being handled in a much healthier and stronger way.

REFERENCES

1. De Angelis, T. (1990, February). Counter-transference disclosure is debated. *APA Monitor*, 24.
2. Jourard, S. (1960). Some implications of self-disclosure research for counseling and psychotherapy. *Counseling Center Discussion Papers, 8*, 14.
3. Jourard, S. (1961). The phenomenon of resistance in the psychotherapist. *Counseling Center Discussion Papers, 7*, 1–12.
4. Jourard, S. (1964). *The transparent self*. Princeton, NJ: VanNostrand.
5. Whitaker, C., & Malone, T. P. (1953). *The roots of psychotherapy*. New York: Blakiston. (Reissued 1981, Brunner/Mazel, New York).
6. Winnicott, D. W. (1965). Countertransference. In *The maturational process and the facilitating environment*. New York: International Universities Press.

12

GREGORY K. LEHNE

Sexual Trauma and Masochism

B ILL WAS REFERRED FOR therapy by a local gay physician, who was concerned about his patient's recurrent bouts of depression, his poor self-image, and a self-destructive lifestyle that included a history of alcohol and substance abuse.

At our initial appointment, Bill looked defeated and beaten down. Although he was short and slightly stout, with youthful features, he looked older than his age of twenty-nine. He was dressed in a raggedly casual, outdated style of distressed jeans, a studded cock-ring bracelet, and a small gold lambda in one earlobe. His grooming was neglected, his hair was a little long and greasy, and his eyeglasses were dirty and bent out of shape. He was devoid of animation, shuffling when he walked and slouching when he sat. His demeanor silently screamed "Victim."

He spoke rapidly, and his diction belied his working-class background. His vocabulary and syntax were consistent with the college education he aspired to complete. His normally avoidant eye contact was transformed into an intense, compelling engagement as he spoke. His speech was concise, well-organized, and reflective. His language accurately conveyed his above average intelligence. The psychological terminology and analytical framework he used he had gained from a previous year of therapy with a different gay therapist. Listening to his voice, I could easily imagine his skill as a volunteer telephone counselor for a local gay hotline.

Bill offered a complex description of his problems. He said he was burned-out in his job at a local gay-oriented community service organization. Labeling his feelings as intense anxiety, he had been taking an antianxiety medication "on and off," which apparently was not prescribed by his physician. Initially, he did not describe himself as being depressed. In response to questioning, he admitted that at times he heard menacing nonlanguage sounds and had altered visual sensations of things closing in on him and "getting white." At times he thought that people were out to get him. He described some of these episodes as anxiety or panic attacks.

Bill despaired of ever finding a lover, although he had a large number of brief sexual encounters. He said that he defeated himself in love and in life, messing up every time he had an opportunity. He was hypersensitive to criticism from others and was aware that he frequently felt angry and could lose his temper and blow up at a slight provocation.

Bill had a history of alcoholism and substance abuse from age thirteen. He had stopped drinking alcohol three years ago and had stopped all substance use (most recently marijuana and bootleg antidepressant medications) three months ago. He had decided to stop using alcohol and other substances because he suffered from chronic hepatitis. The hepatitis was a potentially fatal and basically untreatable condition, so it was important that he maintain his health. He was able to stop on his own, without any twelve-step programs, and did not report difficulties in maintaining sobriety. He was enrolled in a special National Institute of Health research study for hepatitis.

Bill's goals for therapy were to like himself more and to not set himself up for failure and defeat. He was hoping to ameliorate his frequent episodes of anxiety. He requested that his copayment for therapy be reduced because of his poor financial situation (despite working 60 hours a week on his full-time, underpaid, community service job). While requests for reduction in fee are often therapeutic issues, I told him that in this case I would reduce the charge purely on the basis of financial need.

BACKGROUND HISTORY

Bill came from a stable, working-class family. His father was an illiterate factory worker. He described his father as sometimes nice and weak, at other times an ogre. He was the family disciplinarian and could become domineering and abusive when angry. Bill's mother was a homemaker, whom he described as a sweetheart, always nice. She reportedly blamed herself for everything and set high standards for herself and everyone else, standards which were rarely met. Bill was the middle of three sons, each less than a year apart in age.

Bill thought that his mother had wanted a girl when he was born, and he considered himself his mother's girl. Family members, including his brothers, were protective of him, and he tended to adopt a goody-goody role. As a child, he was quickly labeled in the neighborhood as a "fag," which was an embarrassment to his family long before he understood its meaning. He recalled having a crush on his uncle when he was five.

Family relationships were demonstrative, with displays of physical affection. Bill remembered being upset and angry whenever he heard his parents' loud and active sex life in the bedroom next to his. At times he would get so anxious that he dreaded going to bed and would sometimes feel on the verge of throwing up. He imagined that his parents' sexual activities were violent and that his father was hurting his mother. When he could, Bill would try to blank out in his mind his parents' sexual activities.

Bill's younger brother initiated him into rough sexual exploration while they were prepubescent. All of Bill's early associations with sex were that it was supposed to hurt. His earliest vague sexual fantasies, which slightly preceded puberty, were of men doing things to him, like what he imagined his father did to his mother or what his brother did to him.

Bill was a good student in the local public school and was helpful around the house. He was better behaved than his brothers or other children in the neighborhood, and he was positive, outgoing, and rarely in trouble.

On the day before his twelfth birthday, Bill was forcibly raped on his way home from a late afternoon movie. He was taking a shortcut down an alley when a middle-aged man grabbed him and pointed a gun at him. The man reeked of alcohol and was smoking a cigarette. He blubbered that Bill "deserved it, wanted it" as he took his pants down and tried to get Bill to fellate him. Bill resisted. He then smashed Bill's face to the ground, burned him with the cigarette, and anally raped him while calling him a "fucking little faggot, you wanted this now you're going to get it, you're going to like it." The man threatened to kill him if he told anyone.

After the rape, Bill went home. He lied to his parents by saying that he had gotten into a fight. His parents punished him for being late and sent him to his room without supper. He was too ashamed and afraid to tell them what had actually happened. He also felt responsible for the rape. Bill thought that he had seen the man before and that he had been sexually attracted to him. His shame and worry intensified over the next weeks as his body ached and he had rectal bleeding. Still, he did not tell anyone of his experience. He said that he felt it was his fault.

Bill's life changed. He lost interest in school. He did not seem to care about anything. He got more angry at his parents and started getting into trouble. By age thirteen, he was drinking alcohol regularly and using a variety of street drugs. He began hustling older males on the streets, selling the use of his body for small amounts of money that he did not need. His preferred partner was a middle-aged man who would play the top role; they would have rough sex, with Bill receiving anal intercourse. His sexual fantasies were exclusively homosexual and masochistic, which corresponded to his experiences.

Bill experienced flashbacks and fantasies based upon his rape experience that were sexually arousing for him. These flashbacks also occurred sometimes during sexual relations with men. What had been his private tragedy had now become his erotic turn-on. He could not imagine the face of the man who had raped him, but he could remember most of the other details of the experience. He sought out a multitude of sexual partners and sometimes thought that he was picking up the very man who had raped him.

Despite his change in attitude, Bill did graduate from high school. He gained about fifty pounds. He could not stand to be touched by others, except during rough sexual activities. He worked as a waiter and also took classes at various community colleges. He did well in some courses but often had crises that would result in his failing exams or being unable to complete the coursework for credit. Despite nearly ten years of taking classes, he had made little progress toward a college degree. He moved out of his parents' house and lived in cheap efficiency apartments or rooms. He drifted in and out of living-together relationships with men he knew only briefly. Because he was always run down, he caught a lot of colds and had other transitory health problems.

He continued hustling, but with progressively less success. He found more and more of his sex partners among the older gay men who frequented local leather bars. Heavy drinking and drug use preceded most sexual encounters. He was always in the bottom or masochistic role and received anal intercourse from men who might tie him up, verbally abuse him, or physically abuse him to the point of minor injury.

Bill was openly gay, with no expressed discontent except his complaint about his difficulty in maintaining a relationship. He did volunteer work for a local gay community organization. Eventually this work led to a full-time job, where he was overworked and underpaid. He would develop resentment and anger toward fellow staff workers who he thought got more status or rewards than he did. He fell into a pattern of sabotaging his effectiveness at work.

COURSE OF TREATMENT

Bill was seen for a total of 24 sessions of individual psychotherapy, with follow-up sessions one, two, and three years after the termination of treatment. Bill's history, as described above, was readily elicited in the first session, which was largely devoted to history-taking. Little additional or modifying information was obtained in later sessions.

Bill accepted his homosexuality, including his masochistic interest in sexual relations with older men. He claimed to have worked through his juvenile rape in his prior therapy—"I know I wasn't responsible," he said. Having studied psychology and social work in school and worked in a social service agency, he had his own conceptualization and agenda for psychotherapy. Bill wanted to address the issues of anxiety and depression without the use of medication, improve his self-concept, and curb his self-sabotage. He wanted a short-term, present- and symptom-oriented therapy—he did not want to reexamine his history in therapy.

As a therapist, I am eclectic but typically use a cognitive-behavioral approach for short-term psychotherapy. Cognitive-behavioral therapy starts by elucidating and examining the patient's cognitions (beliefs, thoughts, attitudes, and informational conceptualizations). This involves an active, questioning role on the part of the therapist. In therapy, cognitions may be reorganized and reconceptualized through a process called reframing. Behavior patterns are described and recommendations for change are made. Behavioral tasks may be prescribed either to induce experiences which conflict with cognitions or to change behavior first, which leads to changes in beliefs and attitudes. Cognitive-behavioral techniques are described in the work of Aaron Beck and his colleagues, and a similar approach is described as rational emotive therapy by Albert Ellis and his associates.

In our early sessions, Bill and I discussed the day-to-day events of his life. We analyzed the roles he played, both at work and socially (Beck, 1976). As a gay therapist, I lived and worked in the same general gay community as Bill did, although not in the same friendship circles. This commonality made it relatively easy for me to develop a realistic understanding of his situation and the accuracy of his conceptualizations. My knowledge of his social and vocational milieu facilitated reality-testing and reframing of his cognitions (Beck, et al., 1985; Ellis, 1973).

In order to help him command the respect and cooperation from others which he desired, we rehearsed scenarios for handling situations that might occur. We discussed his expectations and how they interacted with his negative world view. By expecting others to disappoint him, he would do tasks before others had a chance to do them and then he would feel exploited. Or, he might be hypersensitive to remarks made by others and lose his temper before others could explain their point of view or help him with the activities at hand. We examined the information he communicated to others through every modality, including his body posture, style of dress, and speech patterns.

Each of our discussions was followed up with behavioral tasks to put the cognitive learning into practical action. These activities were also designed to facilitate self-concept improvement. For example, one task relating to his patterns of self-sabotage involved collecting all of his college credits, analyzing them, and transferring them into one college degree program along with a plan to finish that degree program. Other tasks required personal assertiveness, such as practicing saying "No" to requests at work which were outside the normal scope of his job. Some of these activities resulted in negative responses from others, which provided as much important learning for Bill as tasks that produced positive rewards.

Both success and failure were threatening. Because he was excessively agreeable and compliant, people liked Bill, which proved to him that he was worthless because they only liked him when he demeaned himself by meeting their needs. The more people liked him, the worse he felt about himself and the more he was tempted to sabotage his success. Conversely, being disagreeable and disliked confirmed Bill's worthless self-concept and supported his beliefs that the world was a negative place where nothing turned out right and people were only out to take advantage of him.

As cognitive-behavioral therapy progressed, Bill began to experience more anxiety attacks and more anger outbursts. Despite the effective use of the therapeutic techniques, the patient got worse. As the therapist, I felt defeated. And yet, as things got worse, Bill acted more positively toward me. It seemed like he relished the apparent impotence of my professional skills.

Even though I had only seen Bill for six sessions, I became exhausted and discouraged with his situation. I resented the fact that I was seeing him for a reduced fee. I felt manipulated and trapped when he changed appointments to times which were inconvenient for me. I felt like shaking some sense into him or yelling at him for not getting better. Of course, I did not do any of these things. But it became easy for me to understand how people came to abuse him. It seemed only natural and easy to blame the patient for his condition. Bill was a masochist and it would be a masochistic triumph for him to get his therapist to abuse him psychologically in sessions. I wondered who was controlling our sessions, Bill or myself?

Reflecting upon my feelings provided additional input for my analysis of his condition and treatment planning. In some cases, I would have directly shared the experiences described above with my patient as examples of the effects of his behavioral style on others. In some ways, the therapeutic relationship is a model of other relationships in a patient's life. As a therapist, I could use the example of our relationship to illustrate how he made other people feel. However, I did not share my feelings with Bill at that time. On the one hand, I was afraid that this might lead him to reject me and abandon therapy or that if he stayed it would make him feel that therapy was unsafe and nonsupportive. Conversely, I was also worried that if I gave him much personal negative feedback, this might transform our relationship into a sadomasochistic struggle.

Instead, I decided to modify the treatment plan. I hypothesized that there were unresolved, underlying psychodynamic issues which must be resolved before cognitive-behavioral techniques could help this man. The psychodynamic, I suspected, was to be found in his rape at age twelve and in an orientation toward masochism.

We were three weeks away from Bill's thirtieth birthday, which was the virtual anniversary of the rape 18 years ago. I began to elicit more details of the rape from Bill. Money calls this the "sportscaster's technique," where every item of descriptive, play-by-play information about the initial event is recounted. Bill reported enough minutiae to allow me to have produced a film reenactment, with the exception of any description of the man's face. At times, Bill also appeared to become "spacey" or dissociated and sexually aroused when describing the rape. He said that the details of the rape flashed into his mind during sexual encounters and during masturbation. Bill began trying to visualize the man's face. He reported that for years he had been obsessed with trying to recall the man's face or with fantasizing that the men he had sexual relations with were the man who had raped him as a child. Bill's panic attacks increased in frequency, which seemed directly related to the psychologically threatening content of therapy sessions.

The decision to directly pursue threatening content in therapy is difficult. Many therapists will not do it but will rely upon the patient to bring up all the relevant material. One concern is that the therapist could be iatrogenically reabusing the patient through the repetitious detailed description of earlier traumas. Another risk is that the material may be so threatening that the patient will terminate therapy in a worsened and unstable condition. I also think that many therapists are afraid to directly confront scary or unsavory material in sessions. My clinical judgment in Bill's case, which I discussed with him at the time and sought his agreement on, was aggressively to pursue the childhood rape in order to speed the course of therapy. This decision was feasible because Bill had developed a sense of confidence and safety with me and in my office. If I had provided him with negative feedback about his interpersonal style, as I had considered earlier in therapy, I do not think he would have felt safe enough with me to have pursued the rape content so directly.

I used the paradoxical suggestion that he should, while in the privacy of his home, deliberately masturbate while imagining the rape in full detail. The use of paradoxical suggestions is a technique derived from the strategic therapy techniques developed by Haley and his colleagues (Haley, 1973). Bill initially said that he was not able deliberately to fantasize about the rape during masturbation but gradually admitted that he could and, in fact, frequently did that. I suggested that he extend the imagery as far as it would go, always trying to find out what would happen next in the imagery story.

As the anniversary of the rape neared, I encouraged Bill to revisit the actual location of the rape. He had not returned to the alley since the rape, although it was only several blocks from the house where his family still lived. He did not follow through on my suggestion, and I began to wonder whether I was moving too fast for his well-being.

With psychotherapy intensifying at this critical period, Bill stopped coming to therapy sessions. For one month, he would call and leave messages on the answering machine, canceling each session with one excuse or another. He never called when my office manager or I might personally answer the telephone. He always took care to say that he was OK, but I was not certain how much trust I could put in those tape-recorded remarks. When I discreetly checked on his condition, however, there were no reports of any evident problems. I worried that he was trying to drop out of therapy or get me to terminate with him for his excessive cancellations without adequate advance notice.

When he resumed therapy sessions, he gave no explanation for the treatment lapse. He still had not visited the site of the rape. In an emotionally charged session, we again reviewed the rape in painful detail. But in this review, something had changed. Bill could now remember the end of the rape—he had gotten aggressively loud, the man lost his erection without ejaculating, got off Bill, and left. Bill had shut him off, overcome him—first when he had initially refused to fellate him and would not open his mouth, and then when he frightened him off so he did not ejaculate during the anal penetration. The rape was now reframed in therapy: Bill was the strong one, the man was weak. The man sought to control and overpower, but Bill was not compliant as he had expected and in the end Bill had asserted control.

This led to a new phase of increased personal power and effectiveness, as reported in our therapy sessions. Things seemed to go well. Bill was able to discuss the rape with others. For the first time, he felt the anger and injustice of not being able to tell his parents about it. Therapy focused on cognitive-behavioral strategies for day-to-day living. He got a significant promotion and raise at work. He was accepted, with scholarship aid, into a college degree program. But there were still some bouts with depression and feelings of inadequacy.

Following my vacation, Bill resumed therapy feeling much more depressed than he had ever been before. I had never seen him look so poorly. He was full of rage and was afraid he was going to explode or have a nervous breakdown. He was making arrangements to start on antidepressant medication, which he had previously rejected. He was also starting a support group for male victims of rape.

I saw Bill three times that first week. Rather than retreat from the feelings of anger, rage, and depression, we decided to tackle them head on. Medication was deferred. We agreed to do some implosion therapy sessions to reprocess the rape experience. After discussing hypnotic techniques, Bill also agreed that we would utilize hypnosis to facilitate the implosive reenactment of the rape.

Implosion therapy involves recalling and reliving, in imagery, the original, traumatic situation (McMullin, 1986). The patient experiences the perceptions and feelings, and sometimes sensations and physical movements, which were imprinted at the time of the trauma. Dissociation is

often a defense which was part of the original experience and may occur again during the reenactment. Hypnosis, which is akin to a dissociative process, is sometimes used to facilitate the implosive reenactment.
Traumatized patients, particularly those with post-traumatic stress disorders, do not usually have much difficulty getting into a reenactment state.
Even without a formal hypnotic induction, many easily go into hypnotic
states. The therapist may set the stage for this state through suggestive
imagery.

The theory behind implosion therapy is that the reenactment or rework-
ing of the literally encoded experience may allow it to be integrated into
the present mental state and understanding. To implode is to literally burst
something inward upon itself and make it disappear without destroying
anything else around it. I think of it as going into the memory storage and
exploding it, so that it has to be stored anew in a different form, in different
memory spaces. Thus the traumatic experience/memory can come under
the control of more developed psychological defense mechanisms, where
it causes less interference with the patient's functioning.

Implosion therapy can be a dramatic and frightening technique for the
therapist. The patient may scream out and thrash around, as he or she did
during the actual experience. Fears of violence that might involve the
therapist or office furnishings loom on the one hand, contrasted with
the desire to spare the patient the apparent pain of the reenactment. A
soundproofed space is important or a warning to others within shouting
range not to interrupt the process if they hear screams from the patient. I
have known of cases where patients had erections and ejaculations during
implosive processes. Given the current climate surrounding sexual miscon-
duct against therapists, the possibility of a sexual response occurring during
the session was also worrisome to me. It is important that the patient give
informed consent to the use of this type of procedure.

I had enough information about the rape from our previous sessions to
be able to provide any necessary triggering stimuli. The sessions were set
for an open-ended time, the end of the day on Friday and a follow-up on
Saturday. Bill said that he thought he would feel safe and comfortable
reexperiencing the rape, including any responses he might make, in my
office.

Bill readily went into a trance, with a brief, conventional induction. I
used embedded suggestions of early experiences of gaining control and
mastery such as learning to read or ride a bike. Embedded suggestions are
metaphorical or storytelling techniques used during hypnosis, based upon

the work of Erickson (Haley, 1973). The purpose was to instill the patient with a sense of personal efficacy, power, and control. In the early life stories which I made up in detail for the circumstances, the child is initially afraid and confused by the learning task but is able to master it and perform it almost unconsciously, even though the child cannot describe the actual learning process or tell others how to do it.

We progressed through visualizing and reenacting each detail of the rape experience in chronological sequence. Bill yelled, and his body contorted. Then, we used guided imagery to collect the rage and move it through his body, until he collected it in his chest and released it through exhaling and vocalizing. This use of guided imagery has gained increasing popularity, through the writings of the Simontons (Simonton, Mathews-Simonton, & Creighton, 1978) and Louise Hay (1984), for dealing with physical health complaints. The specific imagery is tailored to the sensory modalities which the patient uses in metaphorically describing his experiences. Bill imagined the rage as being in his muscle tension and would tense muscles and relax them sequentially "pushing" the rage into the chest where he imagined it was exhaled, expelled out of the body by the muscles of the lungs and vocal chords.

I reframed the rape sequence by expanding it to include the sequel when he went home afterwards. Reframing is basically a way of changing the conceptual context of an experience. In Bill's case the rape memory had begun with the man attacking him and ended with Bill facedown on the ground, crying. In the reframing, we progressed through Bill overcoming the impotent man, scaring him off, and defeating him in that he was unable to get what he wanted (a sexual orgasm with Bill). Then, I helped Bill move through the rest of the sequence—going home, full of anger and shame, and facing his parents, who punished him for being late by sending him to bed without supper. Bill had been retraumatized by being unable to tell them what had happened to him. In this reenactment, he was able to see that his parents were wrong in their anger toward him and that it was unjust.

After bringing Bill out of trance, we reprocessed parts of the experience. He was drained of emotion but was calmer, less tense, and did not feel anger or rage. He later described this experience and the time after as "one of the most elated periods in my life, like when, after being caught underwater, you finally come up."

At his next two regular weekly appointments, Bill reported almost hypomanic levels of energy and positive mood. He said that he felt lighter now that he had finally expressed and come to terms with his anger about the rape. He recognized that he had repressed his anger in the process of concealing the experience from his parents. He could also acknowledge his anger at being treated unfairly by his parents after the rape. Yet he understood that it would have been too traumatizing for his parents had he told them about the rape, either then or now. In essence, he had taken it upon himself to behave strongly because he did not think that they were or are capable of such strength in dealing with the fact of his rape. Realizing that he had actually overcome the rapist may have led him to acknowledge the high level of control which he had in his masochistic and self-sabotaging activities. This seemed to free him to use his personal power in more beneficial ways.

Bill also sorted through his ambivalence about enjoying the rape fantasy, although he had not enjoyed the actual experience. What had been an erotic tragedy had become an erotic triumph, in that his pain had become transformed into a source of sexual arousal and pleasure. Bill reported that flashbacks of the rape no longer intruded into his cruising, sexual experiences, or masturbation. However, he remained primarily masochistic in his homosexual interests, but with more flexibility in his role playing and sexual activities. He learned to be a "top" in sexual relations and to enjoy it—he eventually came to prefer it. He became less compulsive about going to gay bars and picking up men. He described the way he felt before as "being driven to do something that makes you so frightened." Now, he had lost his interest in having sex with many different partners. He said that he could "walk into a gay bar and see the whole room now, not just the creepiest guy in the corner." He could recognize and acknowledge the interest which handsome men might have in him. Also, he became more able to open up to his partner with affection. He began to experience falling in love or bonding in relationships.

Bill's very rapid improvement continued to progress and maintain itself, as we shifted to biweekly and then monthly sessions. Physically, he looked better than I had ever seen him, and others commented likewise. His posture straightened up and became more confident. He improved his style of dress. He had lost that victim look and was more positive, assertive, and outgoing. He did well in his classes and changed his job.

At follow-up appointments one, two, and three years later, Bill maintained his excellent progress. He subsequently has read this description of his case history and said that it is accurate. At our last meeting, he said that his younger brother had died of a drug overdose. His brother's history had mirrored Bill's in so many ways that he considered his brother's death as an indicator of what might have happened to him if he had not changed his lifestyle. On the more positive side, Bill had miraculously responded to an experimental treatment for the rare type of chronic hepatitis he suffered from. The disease, which had a 98% chance of being fatal, had gone into remission. Bill continued to be very positive about his future.

DISCUSSION

Bill is a homosexual masochist. This was not his presenting problem when he began therapy, and this was still his sexual orientation when he success-fully terminated therapy. This case of treatment of sexual trauma and masochism raises issues about the distinctions between the genesis and treatment of sexual disorders and homosexuality, which is not a disorder. For example, how did the rape relate to Bill's homosexual masochism? Can Bill's treatment be considered completed or successful if masochism still remains as a significant sexual interest? If his paraphilic masochism changed in treatment, is it also possible to change his homosexuality?

Bill's early history parallels the history of many gay men: an avoidance of typically boyish juvenile activities, early social recognition of his gender-role nonconformity (being called a "fag"), and reported early crushes on males (Green, 1987; Money, 1988; Saghir & Robins, 1973). Bill's homo-sexuality was immutably set before the rape and was not an issue for therapeutic change. My belief is that it is not possible to change a person's basic sexual orientation. In therapy one may only help an individual in-crease their options for sexual behavior.

I believe that there were two components to Bill's masochism that were superimposed upon his homosexuality, which need to be considered separately. One aspect of Bill's masochism was an integral component of his prepubertal homosexual lovemap (c.f. Money, 1986; 1988). The other aspect of his masochism was a sexual disorder (paraphilia) related to his rape experience (c.f. Money & Lamacz, 1989).

A lovemap is Money's term for the internalized representations or men-tal structures that depict the personally appealing spectrum of idealized lovers, love affairs, and sexual activities. The lovemap is a multidimensional mental structure incorporating sexual orientation and a diverse field of sexual content, regardless of whether any of it is acted upon. The multidi-mensional lovemap is in contrast to the Kinsey scale, a unidimensional conceptualization of sexual orientation from exclusively homosexual to heterosexual. The Kinsey scale does not describe any partner characteristics other than gender and does not describe any other romantic and/or sexual activity interests. Lovemaps incorporate both fantasies and experiences which are represented in imagery.

Sexual fantasies significantly precede sexual behavior and interact with developmental experiences in the process of understanding and expressing a sexual orientation (Lehne, 1978, 1988a). Bill's earliest sexual fantasies, which preceded his rape experience, were exclusively oriented toward males and were masochistic. He has continued to have these types of fantasies through the present time.

Bill's prepubertal and pre-rape associations with sexuality incorporated the idea that sex involved domination. This was most salient as his juvenile interpretation of overhearing his parents' sexual activities. He psychologically put himself in his mother's role as the one who was dominated. He was also actually dominated and physically hurt when his brother involved him as a partner in sexual activities. Sex was domination, not "lovemaking": this sensory information was encoded onto the lovemap in his juvenile brain. As a child, Bill was of slight build and the victim of teasing by others—his self-concept also incorporated victimization. In Bill's case, masochism would most likely have been a component of his sexuality, regardless of whether his sexual orientation was gay, straight, or in between. (As an aside, Bill's brother appeared to have developed the complementary, sadistic lovemap, perhaps putting himself in his father's role in his interpretation of family sexual activities.)

Paraphilic masochism as expressed through fantasies is very narrowly focused, ritualistic, and repetitive—it has the quality of a specific memory recall. These obsessional and compulsive qualities are the basis for considering it a sexual disorder. It lacks the capability for variation and experimentation which other sexual fantasies can possess. Many fantasies can function as a rehearsal for a variety of different activities, in contrast to paraphilic fantasies which are scripts which must be followed in exact detail every time they are replayed. The compulsive quality of paraphilic sexuality makes it difficult to control in behavior; the obsessional quality dominates thinking.

In Bill's case, the specific recalled imagery of the rape constituted the paraphilic imagery. This imagery would seem to insert itself into Bill's consciousness during sexual activities, and he would be unable to eliminate or control it. Paraphilias commonly incorporate content associated with eroticized incidents of prior sexual trauma, although frequently experiences at younger ages than Bill was at the time of his rape (Money & Lamacz, 1989). The content of paraphilic imagery is not necessarily consistent with the content of the rest of the individual's sexual orientation or lovemap. For example, I have seen forms of paraphilic homosexual content in men who were otherwise heterosexual, which were associated with a history of a severely traumatizing homosexual experience occurring in early adolescence. In Bill's case, it was perhaps simply by chance that paraphilic imagery of rape got superimposed on an already homosexual masochistic lovemap—or perhaps it was his prior sexual victimization by his brother that made him more vulnerable to paraphilic imprinting of the rape.

In some cases, the hypothesized acquisition of a paraphilia may be akin to a post-traumatic stress disorder. In these disorders, the original trauma is virtually imprinted intact in the individual and then is revitalized under certain circumstances. Perhaps for some individuals, traumatic sexual experiences are associated with cues (such as sexual arousal) that cause the experience to be imprinted into a sexual schema (or lovemap), where it may be compulsively acted out but never integrated into the rest of sexuality, or resolved and eliminated. Part of the treatment plan in Bill's case involved using techniques most frequently applied to post-traumatic stress symptoms, such as hypnosis and implosion techniques.

If the paraphilic masochism (the fantasy of being forcibly raped by an abusive, older man) had been the primary focus of treatment, I probably would have tried the same techniques I actually used with Bill. But if the compulsive sexuality was not under control, other modes of treatment including the use of medication might also have been used to minimize the dangerous reenactment of the paraphilia during treatment. Some masochistic paraphilias can be life threatening. For example, I might have considered the use of Depo-Provera if Bill had been more at risk of acquiring HIV infection through dangerous sexual practices, or if he repeatedly found partners who seriously injured him. Depo-Provera is a synthetic hormone which lowers the frequency and intensity of compulsive sexual urges so they can be controlled. It is effective with paraphilias but has little effect upon more conventional homosexual or heterosexual behavior (Lehne, 1988b).

In the absence of evident risk at the time of treatment, it was not within my role as therapist to be judgmental about Bill's sexual practices. However, it was fortunate that in the course of therapy the compulsive aspect of his sexuality was brought under control and eventually eliminated. The remaining components of his masochism were well within socially acceptable standards for Bill and his subculture. Reduction of these masochistic interests was never a goal for Bill's treatment.

Improving the quality of Bill's interpersonal relationships was a treatment goal, as Bill wanted to find a stable lover. Paraphilias do interfere with establishing bonded relationships. In Bill's case, when he was acting out his paraphilia, it would always be with a man who was not a good candidate for a relationship. Bill would always be the victim who was raped. His partners were chosen based upon their degrading and abusive qualities. There was no affection or expression of caring in the context of sexual behavior. With the elimination of the paraphilic component, Bill was able to get involved in relationships. Within those relationships, he could choose to act in a variety of different sexual ways consistent with his lovemap, which included masochistic and more typical homosexual sexual activities.

The distinction between paraphilic and noncompulsive components of sexuality is important. It is like the difference between repetitively reciting a memorized phrase in a foreign language and speaking in one's native language. To forget the memorized (and not understood) phrase is not to eliminate or change one's native language. In some cases, the ability to change or eliminate a paraphilic compulsive component of sexuality does not mean that underlying sexual lovemaps (such as those which are primarily homosexual) can be changed. Changing or controlling a paraphilia is not the same as changing or controlling sexual orientation. While the origins of homosexuality and heterosexuality are not clearly known, they are not paraphilias and are not caused by early traumatizing sexual experiences.

REFERENCES

1. Beck, A. (1976). *Cognitive therapy and the emotional disorders*. New York: International University Press.
2. Beck, A., Emery, G., & Greenberg, R. (1985). *Anxiety disorders and phobias*. New York: Basic Books.
3. Ellis, A. (1973). *Humanistic psychotherapy: The rational-emotional approach*. New York: Julian Press.
4. Green, R. (1987). *The "sissy boy syndrome" and the development of homosexuality*. New Haven, CT: Yale University Press.
5. Haley, J. (1973). *Uncommon therapy: The psychiatric techniques of Milton H. Erickson*. New York: Norton.
6. Hay, L. L. (1984). *You can heal your life*. Santa Monica: Hay House.
7. Lehne, G. (1978). Gay male fantasies and realities. *Journal of Social Issues, 34(3)*, 28–37.

8. Lehne, G. (1988a). Erotosexual orientations: Understanding and treating homosexuals. In R. A. Brown & J. R. Field (Eds.), *Treatment of sexual problems in individual and couples therapy*. New York: PMA Publishing Corp.

9. Lehne, G. (1988b). Treatment of sex offenders with medroxyprogesterone acetate. In J. M. A. Sitsen (Ed.), *Handbook of sexology, Vol. 6: The pharmacology and endocrinology of sexual function*. Amsterdam: Elsevier.

10. McMullin, R. (1986). *Handbook of cognitive therapy techniques*. New York: Norton.

11. Money, J. (1986). *Lovemaps: Clinical concepts of sexual/erotic health and pathology, paraphilia, and gender transposition in childhood, adolescence, and maturity*. New York: Irvington.

12. Money, J. (1988). *Gay, straight and in-between: The sexology of erotic orientation*. New York: Oxford University Press.

13. Money, J., & Lamacz, M. (1989). *Vandalized lovemaps: Paraphilic outcome of seven cases in pediatric sexology*. Buffalo, NY: Prometheus Books.

14. Saghir, M., & Robins, E. (1973). *Male & female homosexuality: A comprehensive investigation*. Baltimore, MD: Williams & Wilkins.

15. Simonton, O. C., Mathews-Simonton, S., & Creighton, J. L. (1978). *Getting well again*. New York: Bantam.

13

APRIL MARTIN

The Power of Empathic Relationships: Bereavement Therapy With a Lesbian Widow

Eva, 43, SOUGHT TREATMENT in September 1988, one month after the death of her lover of ten years. Her lover, Joanne, had died of cancer after many months of illness. Eva had been at Joanne's bedside constantly throughout the ordeal. She described their relationship as "super beautiful" and cried throughout the initial consultation.

Eva complained that since Joanne's death she was overeating, drinking too much alcohol, and spending money compulsively. She was unable to function effectively at work, had headaches she couldn't get rid of, and cried all the time. She felt she was having a breakdown. She had given the eulogy at the funeral and now found herself reciting it compulsively in her mind. She was clearly suffering a great deal. She rejected the suggestion of a bereavement support group, describing herself as someone who never confides in people. It had taken desperation for her to seek therapy.

RECENT HISTORY

Eva and Joanne had had a very loving relationship. Though they maintained separate apartments, they had spent almost every night together during their ten-year relationship. Together they owned a country house and two dogs. Eva described her relationship with Joanne as extremely supportive, with each actively encouraging the interests of the other. They were wonderful playmates and found a great deal of pleasure in recreational activities and socializing. There was never any question that this was a lifetime commitment for both of them. Eva had only positive memories of Joanne and their life together.

Nine months before Eva sought treatment, Joanne had been diagnosed with a brain tumor. The diagnosis had been made right after Christmas. Though surgery was performed, the cancer had already spread throughout her body. With the exception of a few days here and there, Joanne spent the next eight months in the hospital going through a nightmare ordeal of tests, several major surgeries, radiation, and chemotherapy. Eva spent every night and every minute after work at Joanne's bedside. Joanne made the decisions and Eva supported them. Again and again Joanne decided to pursue another operation, procedure, test, change of doctor, or treatment method. Whatever Joanne wanted was what Eva wanted for her. When Joanne could barely eat, Eva ran around to find the one or two foods she knew she could tempt her with. Eva also went into substantial personal debt trying to pay for nursing care and medical expenses that weren't covered by Joanne's insurance. She washed her, fed her, talked to her, helped her walk, called her from work several times a day (including calls from China and India when a business trip required that she be away), kept her amused, kept her spirits up, and made her comfortable in any way she could. Her devotion was remarkable and very moving. She had cared for Joanne with complete disregard for her own feelings and needs. In her mind, though, there was no sacrifice involved. It was simply what you do for the love of your life.

Eva worked in a high-level job in business. She was a self-made businesswoman who had earned her way to her position with shrewd decisions, a willingness to learn, experience acquired through good career moves, and a personal warmth and appeal. She made an excellent living and used it to live well. She knew how to enjoy herself. Her passions were for physical activity and she engaged in many different kinds of sports with great gusto. She was also very close to her brother's children and enjoyed taking her niece out on the town. During the past year, Eva's priority had been Joanne's care and everything else, including her work, had taken a back seat.

EARLIER HISTORY

Eva had grown up in a middle-class Jewish family with a brother two years older. The mother had married at 16. Eva's brother was born when the mother was 19, and Eva was born two years later. Her brother had been the apparent favorite. Eva said her mother didn't know she had a daughter until Eva was 13. Her father was described as being wrapped up in his work and largely uninvolved in the raising of the children. Eva denied any feelings of deprivation about her lack of support growing up. On the contrary, she said, it had helped her become more independent. She felt she had learned to rely on herself since there was never any one who could be counted on.

As a child, Eva's passion had been sports. She had no interest in the clothes and glamour that her mother cared about. She said that with a different set of parents, she would have become a professional athlete in either golf or tennis. She had wanted to turn pro as a golfer in college but her parents wouldn't support it. She had worked since the age of nine, making hamburgers at a drive-in restaurant, to pay for all of her own athletic training.

Eva's paternal grandmother had shown real interest in her. Eva described her as feisty and unconventional and the only one to whom Eva could talk.

THE WORK TOGETHER

My heart went out to Eva at our initial consultation. She was in tremendous pain. She was also not used to asking for help. She felt proud of having always managed her problems without having to talk to people about them. She would not have come if she hadn't felt overwhelmed. She would also not have come if she hadn't heard that I was a lesbian and that I do a lot of bereavement work.

I have done a fair amount of bereavement work in recent years. This is work I could not have done when I started practicing 15 years ago. Back then I knew people who had died, but I had not yet had a close personal loss. Eight years ago I lost a son to Sudden Infant Death Syndrome. Three years later I lost my father. In the past six years I have lost many friends and patients to AIDS. What I have learned through my own processes of mourning I could never have acquired through books.

Mourning, if unimpeded, is a healing process. A bereaved person, if given a great deal of support, will go through the work of sifting through memories and grief, acknowledging angers and guilts, and reliving warmth and fondness. He or she will take account of the impact the loved one has had on his or her life, cry long and hard, say what never got said, and experience life without the loved one. Little by little, as the holidays come and go and the seasons change, the bereaved's heart will gradually open to life and to love again. Without support, the process of mourning will likely be aborted prematurely, with all the feelings tucked away and frozen in a closed corner of the heart.

When the dead person has been hated as well as loved or when the relationship has been difficult, the mourning is more likely to run aground. Angry feelings, feelings of relief at the person's absence, and guilt about those feelings make it hard to let the sadness flow. Reconciling widely disparate images of the same person, in one instance adored and desired and in the next feared or despised, is very difficult work. This type of mourning is like the healing of an infected wound. It probably will need some intervention to heal properly. The therapist will need to work with defenses against guilt and rage, as well as grief.

When the relationship has no more than ordinary ambivalence, however, that is, when deep love and attachment are the predominant feelings, the wound is clean. The pain is deep and suicidal feelings are common. It seems for a time that life can't go on. Yet even in the midst of that anguish, the healing is proceeding gradually. The therapeutic work with this type of bereavement is less interpretive; it is mainly just the offering of empathy. The bereaved person needs someone who is willing to hear the pain, willing to get close enough to it to feel the anguish of it, and able to have confidence in the ultimate recovery without a need to hurry the process or to make the feelings better.

Very few friends and family members of someone in grief are able to just allow the person to have his or her feelings without trying to "fix it." People can often hear the initial pain at the time of loss and respond with great gentleness and sympathy. But those same people may not be able to tolerate complaints that are made months later. The bereaved may still say that he or she is depressed or angry, that life is not worth living. He or she may be doing poorly at work or be still unwilling to see friends or begin to date. Friends often want to tell the bereaved what to do: "You should put it behind you, get out more, take a vacation, don't dwell on it." The bereaved comes away feeling vaguely criticized for feelings that simply won't go away. He or she may feel that no one wants to hear his or her pain. He or she may even feel there is something wrong with not being over the grief by now.

Unfortunately, some therapists also need to try and stop the pain. They may smother the patient with comfort when the most healing response would be a quiet acceptance of just how bad it feels. A patient's desperation and anger may invite the therapist to try and "do something." It can be hard for a therapist, as for anyone else, to hear someone say in angry, demanding, and heartbreaking tones that she can't stand another minute of the anguish and something has to be done. It makes us anxious. We may be afraid the patient will kill him- or herself. We may be afraid he or she will think we don't care or that we are ineffective. We may wish to see the pain relieved because it activates our own pain. We may be afraid of feeling our powerlessness over life's suffering. At those moments, I draw on my own experiences with grief. I remember that it felt unbearable, and yet, somehow, I lived through it. I remember how helpful it was to have someone willing to listen to my rage at the gods, my fears that life was over, my hopelessness. I recall how it ultimately soothed me that someone else wasn't frightened by the feelings. It gave me hope that I might recover from this dreadful state.

Eva's loss certainly seemed to be of the uncomplicated, unambivalent variety. Though it was clear in the first session that the relationship with Joanne was somewhat idealized and that some ordinary ambivalent feelings were noticeably absent, this was basically love at its best. The bigger problem for Eva, as I saw it, was that she was so reluctant to really let someone else in on her suffering. Both her pride in her self-reliance and her expectation that people can't be counted on prevented her from getting the support that she needed. If there is ever a time when someone is in need, it is after the loss of a loved one. Yet Eva was conscious of not wanting to burden her friends or family with her pain. I was very glad that she had entered therapy. Paying a professional for help allowed her some of the distance she needed to accept support, though even then she expressed many fears about how draining it might be for me to deal with her feelings.

In the early sessions I encouraged Eva to talk in detail about Joanne's illness, death, and funeral. I remember that when my son Michael died, it was so important to have people willing to hear the details of where it happened, how we found him and rushed him to the hospital, and all the rest of the nightmare. She recited to me the eulogy which she had given at the funeral, and which was now haunting her mind. As on so many other occasions with her, my eyes filled upon hearing it. For every event she recounted of her ordeal, I relived the ordeal of losing my baby, of burying him, of getting through the days following the funeral, of disposing of his clothes and toys, etc.

I don't make a big deal out of the tears that may run down my face during a session, nor do I try to stop them. They are always a combination of empathy for the sadness of my patient and the product of the many griefs of my own life. It seems that every loss we live through awakens all the old losses. They all flow into the same river of sadness. Though the healing process restores the capacity for joy and creativity and removes the sadness from the foreground of consciousness, one can still always journey to the waters of grief. I don't know how one could do bereavement work without allowing easy access to one's own tears.

While I listened to Eva's pain at her separation from Joanne, I allowed my awareness to wander to the losses of my life. People have sometimes asked how I can stand to have such painful feelings evoked. I honestly don't know, because it certainly is painful. But for the most part, it isn't frightening, and the awareness of its healing potential for someone else is a strong pull. The one area in working with Eva's loss that I did find difficult, though, was that it evoked terror about the possibility of losing my lover.

Eva and I are both in our forties. This past year I have heard about quite a few lesbians who lost their lovers to cancer. When I hear of women dying of ovarian cancer, breast cancer, and brain cancer, I feel acutely vulnerable. My lover and I have been together for twelve years, since the year before Eva met Joanne. My sessions with Eva, usually the last sessions of my workday, would often evoke frightening thoughts of what life would be like if my lover were to become ill. It is not in my nature to worry as much about getting ill myself. The worse terror for me would be losing the love of my life. I often said goodnight to Eva, walked down the flight of stairs that separates my office from my apartment, and spent the last hour or so before bed trying to deal with awful fantasies about what could happen to my happy home.

I asked Eva to bring in pictures of Joanne, which she did. Together we looked at photos of summer days and good times. I wanted her to really let me feel how special their love was. When Michael died I was so grateful for the people who had known him personally. People who had had a sense of his uniqueness, even in his short four and a half months of life, were especially helpful to me in feeling less alone with the grief. Also, I felt that people who had children themselves understood better what I felt. In order to understand Eva's loss, I wanted to get a detailed sense of what they did together, talked about, ate, saw, laughed about, argued about. I wanted a feeling for Joanne as Eva had known her. It was important to understand the impact Joanne had had on Eva's life in order to begin to grasp what the loss of her must mean.

Although Eva struck me as being closed, intensely private, and even somewhat guarded, I came to understand that she was vastly more open than she had once been. Before her relationship with Joanne, she said, she never talked about herself, rarely even mentioned what she does, and never confided in anyone. Joanne's sociability had opened her up to the point where she was now able to talk to me, albeit with difficulty. We discovered that her secrecy about herself had its roots in very early experience. For one thing, she knew she was a lesbian from the age of three or four. As with so many other people who have a childhood awareness of being gay, the sense of having to keep a secret became a constant presence. Sadly, as is the usual case, the practice of keeping secrets may end up extending to all aspects of experience and may become a pervasive part of the character. If one wants to make sure that the truth about one's sexuality doesn't come out, it's safer to not volunteer anything at all that might lead to a personal discussion. Eventually, the practice becomes so smooth and habitual that one may never even bother to discriminate safe situations from dangerous ones, and one simply remains hidden from everyone—sometimes even from one's closest and most supportive friends.

In addition to sensing that her sexuality would not have been supported at home, Eva had other direct experiences of not being supported that contributed to her sense that she should rely only on herself to solve her problems. She had simply accepted it as a given that she should not expect support from her family.

One of the first issues which came up in the therapy was that Eva's parents and her brother and sister-in-law had not even acknowledged Joanne's death. I encouraged Eva to draw the parallels between her marriage to Joanne and her brother's marriage. There was no question that if her brother's wife had died the family would have participated actively and caringly in the long illness, the funeral, and the ensuing mourning. Yet for Eva's spouse, whom the family knew and liked, not a word or a gesture had been spent.

I felt angry on Eva's behalf at such shabby treatment, but Eva had spent a lifetime suppressing her awareness of anger at her family. Early on she had dealt with emotional deprivation by convincing herself that she didn't really need anything from them and therefore had no anger about what wasn't given. This situation was different, however. The pain of widowhood generated intense needs that could not be ignored. Eva's defenses against feelings of anger at deprivation, which had held up so solidly through her childhood and adult life until now, could not withstand the pressure of her current need.

We discussed the possibility of Eva's coming out to her family. It was the family style to avoid direct discussions of emotional issues. It was Eva's defensive style to avoid confrontations and to ask for nothing. Thus, Eva had never said the words "lesbian' or "gay" to her family. Though in all likelihood they knew quite well what the nature of Eva's relationship with Joanne had been, the words had never been said, nor had the relationship been formally acknowledged. I pointed out to Eva that as long as it was kept unspoken, her family might assume that they, too, shouldn't mention it. By not clearly stating that Joanne was her spouse of ten years, she was both encouraging her family's silence about it and letting them off the hook if their feelings about the situation were hostile or uncomfortable. Eva began to grasp the degree to which her silence about her sexuality had created a barrier between her and her family. If she came out to them, she was either going to find some support there, which she badly needed, or she was going to be able to face and deal openly with her anger and disappointment in their lack of it. She resolved to talk to them during her upcoming visit. When she returned from the visit, however, she said she had not been able to do it, and that it scared her more than she realized.

Having been brave enough to acknowledge anger at her family's lack of support, Eva courageously continued to open emotional doors. She started, hesitantly and with much attendant anxiety, to talk about her anger at Joanne. She was angry that throughout the months of illness, Joanne never talked about it at all. Joanne never talked about her own feelings about being sick, and she never even alluded to the fact that this might be having an impact on Eva's life. As these feelings came up, Eva felt intensely guilty, anxious, and disorganized. She complained of drinking more, eating compulsively, and feeling completely out of control on spending sprees. She dared to trust me more and got brave enough to call me a few times at moments of distress. I reassured her that the intent of what she was doing was not self-destructive, even if the effect of it was. She was merely desperately seeking a way to calm the anxiety she had about being angry. She fought through the fear to voice her complaints about Joanne.

Joanne had never cried. She had minimized the entire illness. Eva had thought about nothing but Joanne for those months, but Joanne seemed not to be thinking about anything but her survival. The minute Joanne had gotten sick, Eva had taken out more life insurance on *herself*, so that Joanne's medical care would be provided for if something should happen to Eva. Eva went into substantial debt for Joanne's care, wiped out her savings, and picked up all the bills for nursing, aides, etc. Joanne had had no money of her own, and her only life insurance policy was made out to her family. They had never talked about Joanne's impending death or the fact that Eva was going to be left widowed and in pain, and without funds. At the time, Eva had suppressed all resentment about it. Any fleeting thought of wanting more from Joanne was replaced with more attention to what Joanne needed. Eva felt her goodness was helping to keep Joanne alive. She couldn't risk the guilt and fear of what an angry thought might do. Now, with much anxiety, she was beginning to get in touch with the feelings.

Eva came to realize that Joanne, in her way, was also a very closed and private person, who also felt she had to handle everything on her own. In addition, Joanne's own difficulty with being gay was reflected in her failure to provide for Eva. Joanne had never come out to her family. Her motive for naming her family as her beneficiary on her life insurance, etc., was not to deprive Eva, but to keep up the appearance of their being no more than "good friends." Joanne had been able to take advantage of employee stock options through her job because Eva had given her the money to do so. The stated intent was for the stock to be jointly owned. Yet, somehow, Joanne never managed to arrange it that way and, instead, left her family to benefit from it. The family members, who no doubt knew very well the real nature of their relationship but had never had to formally acknowledge it, also accepted as their due the assets that were left to them, never offering to help Eva. During Joanne's illness, the family indicated to Eva that they were grateful and would help her out. After the death, however, they cleaned out Joanne's apartment without inviting Eva to choose things she wanted as remembrances.

Eva felt Joanne's presence palpably in her life. Joanne was there, watching her, aware of her. Joanne was angry at her for expressing criticisms of their relationship. Joanne was disapproving of Eva's talking so openly about personal matters. Eva sometimes felt as if Joanne would not release her from her hold. At other times, she could not bear the thought of feeling any more separate from her. I encouraged Eva to talk to Joanne. For a long time after someone close dies, she or he is still present in one's life. People in grief may criticize themselves for continuing to relate to the dead person and may try to stop themselves from doing it. They may also carry on conversations secretly with the one who died, fearing that people would think them crazy if they knew. It seems that if the continued relationship with the deceased is supported, though, it gives an opportunity for the gradual loosening of those bonds over time, as things get worked through. I encouraged Eva to tell Joanne how much she missed her, how upset she was that they never talked more, and to let her know just how hard things were for her now. I also suggested that she ask if Joanne was all right and find out what Joanne wanted of her now.

The hardest part of the day started just before leaving work. They had always had a phone call at that hour and always had dinner together. Eva had been drinking a bottle of wine nightly to get through those awful hours. I was very concerned about her drinking pattern and strongly suggested she go to Alcoholics Anonymous. She felt she did not have an alcohol problem and hated the idea of going to a group meeting. She was not yet willing to give up the wine but did cut down by half. She had no history of chemical substance abuse, nor did her family's history put her at high risk for alcoholism, so I decided not to take too hard a line about it and see how it went.

At about this time, because she seemed better able to tolerate her feelings, I suggested that she begin keeping a diary. She returned saying that she had learned from what she'd written that "I'm not just angry, I'm *very* angry."

She was angry at the doctors who had put Joanne through surgery after surgery and caused her unimaginable anguish, when they were well aware that none of it would really prolong Joanne's life or even ease her suffering. None of them had spoken openly about Joanne's dying. Joanne had gone along with whatever they recommended. Two weeks before she died, Eva had been there while Joanne was screaming in pain from yet another procedure to remove fluid from around her heart. The memory of that screaming burned in her now.

She was angry at Joanne's family. They had minimized and denied the entire thing. They never accepted the seriousness of it. Joanne's mother never went to the hospital or the funeral, presumably because she "couldn't handle it," and she maintained only telephone contact. When the doctors had told Eva to tell the family how serious it was, Joanne's sister had become angry at Eva for making such a big deal out of it. Eva was even more angry now at her own parents for doing nothing.

At about this time Eva threw out Joanne's toothbrush. Though it was a small item, it was a symbolically powerful event. It both marked that another fiber of connection to Joanne had been loosened and also propelled Eva into an even more intense phase of the mourning. It had been about three months since Joanne's death, and Thanksgiving was approaching. Her anger at Joanne was about her silence. She had died in silence, without a word of comfort or support for Eva. The intensity of these feelings brought up old wounds from childhood, and Eva now let me in on things she'd never discussed with anyone before.

Her brother had been violent with her while they were growing up. He used to beat her viciously, unmercifully, and repeatedly. Her mother had looked the other way. There had been no protection or support. The mother would protest weakly that "If you don't stop I'll tell your father." Her father didn't do anything and Eva just assumed that he also didn't care as he surely must have been told. The beatings went on for years. Her father only found out about them accidentally when Eva was twelve, and he came home unexpectedly one day to find a beating in progress. Her father was enraged and demonstrably came to Eva's aid at last.

In addition, there was sexual play with her brother and a group of cousins and friends, which turned into sexual abuse and then into repeated gang rape. This was very hard for Eva to talk about, and there was a great deal of minimizing of the impact of all this on her. The one effect she was able to acknowledge, however, was the profound sense of being alone and unsupported. This was the nature of the old wound that her current anguish reawakened.

Eva was facing a business trip to the Orient over the holiday—her first time out of the country since the loss. It reminded me that, about three months after Michael died, I had to fly to Indianapolis for a few days. The geographic separation from my home, from Michael's home, had provoked a degree of pain and fear that were astonishing in their intensity. I was seized with spasms of sobbing on the plane and then again in the hotel room. It was as if I were abandoning him by going so far away. Eva kept expecting that she should be finished with the pain of grieving any day now and was continually surprised and dismayed by the duration and intensity of the experience. I felt pretty sure that the trip to the Orient was going to hit her with a shock of pain she was not prepared for and so, together, we were able to anticipate it. We arranged for her to call me a couple of times during her trip in order to cushion some of the isolation.

When she returned, it was December. I shuddered when she told me that Joanne's fatal illness had begun on December 27th. My baby had died on December 27th. The coincidence felt eerie.

She wrote a coming-out letter to her parents which was both direct and loving. Her mother responded with a loving and emotional message on her answering machine but avoided the central issue. With Christmas and New Year's approaching, Eva had one foot in each of two worlds. She

had bought Joanne a Christmas card as if she were still alive. She planned
to spend Christmas alone at a house she rented upstate, which reminded
her strongly of the house Joanne lived in when they met. She couldn't
bear the thought of socializing or seeing her family for the holidays,
anticipating that it would be too difficult to keep up the necessary good
cheer. At the same time, she talked more about the very good friends
who had supported her so warmly through the ordeal, and she began to
accept some dates that they arranged for her.

Eva told me that before it happened she had had a psychic vision of
Joanne having a long illness, of the funeral being held in that particular
chapel, and of herself giving the eulogy. She confessed her fear that the
vision had not been totally fulfilled yet, because it included her having a
heart attack after the ordeal. She was afraid that the stress she was under
would cause it to happen. I have no personal knowledge of psychic visions;
they don't happen to me. But I've heard enough startling things in my life
that I'm not willing to discount them. I don't know what they mean or
what one should do about them, but I'm not about to dispute their reality.
What I did do with Eva's vision though, was to explore the suicidal feelings
that might be contributing to her fear. Though she could not articulate
much about them, she acknowledged that they were there. This was the
last session before the Christmas holiday.

Eva felt much relief at having survived the Christmas holiday. The new
year brought her new hope. Putting the feelings of wanting to die into
words was the turning point in Eva's starting to live again.

For someone like Eva words are very powerful. Some people hide
behind glib, articulate, intellectualized verbiage. Eva was simply quiet. In
fact, in many of our sessions there were periods of silence ranging from
five to twenty minutes at a time. There were a few sessions during which,
except for greeting and leaving, we were almost completely silent. Eva
was able to tell me that she was often frightened of putting something
into words. Words gave a feeling of reality to something that it might not
have if she kept it to herself. I often pushed her to talk about the fear that
made her not want to reveal something, while trying to respect her need
to keep the content of the issue private. She often responded that even by
talking about the resistance, she would end up revealing more than she
was comfortable with, and so we would accept the silence when necessary.

Over the next few months, Eva did a great deal of work on herself. She
became involved in a relationship, and although she constantly felt torn
by guilt over leaving Joanne, she was able to enjoy a very sweet and loving

woman who came into her life. She dealt with more anger at her family—her father's lack of support for her as a competent woman in business, her brother's favored position—and also came to integrate that anger with the knowledge of their love and affection for her. She got her finances under control and gave up alcohol. She reported that she was talking more to people as a result of therapy and was more able to listen when people talked about personal things. She was finally able to go into the summer home she and Joanne had together and was surprised that it was not as hard to be there as she had feared. She had never removed the sheets from the bed since she'd last slept there with Joanne, but now she cleaned out the place so it could be rented.

At about the same time, she began insisting that she did not want to work on anything else. She complained that the more she said, the more vulnerable she felt, and she did not want to continue in that direction. She was angry at me, though she couldn't quite say why. She was also angry at Nina, the woman she had begun to see but, again, could not say why. We identified a lot of her guilt about betraying Joanne by talking to me and by being with Nina. We also identified the depression which had been underlying her very high-level independent functioning her whole life. Her response to it was "So what? Where has talking about it gotten me? I'm not sure this whole process is any good. I'm experiencing depression I've never allowed myself to feel before." I reminded her that her alternative was to overeat and spend too much money. She said, "Yes, and it sounds good to me. I've spent my whole life pushing these feelings away and I'm not sure I'm going to be a better person for having dealt with all of this—either to myself or to other people. I kind of liked myself before. I'm not liking myself right now."

As a therapist, I am motivated, on some level, by my own childhood needs to relieve the suffering of the people I loved. Therefore, it is hard to hear a patient say that the work we've done together has only made him or her feel worse. However, thanks to good training and lots of experience, I was also able to understand Eva's anger at me as a wonderful step forward in her growth. I could see evidence of her being freer to love Nina and better able to take care of her life in general, even while she was telling me that things were only getting worse for her. It was important that she was no longer taking care of me and my feelings She seemed to have given up her need to protect me from her depression and her anger, which had to mean a greater willingness to accept those feelings within herself.

She opened up the topic of a relationship she had had with a teacher at thirteen. Though she had told me about it before, she now referred to it clearly as having been childhood sexual abuse. The teacher had been a rather sociopathic and destructive woman who seduced several girls in school and was eventually caught. Eva expressed all the appropriate anger at the teacher and at the family who had failed to either protect her or to adequately sympathize with her pain around the experience.

This work took us through Joanne's birthday, Passover, the summer anniversaries of their last good weekend together, and the anniversary of Joanne's death (which, again eerily, was on August 11th, two days away from my son Michael's birthday). Progress continued in every area of Eva's life. The healing process was passing the acute stages as more and more symbolic goodbyes to Joanne left Eva more open to life and love.

By October, we began talking about terminating. Eva said she felt she'd done everything in therapy that she came to do plus more than she ever expected. She was pleased with the changes she had made, with her increased openness as a lesbian, and with her increased openness in general. For several sessions we talked around the issue of terminating without confronting it directly. We kept fishing for new issues to explore. We both seemed reluctant to let go. The therapy had been about recovery from loss, and now neither one of us was eager to experience yet another loss.

I didn't completely catch on to what was happening with us until one session when Eva told me that I reminded her of Joanne. Though she was saying that she felt an affection towards me which reminded her of her feelings towards Joanne, she was also saying that I was a powerful remaining link to Joanne. I realized that some of her avoidance of termination was because this relationship was the last major tie to Joanne. When I told her that I thought a goodbye to me would be a last goodbye to Joanne, she nodded and was silent for a very long while. Then she said, "But it's time."

To myself, I had to admit a reluctance to say goodbye both to Eva and, once again, to Michael. Eva's warmth towards me in general and her empathy for my loss of my child had been a healing experience for me. Though it forced me to relive the tragedy of losing him, it also allowed me to relive the joy of loving him. I sometimes choose to sacrifice the loving memories to avoid the painful ones. With Eva, I let myself open up the past again. I did it, in part, because she needed me to—because it helped me open my heart to her suffering. But I might not have gone quite as far with another patient.

We both observed that Eva's need to take care of me was one of her biggest defense mechanisms. We took note of every occasion on which she was deflecting the therapy away from her own pain or anger out of a desire to not be a burden to me. This was how she had dealt with Joanne, with her friends, and with her family. However, there was an aspect to Eva's nurturing that was not defensive. It was important to appreciate Eva's sensitivity and caring as a lovely and generous part of her nature from which both she and other people derived a great deal of pleasure. I reaped the personal benefit of it by letting her know some of my grief and feeling touched by her sympathy and sweetness. I felt safe with her and accepted by her. The empathy between us had been a powerful force for us both.

14

DONALD L. MOSHER

Scared Straight: Homosexual Threat in Heterosexual Therapists

C AN A STRAIGHT THERAPIST work with a gay client? Maybe. Empathy is required. Gays are adept at passing in a straight world. If you
are straight, do you have enough knowledge and empathy to pass in a gay
world? It's not unusual to ask for empathy; it's not unusual to ask of
anyone. Can you see with gay eyes? Can you hear with gay ears? Can you
feel with a gay heart? Empathy is not unusual to ask of anyone. For a
straight psychotherapist, it's a must.

Yet, most straight therapists are scared by gays. I know I was a scared
straight. Still, after some shameful, threatening, and enlightening experiences, I managed to change enough to work effectively with gay men and
lesbian women. Here are some of the highlights of that transformative
journey.

SCENES FROM THE SOUTH

Sheffield, Alabama is a small, working-class town perched on a cliff above
the Tennessee River. I grew up there (from 1942 to 1953) and left for
Butte, Montana, the night I graduated from Sheffield High.

We called gays "queers." I don't think that I knew a queer in Alabama.
All the good old boys were macho. Friday night football was the be-all
and end-all of Southern life. I was an all-American boy, small but aggres-

I wish to thank Susan B. Bond, Ph.D. for her helpful comments on this manuscript.

sive, with athletic letters in three sports as halfback, point guard, and sprinter. But I was more than a jock, I was a reluctant leader, an eager reader, an Eagle Scout, the most scholarly boy in my class. I was more or less accepted—I may have been a bit too bright, a bit too goody-good, a bit aloof.

I can't say when I first learned of queers, but I know it was with revulsion. Being queer embodied all of my fears of being unmanly. I knew I must be a man. Being a boy was a struggle against learning not to cry when hurt, not to be afraid when danger loomed. It was a struggle I often seemed to lose, shaming me until the shame became more intolerable than distress or fear. Knowing that I had to dive in, or get thrown in, or be shamed in, I learned to plunge in—even became brazen enough to enjoy it. I waded awkwardly into heterosexuality at seventeen. Feeling the peer pressure about my virginity, I pressured a girl who liked me and deserved better into my first sexual experience. I had to in order to be a man, even if it left me—still a boy—feeling guilty, exploitative, and sinful.

I know I had learned about queers before then. Two memories from my adolescence stand out. My best friend's father told him (he told me), "Don't ever let a queer suck your pecker. He'll suck the marrow right out of your backbone." Now, there's a warning to be heeded. A man needs a backbone.

One of my boyhood idols, a sports star, joined the Navy. He brought home a couple of sailors, full of beer and sailor stories. A couple of them— I couldn't believe this of my friend—had been picking up queers who gave them money to let the queers blow them. I couldn't make heads or tails of this. They seemed proud, like they were getting it over the queers; they bragged how they would beat the queers up if they tried to kiss them. How could you let a queer do that to you for money? How much is a backbone worth?

SCENES FROM BUTTE

Such stories from the more cosmopolitan world of Memphis prepared me for the unexpected during my family's move to Butte in 1953. Montana was lovely, but Butte was hell for a Southern boy from dry, tranquil, fundamentalist Sheffield. Butte was once a mining town for gold and silver and now for copper; it proudly claimed to be a mile high and a mile deep. The hill was a patchwork quilt of mining derricks, assorted churches, and western bars randomly stitched together. The ethnically diverse people were proud to be cowboys, mountain men, or miners, calling themselves "Butte rats." Their names weren't familiar to my Southern ears, like Mason or Dixon, but were funny sounding names, like Borkovich or Flaherty. Not only that, if you dared go far enough up Main Street, there were pachuchos (a Chicano gang).

Butte had closed its cribs, but had left a respectable cathouse in town so a man could still get a poke. Butte rats gambled illegally in the backs of the bars, tossing their silver dollars on the tables, tossing their shots in their mouths, and throwing the bird or a shot at anyone who didn't like it. Everyone drank, everyone fought, everyone fucked, everyone shot Bambi.

While my parents looked for a house to rent, we lived in the Butte Hotel for six weeks. The circus came to town. At the hotel, I met an athletic looking guy in his twenties from South Africa who walked the tightrope. I was lonely, he was friendly. He asked me if I liked sex. I said yes, even allowed I wasn't a virgin, with more blush than boast. He had me show him where the cathouse was.

On our walk, he suggested that later on he'd go into a bar and pick up two women for us. He'd show me where his room was now. Later, I was to wait in the lobby and follow him up to his room. He said the women might come up separately to fool the desk clerk.

In his room he had a number of sexual stories to tell; he showed me some sketches of nude women. But his stories included a story about sailors—yes, those wicked guys again—fucking one another in the ass on the wing of an airplane aboard an aircraft carrier. He'd caught them in the act, and they asked him to join in. He said it was better than jacking off. He speculated I'd jack off if he didn't get the girls, wouldn't I? I allowed as I would; I had an erection. He reached over to feel how big I was. He judged I was not very big; I defended the size of my penis as that of a still growing boy. He said cocks stopped growing at fifteen.

His touching me like that made me feel uncomfortable and suspicious (as well as small). I decided he was a queer; even though he didn't look like a queer, he told queer stories, and feeling peckers was definitely queer. So I played it cool, saying I would meet him later like we planned. Instead, I flew squawking back to the safety of my roost like a chicken spared from the hawk. I don't remember whether I masturbated, but if I did I thought of girls. Just my luck to meet a size queen who left me feeling not only gullible but also smaller than average. I didn't even go to the circus.

FROM SIN TO PERVERSION

Back in Alabama, I had started reading Freud. I was curious about people and even more curious about sex. Freud was, too. I first learned of homosexuality (as opposed to "queers") by reading psychiatric texts. Like my friends in Alabama and Butte, many psychiatrists regarded homosexuality as a fate worse than death. Given his belief in humankind's bisexuality, Freud regarded homosexuality as a fate to be accepted, if not cherished. But, in my mind, psychiatry replaced sodomy as sin with homosexuality as perversion.

As an undergraduate at the University of Montana, I read the classic *Psychoanalytic Theory of Neuroses*, by Otto Fenichel (1945). Fenichel's account emphasized the motivating force of castration anxiety as causing homosexuality. He believed homosexuals either identify with their mother to avoid castration or transform this fear into a wish to be passive-receptive partners in anal intercourse.

It was bad enough to learn from Freud that I unconsciously wanted to have sex with my mother and kill my father; it seemed even worse to have a homosexual perversion. And how could you be sure this strange *otherness* wasn't latent, forever lurking?

If I was safely heterosexual, I must still watch out not to become fixated on either oral sex or anal sex, rather than on genitally mature heterosexual coitus. And I definitely wanted to be both heterosexual and genitally mature—even big.

MY SEXUAL GUILT

Whether in Alabama or Montana or Ohio, I just couldn't handle my sexual guilt. I reacted to the move to Butte by deciding to become a preacher and save those lost and sinful souls. I went to "the U" in Missoula, studied psychology, and then returned to Butte on weekends to preach. But I remained pinioned between sexual desire and sexual sin: infrequent sexual experiences still filled with shame and guilt. Still, psychology's conception of sex and guilt seemed kinder to me than did the harshness of my fundamental religious beliefs. In college, my identity transformed. The ideological polarity flipped within me from normative intolerance to humanistic tolerance, but the guilt lasted longer.

After entering graduate school at Ohio State, I rushed into a marriage. Marriage was what a man did after he reached adulthood; marriage would rescue me from sexual guilt. I thought that I, the Southern gentleman, was rescuing the woman that I married from poverty and hardship. My choice was more of marriage than of partner: a choice powered by romanticism, conventionality, and a macho man's need for sex that was, for me, also guilt-ridden.

Graduate school was my first academic challenge, and I loved it. I studied consistently, worked hard, and graduated early. In my dissertation, I developed an inventory of guilt, including sexual guilt. What a surprise.

MY PSYCHOANALYSIS

Now, I owed the U.S. Army two years of my life. I served as a clinical psychologist at Walter Reed General Hospital. Soon after arriving in Washington, D.C., I called the local psychoanalytic institute. So anxious I could barely breathe, I had the good fortune to become a reduced-fee case for an analyst-in-training who worked at Chestnut Lodge in Rockville. Four mornings a week, at 6:30, with legs crossed, arms folded, dressed in my class A uniform, I lay rigidly on his couch, alternating boastful ingratiation with silent passive resistance. My analyst, the blank projective screen, bided his time in silence.

I told him my dreams, complete with brilliant interpretations. After all, I had read Freud's *The Interpretation of Dreams* by age 16. The analyst did not find this too helpful; he had me stop bringing in my precious dreams. Finally, with much apparent trepidation, I offered the secret of my childhood sexual play, convinced this trauma could earn me the dreaded epithet of "latent homosexual."

At age five, under the side stairs of the weathered frame duplex where we lived in Columbia, Tennessee (the mule capital of America) a roguish, older boy suggested that I put my penis in his mouth and then he'd put his in mine. It must have sounded interesting at the time, so I did. His tongue tickled mine. When he put his penis in my mouth, he pissed right in my mouth. I still remember the taste of that warm urine with disgust. I stuck my T-shirt in my mouth, trying to get rid of that taste. What a dirty trick.

Not only that, he talked me into doing this a second time, with the same ending—an unwanted golden shower. Fool me once, shame on thee; fool me twice, shame on me. Yes, I felt foolish, deeply ashamed of being so easily tricked, and guilty because I knew it must be kept a sexual secret. Never again, says me.

Of course, at age five I had not yet heard of queers. But when I did, I knew that this event posed a definite problem for my heterosexual history. I did not know the word "macho" back then, but I yearned to be a heroic man, not a humiliated queer.

My analyst, to my surprise, did not make too much of this riveting confession. My analyst, despite my stereotyping, saw this as simple childhood sexual play—of little interest and significance. He gave me a great vote of confidence as being safely and securely heterosexual. I was a psychoanalytically certified straight.

THE BLIND SEXUAL SOPHISTICATE

At 34, I became a full professor, my own man, more macho, less guilty. I naively believed I was a man of the world. I thought, at last, I really know about this sex stuff. I was becoming recognized as a sex researcher. When I was invited to do research for the President's Commission on Obscenity and Pornography in 1969, I became an expert on smut. I saw a lot of dirty pictures, even gay ones.

Then, in the early '70s, it happened. There I was—a macho, Southern gentleman, sexual sophisticate; there he was—a Southern black homosexual. We were professor and student—the situation contained the ingredients of melodrama or farce. I saw him as sensitive, intelligent, caring, and caught in an existential crisis. Without my realizing it, he saw me as the man of his dreams—a hunky, honky dude.

Wanting to nurture his talent, I was sensitive, intelligent, and caring. Wanting me as his lover, Walter began to court me.

When he went back to his grandmother's home in North Carolina over Christmas break, Walter wanted to know if he could call me. That is a bit unusual, I thought, but OK, what's the harm? We didn't seem to have much to say over the phone; I didn't have a clue what was going on. Then, he brought me back a small, cedar box filled with sea shells he had painstakingly found for me on the beach. I thought it was an unusual gift, but maybe he didn't have any money for a Christmas present.

Lovesick as he was, blind as I was, we muddled along: professor and student, friends? Densely polite, I regarded him as offering me a friendship, without seeing his efforts to define our relationship as true love.

Now you may find this next part difficult to believe, given I was a professor, fellow, and diplomate in clinical psychology at the time. But Freud did get the part about denial and repressive defenses right.

Walter invited me over to his place for a drink. We sat on his couch (his roommates were gone), had a drink, and talked. There was still no glimmering on my part. Then he said, "Would you like to see my bedroom?" Equally polite, I said, "Sure." We walked in, with me expecting some interesting architectural detail or a fascinating collection of sea shells he wanted me to see and with Walter expecting me finally to embrace him. Once there, the bedroom was bare, except for a mattress on the floor.

He turned to me, looking into my eyes expectantly. Suddenly the clouds parted and calling on a vast native intelligence, a formidable background in psychological science, and an erudite, perceptive knowledge of erotic cultural mores, I instantaneously concluded, "This is a sexual invitation." Muffling my cry of "Eureka," I mumbled, "Nice room." And I walked out, back to the couch, and soon out the door without daring to say a single word about his unmentionable love that has no name. My defense of last resort was to deny that the whole thing was happening.

Each time I remember this scene, I am chagrined. I was not prepared to deal with Walter's feelings or my own. I was too scared to acknowledge what was going on, too frightened to be kind, too terrified to comfort. I was at a loss for words and was lost in fear.

Now that I saw the light, I knew it was a torch. Yet I was still lost in my own experience, not in Walter's. I knew I was straight; he knew I was straight. Still, how could I have missed all these cues? What the hell was I going to do? Talk about homosexual threat, I was a paradigm case.

We had made a date—yes, that was the word—to meet in my office the next afternoon, but I fled, leaving a note on the door about feeling sick. I was sick all right, scared shitless. Uptight. I was one scared straight.

What was I so frightened of? Could it be that my blindness bespoke of suppressed homosexual interest? Maybe. Yet, I knew I had no desire to take a male lover; I couldn't make any erotic pictures in my mind of such a scene. Yet how could I be so blind, so stupid, so obtuse. All too easily, it seemed.

SELF-DIAGNOSIS AND SELF-THERAPY

Like women must feel when they are courted by men they like as people but do not find sexually attractive, I did not want to hurt Walter's feelings by rejecting him. Yet, is there anything more unkind than to not even acknowledge his sexual invitation for what it was?

That he was black brought out my liberal guilt. I remember when I was five, the Klan burned an abandoned house in my white neighborhood in Columbia because colored squatters had moved in. I remember playing with this black boy for a day or so, before the fire, until I was told not to by my parents. Apprehension and racial tension permeated my young life, confusing me. My college days were filled with trying to sort out issues of race.

Yet, I had to confront the issue with Walter. So I did—not as gracefully as I would have liked, but as best I could, given my own limitations.

My self-diagnosis: heterosexist egocentrism, motivated by homosexual threat. My self-psychotherapy: *in vivo* flooding and cognitive restructuring, leading to a further reversal of polarity in sexual ideology and to a commitment to advancing sexual freedom.

First, I told Walter that I liked him and wanted him as a friend, but only as a friend. I learned that I could be a caring friend without being sexual. Walter was sensitive, intelligent, and caring. I am sure he helped me through it all. It is so nice to have a younger, wiser head around to help you through your awkward adolescence at 30-something. Although more powerful, but not wiser, the oppressor requires educating by the oppressed.

Walter began graduate school, and our friendship continued. I visited him at his mother's apartment in New York City. He took me to the gay bars and introduced me to the scenes. He educated me, desensitized me, and instructed me in the mores and motives of the gay life. Having developed a sympathy for him and the gay life, I wanted to understand the lifestyle. I wanted to understand myself. Perhaps it is always less threatening for me, the professor, to deal with the abstractions of ideas than the concrete realities of people interacting with me in scenes that seem unmanageable.

The sense of shame within me at failing to understand, at failing to know, at failing to care—in the way that fits—runs deep. Throughout my life this embarrassing blindness has preceded my eventual enlightenment. The shame yields and insight comes, but shame lingers at the memories.

I danced with Walter in the gay bars. He told me about his love of the men in the baths. I slept on the couch with one of his former lovers; I know I slept soundly. I knew I was safe, once I knew who I was, what I wanted, how to say "No."

Because I grew up in a world that was racist, sexist, and heterosexist, I have been every self that I fear; I still fight against being each of those feared identities. It is a struggle I win more often than not, yet it is still a struggle. The feared identities and their polar opposites were interwoven in my childhood tapestry of life as lived in the South in a fundamentalist family of that time around the Second War. My parents—good, decent people—loved me as I love them. But they love their fundamentalist vision of God, too. I was a good child, accepting and conventional. Much of my personal psychology has entailed a series of confrontations between the social and religious ideology of my parents and the South with the ideology of scientific humanism. It is no accident that I study sexual guilt, given my concern with sexual sin. No accident that my master's thesis studied ethnocentrism. No accident that I study macho men.

During college, I struggled to form a personal identity differentiating myself from my parents, leaving behind and carrying forward blended parts of them with parts of me. I struggled to see the invisible, to discern its form, to transform my view of the world and myself. I became a scientific psychologist, conventional in method, but I challenged psychology's restricted subject matter, daring to study sexuality. The emotions of humans caught in personal and interpersonal conflict intrigued me, just as my own sexuality, rage, and guilt did in everyday life. *I study who I am that I might become who I want to be.*

My blindness to Walter's love and desire was heterosexism in its subtler aspect. Perhaps it is heterosexism, not homosexuality, that is blatant or latent. Although I was past the point of obvious homosexual prejudice and discrimination when I met Walter, I still did not understand my own denial and lack of acknowledgment of gay lifestyles, including the right to have a sexual interest in and to invite a straight to share a gay's sexual preference.

In his editorial role, Charles Silverstein reminded me that, not withstanding my claims of innocence, others will claim that I am a closeted gay man. Why else walk into bedrooms and dance with gay men? If so, so be it.

But if gay men make the claim, I invite them to examine their own homosexual egocentrism. Some gay men take comfort in believing straight men secretly envy their sexuality and lack the courage to come out. If straight men accuse me of being gay, is it not to oppress both gay men and me as a straight man for not being as homophobically oppressive as they are?

IDEOLOGY AS BLINDING

The institutional and personal power of WASP men permits them to spotlight their own pervasive ideological preferences as *the* perceptual figure. Simultaneously, they reduce the ideology and alternative lifestyles of underclasses to the perceptual background. Thus, the gay man and his lifestyle remain mere shadows, unseen on the wall of the cave, whereas, officially in law and unofficially in practice, the powerful, Anglo, macho, straight hero defines goodness and truth in his own image. Victor dominates vanquished; then he writes his version of history.

Next, reality is defined and constructed; it must be seen as *the real*, as the only possible reality. The truth of reality cannot be questioned unless first it is deconstructed. Thus, gay men must struggle through the stages of coming-out to develop their personal acceptance and integrity.

Many conservative straights accept and enforce the dominant social definitions of homosexuality as sin, perversion, and threat to the dominant lifestyle. But even a liberal straight, like me, must struggle to identify and reidentify his heterosexism. Too many heterosexuals are *egocentric* in Piaget's sense—comprehending the world only from the heterosexual point of view, without awareness of the existence of other perspectives.

As a scared straight, I was so trapped by my egocentric, subjective self-definition as straight and so frightened by a feared identity as homosexual that I failed to see any of the obvious, objective features in that family of courting scenes. Only the most objective prototype of sexual courting—the bare mattress on the bedroom floor—could break through my subjective, egocentric denial. Blind, I did not see. Deaf, I did not hear. Insensitive, I did not feel. But, empathy is not too much to ask of anyone.

BECOMING A FELLOW-TRAVELER

I continued to read the gay literature, from gay pride to gay pornography. As I read, I thought about what I might feel living this stigmatized gay life. I nurtured friendships with gay men and lesbian women. I treated some gay and lesbian clients, but not for their homosexuality. Their psychotherapy was for the everyday problems of living, complicated by a culturally stigmatized sexual orientation. Every gay or lesbian I met was a *person*, possessing the same emotions, the same humanity, the same autonomy as me. Each was a distinct individual; each had as much claim to model the prototype of "person" as I did.

I thought about psychology as an agent of social control, conservatively containing deviance while maintaining a racist, sexist, heterosexist culture. Was this the psychology—the sexology—I wanted to represent? I grew more knowledgeable about gay issues, more understanding of gay life, more critical of American culture as sexually negative. I became less psychological and more sexological in my scientific orientation.

I had published an MMPI study in 1968 (Oliver & Mosher, 1968) in which I had labeled "wolves" and "punks" in prison, "homosexual inserters" and "homosexual insertees," respectively. Gonsiorek (1982, p. 66) chided me, with good reason, for my poor choice of labels. The "inserters" were heterosexually-identified macho men raping or exploiting vulnerable men, only a few of whom identified themselves as gay.

Morin's (1977) citation of heterosexual bias in research on gay men and lesbian women also sent me a message. I decided my future research would be more sexologically informed. It would either focus on antihomosexual prejudice in straights or more carefully consider the social and political predicaments of sexual minorities within its design and discussion. Mainly I would continue my studies of sexual guilt and concentrate on understanding the aggressive sexuality of macho men. At least, I would do no harm to gay pride and gay rights. Perhaps, I could be a friend.

HOMOPHOBIA AND MACHO MEN

The term "homophobia" is, with rare exceptions, a misnomer. Underlying my own heterosexism was a homosexual threat to my heterosexual identity. I had no homophobic fear of homosexuals as a boy; I regarded them as unmanly wimps and sissies. In researching homosexual threat (Mosher & O'Grady, 1979), we identified three components: (a) antihomosexuality to bolster hypermasculine esteem, (b) fear of and attraction to homosexual behavior, and (c) prejudice against homosexuals. The predominant affects of macho men toward gay men are anger, disgust, and contempt. They want the gay man to be *machophobic*—to fear their violence.

Macho men are socialized to magnify the importance of excitement, surprise, anger, disgust, dissmell as warrior affects in a macho personality script (Mosher & Tomkins, 1988). This script resonates with an ideology celebrating the power to live a dangerous, callous, violent life. Hypermasculine esteem is threatened by any challenge, any dare, any loss of masculine face. Solutions to conflict are preemptively physical. Every macho man is potentially violent when threatened.

Gay men threaten macho men's idealized, magnified, hypermasculine gender identity by being "effeminate sexual freaks." In contemptuous macho eyes, the gay man is neither man nor woman. Given this contempt for the unmanly, being not truly "masculine" means being undeserving of respect. On the other hand, macho men believe all lesbians just need to be fucked by a real man to become feminine women again. For the macho man, the homosexual man, weakened by the dubious enjoyment of sex shared with other men, should be found trembling in fear and left crying in defeated distress. Macho pride requires gay shame.

KNOW THYSELF

Just as the straight, white male therapist must understand his own sexism and racism he must also understand his own heterosexism. Many men who are heterosexually-identified have a history that has mixed participating in homosexual acts with scenes of antihomosexual prejudice. Some homosexual threat may remain in any straight therapist, whether man or woman, perhaps as blindness, perhaps as ignorance, perhaps as confusion. My advice is to dig deeper into yourself while seeking social contacts with gay men and lesbian women. Discover the uniqueness in each individual, how little sexual identity matters in friendship. Desensitize your homosexual threat first. Then, you can learn to appreciate diverse expressions of sexuality as human variations, nothing more and nothing less.

Helping gays and lesbians develop self-acceptance and self-integration fosters their growth and development as persons (Coleman, 1982). Developing self-respect requires the help of the gay community, both as role models of self-respect and in instilling pride and a sense of gay history. Developing self-respect in a heterosexist world that denies respect is a major treatment goal for gay men and lesbian women. A straight therapist must know about, be able to call upon, and move comfortably within the gay and lesbian community. We must be acquainted with the gay life, its slang and its mores. We must be knowledgeable about HIV and the transformation in gay life resulting from AIDS. We must mourn the death of a generation of gay men who had no warning—good men, irreplaceable men, men like Walter. We must preserve the health and welfare of the next generation of gay men.

If being a straight therapist has any advantage in treating gays and lesbians, it may be that respect from a representative of the in-group helps heal the wounds of the out-group. Genuine respect and concern from a heterosexually-identified therapist fosters self-respect in homosexually-identified clients. If the straight therapist respects gay and lesbian clients as persons and also respects their freedom of sexual choice, then gay and lesbian clients may accept themselves more completely. The acceptance of the therapist may even symbolize parental and societal acceptance. All ethically made sexual choices – including a loving gay lifestyle – are worthy, not only of tolerance, but of our full respect.

Sexual orientation is no bar to successful psychotherapy with homosexually-identified clients by heterosexually-identified therapists, and vice-versa. In fact, identification across sexual orientations may be easier for us than identification across sexes. Whether gay or straight, a skilled, empathic, knowledgeable, insightful therapist of any sex can work with either men or women (including transsexuals) who are homosexual, heterosexual, or bisexual. Empathy, concern, and respect for the client, whether gay or straight, and insight into oneself are requirements for all successful therapists, whether gay or straight.

SETTING WRONGS RIGHT

One of the universal human solutions to inner conflict is active mastery of passively accepted experience. Even the traumatic can be transformed in the creative crucible that sets right past wrongs to the self or to others. For me, that meant a duty not just to understand but to transform antihomosexual prejudice into tolerance and to undertake prosocial action. Psychologists, as scientists and professionals committed to promoting human welfare, have a positive duty to end racism, sexism, and heterosexism.

The straight psychotherapist's usual commitment to caring must include an unusual commitment to justice for sexual minorities if he or she is to be an effective therapist with gay men or lesbian women living in our unjust world. We live in a time and place replete with threats to sexual freedom (Mosher, 1988, 1989).

If gay and straight are to live in harmony, the powerful, the prejudiced, and the privileged must pass from intolerance into tolerance, from egocentrism into empathy, from pity into sympathy, and from acceptance into appreciation.

REFERENCES

1. Coleman, E. (1982). Developmental stages in the coming out process. *Journal of Homosexuality, 7*, 1–9.
2. Fenichel, O. (1945). *The psychoanalytic theory of neuroses*. New York: Norton.
3. Gonsiorek, J. C. (1982). Mental health: Introduction. In W. Paul, J. D. Weinrich, J. C. Gonsiorek, & M. E. Hotvedt (Eds.), *Homosexuality: Social, psychological, and biological issues* (pp. 57–70). Beverly Hills: Sage.
4. Morin, S. F. (1977). Heterosexual bias in research on lesbianism and male homosexuality. *American Psychologist, 32*, 629–637.
5. Mosher, D. L. (1988, April). Plenary address: Sexual freedom, gay rights, and AIDS. Annual meeting of the Society for the Scientific Study of Sex—Western Region, Dallas, TX.
6. Mosher, D. L. (1989). The threat to sexual freedom: Moralistic intolerance instills a spiral of silence. *The Journal of Sex Research, 26*, 492–509.
7. Mosher, D. L., & O'Grady, K. E. (1979). Homosexual threat, negative attitudes toward masturbation, sex guilt, and males' sexual and affective reactions to explicit sex films. *Journal of Consulting and Clinical Psychology, 47*, 860–873.
8. Mosher, D. L., & Tomkins, S. S. (1988). Scripting the macho man: Hypermasculine socialization and enculturation. *The Journal of Sex Research, 25*, 60–84.
9. Oliver, W. A., & Mosher, D. L. (1968). Psychopathology and guilt in heterosexual and subgroups of homosexual reformatory inmates. *Journal of Abnormal Psychology, 73*, 323–329.

15

GERALD PERLMAN

The Question of Therapist Self-Disclosure in the Treatment of a Married Gay Man

T HE COLLEAGUE WHO referred Ralph to me said all he knew was that Ralph was experiencing identity problems. I have learned to hear this as a euphemism for conflict about sexual orientation. The first time I met him, my assumption was confirmed. Ralph was meticulously dressed: He looked as if he had jumped off the hanger fresh and pressed from the dry cleaner. I learned later that he laid out his clothing for the morning the night before. He left little to chance and needed to control or have the illusion he was in control at all times.

Ralph was short and stocky, with thick black hair. He had an engaging smile, which showed gleaming white teeth that were as straight as his posture. As he spoke, he punctuated his consonants to compensate for his slight Cuban accent. He had a sense of pride that came from being a member of a privileged class of Spanish ancestry and from having a light complexion. The pride also came from being the oldest and only male child in a family, where he held the role of Prince Charming. He was adored by his younger sister, was confidant to his mother, and felt morally superior to his father.

Ralph, 33, had been married to Maria for eight years; she came from a similar background. He loved her and they appeared to have a mother/

This chapter is dedicated to my daughter Jennifer, and to David, my life partner. Special thanks go to Drs. Jeffrey Rubin and Charles Silverstein, and to Mrs. Pearl Leisten for their help in shaping the chapter's final version.

son relationship. He explained to me that he was experiencing acute anxiety verging on panic and bouts of depression alternating with great feelings of romantic elation. He had fallen in love with a man and it made him feel "crazy." He longed to be with his new lover, but even more he longed to be rid of what he experienced as invasive, distasteful, and disorganizing homoerotic feelings. He wanted to maintain the safe and respectable haven of his marriage while enjoying the excitement, intrigue, and powerful pull of his new relationship with a man. Ralph was tormented by internal pressures to give one up for the other, make space for both, or run away from it all.

Although he wanted quick respite from his pain and confusion and to regain a sense of control, decisions about his conflict would have to wait. It is a cardinal rule of therapy, as well as of other aspects of life, that no decisions be made during a crisis or a clinical depression. By the time our first meeting ended, I was able to reassure him that I understood his pain. Moreover, I convinced him that he did not have to decide between his wife and male lover immediately. And more importantly, for now, he did not have to decide whether he was homosexual, bisexual, or heterosexual.

During our work together, Ralph described how, for years, he would stop off on the way home from work at a known cruising spot. While there, he would have a brief sexual encounter with another man. Yet he never thought of himself as gay. It became apparent that if the idea that he might be gay broke through his dissociative defense system, he quickly dismissed it and assured himself that it was "just something I did." Ralph thought that perhaps he had "special needs" that others did not have. He believed that all men engaged in sex with other men from time to time, but that it was never talked about.

As Ralph detailed these internal dialogues, he demonstrated the depth of his defensive need to deny, compartmentalize, and rationalize his homosexual feelings. It was also apparent how isolated and detached he was from himself and others. Despite his charming, compliant, and congenial manner, Ralph had no close friends, no support network at all.

As I listened to this young man describe his turmoil, I thought, "You've come to the right place." I was sure I could be helpful, but I had to be a neutral, unbiased facilitator and allow him to develop his own self. I recalled Guntrip (1969), who said that the therapist needs to know from his own experience what the patient is going through. I knew, because I had been there. A part of me wanted to tell Ralph that I once sat exactly where he was now. But, do I tell him that I am gay and had been married?

Do I tell him that I too had felt confused and so frightened it made my skin crawl? I knew what it felt like to believe that everything that mattered could be taken away. As the literature on this issue will confirm, coming out as a gay person is a difficult and often painful process (Gonsiorek, 1982). Coming out to a marriage partner and possibly dissolving that union ups the ante. Add children and in-laws to the equation and the decisions and painful experiences may become overwhelming. In addition to all the concerns coming out presents, the possibility of losing a wife you may have loved, fearing that your child may turn from you or be taken away, and losing the cloak of respectability marriage and family provide often feels unbearable. I knew what it felt like to live in terror of ostracism, abandonment, and disgrace.

Any disclosure should be timed to enhance the client's growth. I could not possibly know what impact my self-disclosure would have on Ralph so early in his treatment. I felt that self-disclosing now could only serve my own need to present myself as an understanding and compassionate man. To share my own story would be to unnecessarily burden the patient with my own narcissistic need. It would have been invasive. As it turned out, more than a year would pass before I revealed my own struggle with being a married gay man.

Ralph told me that his world was collapsing. It was a world he had carefully built to bring respect and honor to himself and his family. He had developed a "false self" based on denial, containment, compartmentalization and rationalization. He was unaware of the hysterical components of his personality, nor was he in touch with what he needed or felt. Currently, all he knew was that the rigid defense system he had erected was crumbling and that his life had been turned upside down. He described feeling like a ship that had lost its mooring. As painful as this experience was, it provided the impetus for him to explore his own psyche and dare to change.

He was consumed with feelings of self-doubt, shame, disgust, and self-loathing. Homosexuality represented everything ugly in the world. As with most gay men experiencing homoerotic impulses, internalized homophobia presented a major obstacle to self-acceptance. Ralph echoed the myths I had heard before and, indeed, felt myself: "Being gay is unnatural; it is sick. It's not me." His dissociative terminology brought to mind Sullivan's (1953) description of the loathsome, dreadful, and anxiety ridden personification which he termed "not me"—a part of self so inconceivable that it is dissociated from consciousness and which, when it breaks through to awareness, sends the person into panic. The therapist must be sensitive enough to monitor and ameliorate the patient's anxiety when "not me" experiences emerge.

Ralph expressed the fear that living a gay lifestyle would leave him feeling lonely and ultimately rejected. The idyllic union he had created with Maria was in jeopardy. The illusion of the perfect couple was shattered when he met Alan. Where his wife was a forceful, energetic, and demanding person, his new lover was a meek, isolated, and bland man several years older. Yet he loved Alan, who represented the quiet, gentle, fair haired man who would care for him. Once the triangle of self, lover, and wife was set, respectability, self-rightousness, and clarity about right and wrong were gone. Lost was the perfect "false self," that is, a delusional image and concept of himself constructed around what he felt he should be as opposed to the hated real person he was (Winnicott, 1958). In his view, only the specter of a lonely, denigrated, humiliating, and perverted life lay ahead. Ralph was clear about one thing. "If I'm gay, I'm no good." Despair and suicidal thoughts were now ever present.

I could feel his pain and his sense of helplessness. I felt the urge to tell him that I understood exactly what he was going through. I recalled my own despair. I recalled feeling confused and disoriented, as if there were no way out. Everything I had worked for seemed on the brink of collapsing. I had been certain that all my friends, colleagues, and relatives would desert me. It had felt as though I were falling from a very high place and there was no one to catch me. But if I came out to Ralph at this point in therapy, it would have been out of my need to quiet my own feelings of helplessness. These helpless feelings came from my own recollected past and the momentary desire to help Ralph through his despair. In the course of psychotherapy, the therapist may feel a sense of helplessness in regard to the client. Often, this is induced, that is, the therapist is responded to in a way designed to let him or her know what the client is experiencing in the moment. There is also our human desire to be helpful and try to alleviate pain and suffering. However, in psychotherapy, to act on this impulse is usually not helpful.

I felt that to disclose at this juncture would have prematurely closed further exploration of his fears and assumptions. In the depth of his conflict, any revelation on my part might have frightened him and caused him to question my motives. Had I told him how I resolved my conflict, he might have felt it necessary and expedient to use my resolution as a way out of his torment, or he might feel that I had a vested interest in the direction of his own resolution. It was necessary that he develop and maintain trust and confidence in me and the therapeutic process in order for our work to progress. My neutrality was imperative.

Another cardinal rule of therapy suggests that if you feel compelled to say something, don't. Experience indicates that, most often, allowing the client to sit with his or her feelings of despair and helplessness is more therapeutic than rescuing him or her. I decided I could be more helpful by letting Ralph know that he was not alone in his struggle anymore. He needed to experience what he was going to experience and know that I was available to walk through the pain with him and, if necessary, catch him as he experienced falling through space. Those of us who practice psychotherapy know that the development of trust and a working alliance is usually the first order of business. Trust was an important variable in Ralph's life; he had secrets and no friends with whom to share them. The second time we met, Ralph told me he had left our first session with a feeling that, "I had someone to talk to for the first time in my life." Some time later in treatment, he confessed that, although he had now found someone to confide in, he was not at all sure he could trust me, but he felt he had no other choice at the time.

Ralph revealed how enmeshed he had been in a family of women. His sister, his mother, and his grandmother all adored him. He was their prince. He cried as he told me, "I was never able to trust another man. My father had never been demonstrative in his love. There were never any men for me." We then began to explore his relationship with men in general. He told me that I was the only one who could listen to him without making demands. He then added that this was because of my professional responsibility. My response was that, in effect, he had nullified my caring and receptivity. With this intervention, he began to sob. He said that he felt totally alone in the world. I asked him how he would feel if I hugged him. He said he would very much like that; at least there was one man in the world who could care for and respond to him emotionally. I hugged him. He cried on my shoulder. Some time later in therapy, Ralph let me know that the hug was a critical point in our relationship. He said, "That embrace showed me you really cared. You weren't just bound by professional responsibility to listen. I knew you had a choice. Until then, I had never been able to trust a man."

At that point, I could have told him that I had felt abandoned by men, at an earlier time in my life. I could have shared my own experience of weeping like a lost child and longing to be held and comforted by my own male therapist. I might have described the release I felt from my self-imposed isolation and the relief I experienced when my therapist held me and I knew he was there. I decided not to disclose. I believed that it was more important for Ralph to feel cared for by a man, regardless of sexual orientation. To introduce my own story then would have shifted the focus of treatment from his experience of the hug to his reaction to my disclosure, thus robbing him of the valuable emotionally corrective experience of trusting and feeling cared for by another man.

Although his sense of shame regarding his homosexual desires was diminished, it was still evident. He now understood that gay was not necessarily synonymous with bad, nor did heterosexuality automatically entitle one to respectability. Yet, he continued to feel that there was no one besides his therapist with whom he could talk. He began to express the desire to share some of his newfound self-understanding with others. He could share some things with Alan, but Alan was often part of the problem. He needed peers and friends.

I knew the importance of a supportive network for any stigmatized group, and I felt confident that Ralph had gained enough self-acceptance, so I informed him of the Gay Fathers Forum, which has a subgroup of gay married men. With much trepidation, Ralph joined the organization. During the remaining three years of our work together and after, Ralph was an active participant in the group. For the first time in his life, he was able to share himself openly and to develop intimate friendships. In addition to discussing their sexual orientations and marital situations, the group members shared extended parts of their lives, including outings with wives and children. Ralph came to realize the many, varied possible options open to him.

During the course of treatment, I often challenged Ralph's myths and stereotypes about gay life. At these times, I served as a resource center. I would inform Ralph about organizations, research findings, statistics, etc. Much of what had been imparted during treatment was now being validated by his peer group. After he had been involved with the group for several months, and our work was well into its second year, Ralph noted that I seemed to be particularly well informed about gay issues and organizations. I had emerged from my role as therapist and become a person for Ralph. He wondered aloud, "How come you know so much?" Someone in his group had asked him if his therapist was gay. When he told his friend he was not sure, he was encouraged to ask. We discussed his feelings and thoughts about my sexuality, as well as his hesitance to ask. We explored his difficulty in considering me as a person apart from my role, and then he asked me directly.

I revealed that I was gay and had been married. He was delighted to hear that and felt confirmed in his initial judgment about me. He had suspected I was gay but had been reticent about bringing it up earlier in our work. He felt that if an "intelligent professional man with so much to contribute is gay, it can't be as bad as I've been taught. I'm an intelligent professional man with much to contribute. And I guess I'm okay." He also confirmed my belief that had the issue of my sexuality emerged earlier, it would have been confusing and would have detracted from his own struggles at the time.

Had Ralph asked about my sexuality earlier in treatment, before we had developed a trusting working alliance, I would not have disclosed it. My disclosures would come once he had, at least partially, worked through his internalized homophobia. Only after he had developed enough self-acceptance and self-knowledge, would I be self-revealing. I would not have disclosed until he was capable of seeing me as a whole and real person apart from my role as therapist. I would first have explored his fantasies as grist for the psychotherapeutic mill and then informed him that I did not think it would be helpful for him to know about my sexuality at that time. In other words, I would have been appropriately withholding. However, once the essential elements mentioned above were apparent, I felt my disclosing would facilitate the therapy. I was now confident that revealing specific events and accompanying feelings from my own experience could be integrated and utilized by Ralph, as he saw fit, in the context of his own life.

Self-disclosure is a therapeutic intervention. When, how, and why to utilize a particular intervention should always enhance and promote the client's psychological development. Riddle and Sang (1979) have noted that discretionary use of therapist disclosure can be healing in that it validates the client's struggle. Disclosure can enhance empathic experience and create a positive and respected role model. Malyon (1982) argues that although reassuring during the therapeutic alliance phase of psychotherapy, therapist disclosure is contraindicated when the client has not yet come out or is conflicted about his or her homosexuality.

Any question concerning technique in psychotherapy depends on the patient, the therapist, and the type of therapy within which they interact. Important variables to consider before self-disclosing are the developmental level of the client, the degree of his or her psychological awareness, and the issues being negotiated at a particular time in treatment (Perlman, 1988). Self-disclosure is not for all patients; nor is it for all therapists.

Some people use information about others to hurt and entrap them, or in order to feel superior. Unless the therapist is inclined toward masochism, there is no need to give such individuals ammunition. There are clients who are so oblivious to the person who is the therapist that self-disclosure would truly be experienced as overwhelming. Working on one's own psychology may be enough to deal with at a given point in time; to introduce the therapist's psychological issues can flood the client's psyche. And then there are those, like Ralph, whose doggedly internalized homophobic experience and conflicts engender a great deal of self-hatred. If the therapist too quickly reveals himself to be gay, the client's self-loathing may be projected onto the therapist. The latter possibility devalues the therapist and the therapy, thus hindering the work or making it completely impossible.

Self-disclosure is not for all therapists. Some theoretical models demand a "frame" or a "blank screen," for example. Clearly these models fall apart when self-disclosure is employed as a technique. The language of metaphor developed between client and therapist would become internally inconsistent and thus confusing for both participants. Self-disclosure can hinder treatment if the therapist has not worked through his or her own homophobia and the multitude of issues surrounding his or her sexuality. In particular, the therapist who is working within a psychodynamic framework must anticipate and be prepared to deal with the impact of any self-revealing statements on the transference/countertransference continuum. Self-disclosure is likely to open up a can of worms. Clients typically have a myriad of spoken and unspoken reactions to the therapist's feelings and statements about his or her own sexuality. The therapist must be ready to utilize the client's responses in a nondefensive therapeutic manner. The inexperienced or unanalyzed psychotherapist is better off heeding the advice, "Don't just say something. Sit there!" If the therapist is not ready to reveal his or her vulnerability, self-disclosure can become problematic for both therapist and client.

In a discussion of the general issues of disclosing countertransference reactions, Taney (1989) recommends that a therapist assess what effect a disclosure will have on a client before intervening in this manner. A sense of congruence between the immediate experience of the therapist and that of the client should be apparent. Self-disclosure comprises the revealing of facts about one's life and the accompanying affects; it may also refer to the spontaneous emotional reactions one has in the here and now with a client. Both aspects of self-disclosure may be used for therapeutic gain. Thus, the sharing of the therapist's relevant life experience or crying at the news that the client's lover had died can facilitate the therapeutic enterprise. Spontaneity, unlike impulsivity, implies that some thoughtful process had intervened between experience and action. When such a thoughtfulness has not been manifest, these same interventions may be construed as intrusive, invasive, overwhelming, and in other ways countertherapeutic. Disclosures that will burden the client should be avoided. Disclosures that are impulsive or that one feels compelled to reveal are to be guarded against, nor should a therapist utilize disclosures to gratify his or her own narcissistic needs or to fend off uncomfortable countertransferential reactions.

REFERENCES

1. Gonsiorek, J. C. (1982). *Homosexuality and psychotherapy*. New York: Haworth.
2. Guntrip, H. (1969). *Schizoid phenomena, object relations, and the self*. New York: International Universities Press.
3. Malyon, A. K. (1982). Psychotherapeutic implications of internalized homophobia in gay men. In J. C. Gonsiorek (Ed.), *Homosexuality and psychotherapy* (pp. 59–69). New York: Haworth.
4. Perlman, G. (1988, March). *On therapists' self-revelations*. Paper presented at the meeting of Gay Psychiatrists of New York, New York, NY.
5. Riddle, D. L., & Sang, B. (1978). Psychotherapy with lesbians. *Journal of Social Issues, 34*, 84–100.
6. Sullivan, H. S. (1953). *The interpersonal theory of psychiatry*. New York: Norton.
7. Taney, M. J. (1989, August). *On countertransference validation and disclosure in the therapeutic interaction*. Paper presented at the meeting of the American Psychological Association, New Orleans, LA.
8. Winnicott, D. W. (1958). Metapsychological and clinical aspects of regression within the psychoanalytical set-up. In *Collected Papers*. New York: Basic Books.

16

ESTHER D. ROTHBLUM

KATHLEEN A. BREHONY

The Boston Marriage Today: Romantic But Asexual Relationships Among Lesbians

IN LESBIAN FOLKLORE, there is anecdotal evidence of women in past centuries who chose to live together as married couples. The lesbian novels *Patience and Sarah* (Miller, 1969) and *The Ladies* (Grumbach, 1984) are fictional elaborations of such relationships. Lillian Faderman's book, *Scotch Verdict* (1983), is a factual account of two headmistresses who were accused of lesbianism by a pupil. In her book, *Surpassing the Love of Men* (1981), Lillian Faderman describes the passion, shared activities, and writings of women who expressed love for each other while often married to men or living other conventional roles in society. She states:

It became clear that women's love relationships have seldom been limited to that one area of expression, that love between women has been primarily a sexual phenomenon only in male fantasy literature. "Lesbian" describes a relationship in which two women's strongest emotions and affections are directed toward each other. Sexual contact may be a part of the relationship to a greater or lesser degree, or it may be entirely absent. (pp. 17–18)

In past decades, "spinster" women who lived together and shared their lives were considered to be in a "Boston marriage," a term that reflected the presumed asexual nature of this relationship (the word "Boston" probably referred to the Puritan and thus asexual component). When we read about such women today, we may assume that their relationships were, in fact, sexual. Our assumptions are supported by the above authors, who added a sexual component to the lives of women who existed but about whom little more is known than a few facts documented by newspapers of their era, presexual revolution and pre-Stonewall. Whether or not such Boston marriages were in fact sexual, there is very little question that the women involved would have kept knowledge of their sexuality secret from their community.

The current chapter will focus on the "Boston marriage" today. In lesbian communities there are women who are lovers in every sense of the word except for the fact that they are not currently sexually involved (and may never have been lovers). Sometimes they live together. Often they travel together, move to live in the same part of the country, make out wills for each other, and share long histories. Often, in total contrast to the Boston marriage of bygone eras, these women keep knowledge of their *asexuality* secret from their community.

Blumstein and Schwartz (1983) studied the relationships of more than 12,000 people, including lesbians, gay men, married heterosexuals, and heterosexuals living with a partner. Their results indicated that lesbian couples had sex less frequently than any other group of couples. In a society that defines a lover relationship by the occurrence of sexual activity, we have no word (and thus no awareness of) the intense romantic, but asexual, relationships that some lesbians may form. Consequently, these important relationships may be discounted by the two women involved in the relationship, by the lesbian community, and by therapists. Therapists, even if lesbian or feminist, may define relationships by the occurrence of sexual activity (in fact, the results of Blumstein and Schwartz caused great disbelief among lesbian readers) and thus disregard the romantic nature of asexual relationships.

For lack of current terminology to describe such romantic but asexual relationships among lesbians, we have chosen to reclaim the historical term "Boston marriage." Although romantic but asexual relationships may occur among heterosexual and gay male couples, the former have the option of legal marriage (which then defines the relationship as legitimate, with or without the presence of sexual activity), and the latter have more frequent sexual activity than do lesbians (Blumstein & Schwartz, 1983).

This chapter will describe a case study of two women involved in a modern-day Boston marriage. We will analyze this case from the perspective of both intrapsychic and societal perspectives and then discuss possible strategies for therapists. We have chosen to use a fictitious case study that is a composite of many of the elements found in the Boston marriages we know. We did not use a true case for two reasons. First, as we will discuss later, one or both members of the Boston marriage are often extremely closeted or only marginally involved in the lesbian community. Second, members of the Boston marriage often seek therapy when they are separating, and, at that point, one partner often denies that they were ever, in fact, a couple. For this reason, it is difficult to obtain consent from both partners of a Boston marriage who are in therapy.

CASE STUDY: A BOSTON MARRIAGE

Hilary, aged 41, and Anne, aged 35, describe themselves as a couple of 15 years' duration. Hilary is the principal of a high school and Anne plays keyboard in a jazz group and works part-time in a bookstore. They have known each other for 17 years, since Anne was a student teacher in the music department at the high school in which Hilary was an English teacher. At that time, Hilary was an important mentor to Anne, although they taught in different departments. They met again two years later at a party and shortly thereafter became lovers. Their sexual involvement lasted six months. There was no particular reason for the cessation of sexual activity; Hilary and Anne "drifted" into celibacy. Since that time, for the past 14 years, both women have been celibate.

Hilary and Anne have lived together for the entire 15-year period and recently bought a house together. Although Hilary's income is significantly higher than Anne's, and she is responsible for most of the mortgage, they alternated paying for household appliances and furniture, and each item, as well as their house, is seen as belonging to the "couple." They sleep in the same bed. The second bedroom is referred to as the "guest room."

Hilary and Anne present themselves as a couple when they are with other lesbians. Hilary is more likely than Anne to refer to the couple as "lovers" and to be physically affectionate when they are among friends. Each year, on the anniversary of when they first became lovers, they have a party to celebrate another year together. They are invited to social situations together, give presents together, and speak of themselves as a unit. No one in the lesbian community is aware that Hilary and Anne have been celibate for over 14 years. On the contrary, the longevity of their relationship has become legend in their community, and they were recently interviewed for a book on long-lasting lesbian couples.

Neither Hilary nor Anne is very politically involved in lesbian issues, nor do they attend many visible lesbian events. Hilary is particularly closeted since she is concerned about losing her job in the school system, which is extremely homophobic. However, both women are well integrated into a network of lesbian friends, mostly couples in their 30s and 40s who are professional women and who view themselves as "gay." Hilary has been to a few gay bars, but this is usually limited to times when she is out of town at conventions. She has a great fear that she might run into students or teachers from her school, or into parents of her students. Once, when a friend placed the couple's names on a list to receive a catalog of lesbian books, Hilary wrote to the company and asked that her name be removed.

Anne has known that she was attracted to other girls since she was 16. She dated a boy for two years in high school. Then, as a junior in high school, she was attracted to Betsy, a girl in her class. Although they never had sex, they would frequently spend the night together, sleep in the same bed, and, under the pretense of being asleep, roll over and lie close together. The closeness of Anne and Betsy's friendship was noted by their peers, who jokingly referred to them as the "lezzies." Betsy was so alarmed at this that she broke off the friendship. Hilary is Anne's first and only sexual partner.

Hilary was sexually abused by her stepfather when she was 13. She remembers the abuse vividly but has never discussed her feelings about this period to anyone. Hilary had one brief sexual relationship with a woman in college. Both women were afraid of being caught, and neither woman would have defined herself as a lesbian. She also dated several men in college, but broke off with them when the men wanted to have sex.

Hilary has never come out to her mother or stepfather (her father is dead). When Hilary's mother comes to visit, Hilary and Anne spend several hours "straightening up" the house, removing lesbian books, records, and magazines, and hiding letters they have written to each other. Hilary is sure that it would kill her mother to know about her lesbian lifestyle. Hilary spends Christmas vacation with her mother and stepfather and has never brought Anne along on these visits.

Anne and Hilary have had several repeated conflicts in their relationship. In general, the theme of each conflict is that Anne accuses Hilary of being controlling, cautious, and closeted. Hilary retorts that Anne is impulsive, irresponsible, and immature. One of these conflicts concerns Anne's wish for the couple to spend Christmas together. When Anne contemplates the idea of coming out to her parents, Hilary talks her out of it, stating that Anne's mother, who lives near their town and who does not keep confidences (she occasionally gets drunk and divulges intimate information to her friends and neighbors), may tell other people about Anne and Hilary's lesbianism. Since Anne and her mother have a very distant relationship, Anne has agreed to keep her lesbianism a secret from her mother. A second area of conflict is that Hilary often puts pressure on Anne to lose weight and to pay more attention to her appearance. Of the two, Hilary would be considered the more physically attractive. Finally, Hilary occasionally tells Anne to find a more "serious" profession than music, and Anne resents such advice.

Recently, Anne joined an all-women's jazz group. Hilary has been alarmed that this jazz group is regarded by some people in the town as a lesbian group (in fact, most of the group's members are lesbians). She is particularly upset that the group performed at the local state fair (an event that most of her students and fellow teachers attend) wearing lavender T-shirts.

Anne has become good friends with Ruth, a member of the jazz group. Ruth is involved in many lesbian political activities. A few months previously, she invited Anne to accompany her to a conference on the politics of lesbian sexuality. During the car ride to the conference, Ruth and Anne discussed their own sexual history, and Anne revealed that she and Hilary had been celibate for 14 years. Shortly thereafter, Ruth asked Anne to be her lover, stating that, after all, Anne had not been "in a relationship" for 14 years. Anne is particularly flattered by Ruth's obvious sexual attraction to her physical appearance.

Anne and Ruth have not had sex but have talked about becoming sexual and have been flirting with each other. Anne told Hilary that she was attracted to Ruth. Hilary's reaction was anger and confusion. She felt that she and Anne are a monogamous couple. Anne responded that they have not really been a sexual couple for 14 years. This is the first time that Hilary and Anne have ever discussed their lack of sexual activity. Hilary felt very threatened by this conversation and responded that their bond, their long history of living together, and their love for each other should more than compensate for the lack of sexual activity. For the past several months, Hilary had accused Anne of being sexually attracted to Ruth and Anne denied this. Now Hilary accuses Anne of being a liar. When Anne returned home late after a jazz concert, Hilary experienced severe anxiety attacks triggered by the thought that Anne might be sexually involved with Ruth. Hilary is concerned that Anne may abandon her.

In therapy, both women are clear about the fact that they love each other and that they view their relationship as monogamous. If Anne were to become sexually involved with Ruth, both women would interpret this as the termination of their own coupled relationship. In therapy, Hilary views the current situation as Anne's problem and as something that could be resolved if Anne were to terminate any contact with Ruth. Hilary does not view her own relationship with Anne to be problematic. Both women state that they want their relationship to continue.

In therapy, Anne states that she feels less verbally skilled than Hilary and thus less able to "win" an argument. Consequently, she finds herself agreeing with Hilary's carefully constructed arguments about the nature of their relationship, while simultaneously being unable to express her own views about their relationship. She is feeling "crazy" and confused about continuing a relationship with Hilary without sex.

What Is a Boston Marriage?

Asexual but romantic relationships between lesbians can vary widely. However, they seem to include the following elements:

1. The two members of the Boston marriage are not currently engaged in a sexual relationship with each other. They may never have had sex with each other but, more typically, had a short period in which they were lovers.
2. One or both of the members is still sexually attracted to the other. In this regard, at least for one of the partners, the Boston marriage is different from a friendship.
3. With the exception of the lack of sexual activity, all other aspects of the Boston marriage are indistinguishable from many lesbian lover relationships. The two members may refer to each other in public or private as lovers and be physically affectionate in public or private social situations. They will engage in shared activities (rearing children, buying property, making out wills) that are rarely done by friends (or, if done by friends, are done for a specific and nonromantic reason).
4. The lesbian community is generally unaware that the two members are nonsexual and views them as a couple. Often the romantic nature of their relationship makes them role models for other lesbian couples to emulate and there may be some social pressure on the two members not to break up. When the lesbian community is aware that the two are *not* lovers, they will not be viewed as a couple.

5. Both members of the Boston marriage have typically had no or limited sexual experiences prior to the Boston marriage.
6. Both members of the Boston marriage are likely to be closeted to some degree in their place of employment, with their family, and in their community. If one or both members of the Boston marriage are extremely closeted or only marginally involved in the lesbian community, then they are less likely to refer to one another as lovers.
7. The two members of the Boston marriage usually have little or no direct communication about the lack of sexual activity in their relationship and the nature of their relationship.

Furthermore, we have found that the two members of the Boston marriage assume different roles. We will refer to these as "the woman in Hilary's position" and "the woman in Anne's position," respectively. Although Hilary and Anne in the case study, above, are composites of many Boston marriages, there are a few commonalities.

Usually, the woman in Anne's position is more aware of her sexual attraction to her partner and more willing to talk about the relationship. She is more likely to want continued sexual relations with her partner. Moreover, the woman in Anne's position has less power in the relationship. In the case study, Anne was younger, had a lower income, a less secure job, and was considered less physically attractive than Hilary. She may also provide the spontaneity, risk, and creativity in the relationship, although this may not be viewed as desirable by her partner.

The woman in Hilary's position is usually the one who declines sexual activity, although this is rarely discussed. The couple may "drift" into celibacy. The woman in Hilary's position, however, often perpetuates the image of the two as a couple in other ways. She may be the first to suggest joint activities and may be the one to refer to her partner more often in public. Interestingly, the lesbian community often has the impression that the woman in Hilary's position is more "in love" or invested in the relationship than the woman in Anne's position. The woman in Hilary's position often has more need for control, security, and safety.

It is important to differentiate a Boston marriage from other ways in which women relate. Members of Boston marriages are different from "best friends" in that friendship does not include long-lasting sexual attraction. The women in Hilary and Anne's position's are not ex-lovers in that they still define themselves as a couple and are viewed as a couple by the lesbian community (Becker, 1988). Becker is also in the process of writing a book about a concept she calls lesbian friendship networks, or the close circle of immediate friends that serve the role of "family" for lesbians while not being lovers. For members of the Boston marriage, they are closer to each other than the closest member of their friendship network.

However, Boston marriages may exist in slightly different forms than the one we have described. Two women who feel mutually in love and sexually attracted to each other but who decide they cannot have sex (e.g., for reasons of physical pain or disability, because they have taken a vow of celibacy, because they want to be faithful to their husbands) might be considered to be in a Boston marriage. In other words, it is possible that both members of the Boston marriage are conscious of and comfortable with the asexual nature of their relationship despite their sexual attraction to each other. Usually, women in this category do not seek therapy for their relationship.

What Is a Lesbian Relationship?

The concept of the Boston marriage brings up the issue of what is the definition of a lesbian relationship. In the case study, both Hilary and Anne view Anne's having a sexual relationship with Ruth as a violation of their own relationship, despite their own celibacy. Ruth, on the other hand, does not view Anne and Hilary as being in a relationship, given the absence of sex.

Among heterosexuals, marriage is defined by a legal ceremony. Heterosexual couples are considered to be married until they obtain a legal divorce, whether or not they are sexually active and even when they are sexually active with other people. All other coupled relationships (whether between lesbians, gay men, or unmarried heterosexuals) tend to be defined by the presence or absence of sexual activity. This sex-focused definition of a relationship becomes problematic in the lesbian community, given the relatively lower frequency of sex among lesbian couples compared with gay male or heterosexual couples (Blumstein & Schwartz, 1983). Loulan's (1988) research on the frequency of sexual activity of over 1,500 lesbians indicates that the majority (78%) had been celibate at some point, with 35% celibate from one to five years and 8% celibate for over six years. Loulan states: "The fact that lesbians are raised in a culture that teaches women that they cannot be sexual, and that teaches lesbians their identity is determined by their sexual partner, becomes a double bind. This creates a great deal of anxiety, ambivalence, and pressure on the sex lives of lesbians" (p. 221).

What could account for the lower frequency of sexual activity in lesbian relationships? Blumstein and Schwartz argue that their results reflect the desirability of touching, cuddling, and romance among lesbians, without the presence of males who would value genital activity above nonsexual contact. Given the low frequency of sexual activity among lesbians compared to other couples, this sex-focused definition of relationships in our society denies other ways in which lesbians relate. Given the importance our society places on sexual relationships, many lesbians may feel undesirable or rejected if they are not currently having frequent sex.

What Does It Mean to End a Lesbian Relationship?

All relationships follow a certain mythology and one that is sanctioned by the particular subculture. Similarly, our culture has norms for terminating relationships. Usually we define the end of a sexual relationship by the absence of sex or, if the relationship is monogamous, by the absence of monogamy. In sum, the beginnings and endings of relationships are defined by sexual activity. Is this a valid definition for lesbian relationships?

Gawain (1986) describes the vagaries of such simplistic definitions. She argues that each relationship is a commitment to a set of rules, but that people rarely clarify what these rules are. One rule may be the lack of sex with anyone else, but it is unclear whether sex includes sexual feelings or just behavior. Furthermore, rules may be static, whereas one or both partners will change over time. Rules may exist to guarantee the security of a relationship, but no external form can offer such a guarantee.

What Does It Mean to End a Boston Marriage?

It is rare that couples in Boston marriages seek therapy because they cannot tolerate the relationship or the absence of sex. Couples in Boston marriages often seek therapy when they are "breaking up." The concept of "breaking up" is a difficult one to define in the Boston marriage, since our society defines breaking up by the termination of sexual activity. In the case of the Boston marriage, sexual activity is not present.

It is our impression that such couples come to therapy when one of two things happen to suddenly alter the definition of the relationship: (a)

The woman in Hilary's role is attracted to another person (often a man) or (b) the woman in Anne's role is attracted to another person (often a woman).

The woman in Hilary's position is usually more closeted and thus may be viewed as sexually available by men in her workplace or men she meets in social situations. Furthermore, she may experience more internalized homophobia, which will be discussed later on. The woman in Anne's position is usually more willing to come out in the lesbian community and more interested in a sexual relationship. Thus, she is more likely to consider relationships with other women in the community.

What is particularly painful about Boston marriages, however, is that one partner can change the rules on the other and often does. Although Hilary and Anne had considered themselves to be in a partnered relationship for 15 years, Anne suddenly refers to them (inspired by Ruth) as celibate for 14 of those years. Thus, she is suddenly changing the definition of their "relationship" from 15 years to six months! At the time of the breakup of the relationship, the members of the Boston marriage may discuss their expectations of the relationship for the first time and be considerably surprised by their lack of agreement.

The breakup of a Boston marriage often involves the lesbian community to a considerable extent. First, with their strong focus on romance and external validation, Boston marriages may be the role models of their communities. Thus, the termination of such a relationship may threaten other lesbians who have built up this relationship as the fantasy model. If Hilary and Anne break up without informing their community about the asexual nature of their relationship, the community is likely to side with Hilary. Anne (and Ruth) will be viewed as breaking up an ideal relationship and may lose many of their previous friends. The woman in Anne's position is often blamed by the lesbian community for breaking up the relationship, because she is often the one to have the first sexual relationship with someone else. This will add to her confusion about her own needs for intimacy and passion and perpetuate her guilt for needing and seeking sexual relations. On the other hand, if Anne were to discuss their celibacy with members of the lesbian community, Hilary might receive little support for her "irrational" negative feelings about Anne and Ruth. After all, if Hilary and Anne were not currently lovers, why should Hilary be jealous of Anne's seeking another lover? In this way, the lesbian community would deny the reality of the long-term Boston marriage.

Usually, the two women involved in a Boston marriage have been colluding to some degree, often for years. They may have called themselves lovers while knowing that the lesbian community would not define them as such because of the lack of sexual activity in their relationship. The collusion may continue even as the nature of the couple's relationship changes. For example, one or both partners may be involved in relationships with other people but keep this a secret from their friends and acquaintances. This is especially likely if one partner is involved with a man, yet does not want to be ostracized by the lesbian community. Consequently, neither partner may be able to discuss all the facts of the relationship difficulties with anyone else, and the members of the Boston marriage often have difficulties discussing their relationship with each other as well.

Termination of a Boston marriage is particularly confusing in a situation where only one member of the couple (Partner A) may consider herself to be in a relationship to begin with, whereas the other (Partner B) may view the relationship as a "friendship," but typically may be maintaining the relationship in other ways. Partner A may want to leave the relationship, to the confusion of Partner B, who cannot understand why anyone would want to leave a good "friendship." Or Partner A may be jealous, angry, and confused that Partner B is "leaving her" to have a sexual relationship with a man or with another woman. On the other hand, Partner B, who may have been urging her partner to have sex with other women or men, may be alarmed at her own panic and confusion when Partner A acts on this advice.

GOALS FOR THERAPY

We feel that it is in the nature of individuals to be sexual. Lesbians who are in romantic but asexual relationships may do so for intrapsychic as well as societal reasons. A further issue in the case of lesbians is homophobia, which also may be intrapsychic (internalized) or societal (external). Thus, we will discuss intrapsychic and societal issues facing members of the Boston marriage separately.

The lack of sexual activity in the Boston marriage is rarely the overt issue in therapy. In fact, the therapist may be the only one who even refers to this or views it as a problem. Thus, we will also discuss countertransference issues.

Countertransference Issues

The therapist's own definition of relationships and norms about frequency of sexual activity will affect the course of therapy with women involved in Boston marriages. If the therapist expresses amazement or negativity about the extended period of celibacy, this will reinforce the belief that the couple is not "legitimate" and may also increase the couple's reluctance to broach this subject with other lesbians who may have similar reactions.

It is very difficult not to take sides when two members of a Boston marriage are terminating their relationship. Lesbian and/or feminist therapists may be acquainted with or know about the couple from the lesbian community and thus may be influenced by the strong community reactions to their breakup (especially if the couple is idealized in the community). One or both members of the Boston marriage may have convincing arguments for terminating the relationship. Furthermore, each member of the couple is likely to have extremely different interpretations of the nature of the relationship.

It is very important that the therapist be familiar with the norms of the lesbian community. A homophobic therapist may want to discount this relationship or suggest that the women are not really lesbians. It is important that a heterosexual therapist not equate the Boston marriage with the kind of "best friends" relationship she may be having and deny its sexual attraction component. It is important for the therapist to examine her own values about sex versus affection and not to project these into the therapeutic relationship. The members of the Boston marriage are engaging in their own projections, fantasies, and metacommunications—if the therapist colludes in this it will reinforce indirect communication and perpetuate confusion.

Intrapsychic Issues

The therapist's goal is to uncover what needs each woman has in this relationship and to what degree these needs are being met. This is not an easy process, as neither woman is likely to have thought or talked about her needs in this relationship. The woman in Anne's position has less overt power and may become even more vulnerable if she discloses sexual or affectional needs. She may not be aware of her own anger about the relationship or at having to tolerate lack of sexual activity for years. She may be angry that the couple presents a cover of "normalcy" among friends. The woman in Hilary's position may deny any needs in the relationship.

It is critical for the therapist to help the couple determine the importance of sexual activity in their relationship. Are closeness, intimacy, affection, and shared activities of enough value to continue the relationship in its present form? There are women who are celibate for conscious reasons, who are in tune with these reasons. There were probably women in past generations who lived together in celibacy and were comfortable with asexual but affectionate closeness. From an intrapsychic level, the question in therapy becomes whether Anne and Hilary's celibacy is a conscious choice for one or both women.

Women who have been involved in Boston marriages often have a history of such relationships and may never have been in a relationship that was sexual for more than several months. Frequently, women in Anne's position indicate that many previous lovers were heterosexual or bisexual women, or women who were unavailable sexually (e.g., women concurrently married to men). The therapist can help the couple to explore the reasons why they remain in relationships for extended periods without sexual activity.

For the woman in Hilary's position who becomes involved with a new lover, there is often little discussion of the role that her previous Boston marriage played. Consequently, there may be unresolved issues. For example, the woman in Hilary's position may be withholding sexually (out of guilt to Anne). The woman in Hilary's position often has concerns about being openly identified as a lesbian. Although Hilary would deny this, she may have negative views of lesbians who look 'gay" or who rally for political changes for lesbians and gay men. Thus, internalized homophobia needs to be examined. Hilary may be concerned that she will lose control over Anne if Anne becomes friends with Ruth, and she may specifically be concerned that Ruth will spread information about Hilary being a lesbian.

In the case study, Anne is younger, financially less powerful, and less verbally facile during arguments. Anne is often a woman who makes few demands on the woman in Hilary's position and, thus, is a "safe" partner for someone who needs to retain some control. In the case study, Hilary's history of sexual abuse is very likely to predispose her to want some control in her sexual life. Given Anne's sexual history, she may feel sexually unattractive and feel that she is not deserving of sexual intimacy or that no one would want to have sex with her. Often, women in Anne's position may feel capable of generating love and respect, but not sexual passion.

We may speculate that Hilary represents a secure mother-figure to Anne. Anne has fears of being abandoned, and Hilary's financial and professional security are attractive to her. Nevertheless, the woman in Anne's position frequently becomes depressed during the course of their relationship, which will affect her motivation, self-esteem, and creativity.

Either partner in a Boston marriage may be someone who separates sex and love. If sex is viewed as dirty or immoral, but love is viewed as beautiful and respectful, then two emotions may be displayed towards different people. For example, one or both members of a Boston marriage may have occasional and superficial sexual relations with men or women when out of town, or have rules permitting sex but prohibiting close emotional involvement with other people.

It is possible that women who become involved in Boston marriages may have less rigid boundaries between what constitutes friendship and sexual attraction. The issue of boundaries and definitions for the relationship can be a profoundly important direction in psychotherapy. Many psychotherapeutic theories state that people select sexual partners based on early relationships with their mother and father. Yet we have comparatively less understanding of how people choose friends and how one may project early relationships onto friends as well.

Societal Issues

From a societal level, the question in therapy becomes whether two women can be termed a couple if they are consciously and happily celibate. The irony of the Boston marriage today is that two women involved in such a relationship will be viewed as a "couple" in public more so than in private, whereas historically they were viewed as "just friends" or "spinsters" in public but may have regarded themselves as a couple in private. Today, members of a Boston marriage are sometimes keeping up appearances as lesbians to hide the fact that they are not sexual and, thus, not "technically" in a lesbian relationship. In some ways this points out the gradual social acceptance of lesbians in U.S. society and certainly the fact that lesbian sexuality may be more socially accepted today than is celibacy.

The absence of sexuality presents us with confusion about when two women become "more than" friends. In fact, the phrase that two women are "just friends" indicates how much we devalue friendships compared to sexual relationships in our society. A good question for the therapist to ask members of a Boston marriage may be: "What would you do with a lover (besides sex) that you would not do with a close friend?" Answers to this question provide a more complete definition of a relationship and determine whether it more closely approximates a friendship or a partnered relationship.

The issue of the Boston marriage demonstrates how inadequate our terminology is for defining relationships in the lesbian community. In the institution of heterosexual marriage, sex is not used as the definition of who is married. The lesbian community must examine the ramifications of defining a partnered relationship by the frequency or duration of the sexual aspect of that relationship. Even the term "we are in a relationship" is vague, since lesbians have intimate, nonsexual relationships with many people—friends, ex-lovers, biological family members, athletic partners, etc. Nevertheless, if two women refer to each other as "lovers" and they are not sexual, there is some amount of disequilibrium and extra explanations may be necessary. Just as lesbians once had to define their sexuality in a homophobic society, so it is necessary to define lesbian romantic love without sexuality in a society that currently defines love and romance by the presence of sex. Perhaps if there had been a term for this type of relationship in Hilary and Anne's community, the two women would never have had sex, because there would have been no need to "legitimize" their relationship via sex. Carla Golden (personal communication, 1983) has discussed lesbianism as consisting of three dimensions: lesbian identity ("I am a lesbian"), lesbian sexuality ("I am having sex with another woman"), and lesbian politics ("I support rights for lesbians"). She argues that the lesbian community assumes that all lesbians agree with all three dimensions, when in fact there are multiple variations.

Similarly, the lesbian community needs terminology for the relationships that women assume when they have terminated sexual relationships. Becker's (1988) book on lesbian ex-lovers indicates the variable norms in lesbian communities for remaining friends with ex-lovers. In the case of the Boston marriage, this may be confusing. If Anne were to become sexual with Ruth, Hilary's role in Anne's life may not have a defining term, yet would continue to be very important. Often, to the confusion of everyone, Hilary's role in Anne's life continues to be more important than that of Ruth. Former lovers, now both involved sexually and emotionally with new lovers, may still maintain primary ties and roles that approximate those of the Boston marriage. Quite frequently, this is evidence of a refusal to let go of the earlier relationship and build a new relationship with commitment and emotional involvement. On the other hand, as Becker (1988) points out, the relationships between ex-lovers in a lesbian community may run the gamut from total avoidance of the former lover to the development of healthy enduring friendships and a sense of "family." The therapist, in working with the aftermath of the loss of a relationship, can be of great help to the client in sorting out the motivations behind and realities of the ties between former lovers.

We feel that it is most important not to pathologize the Boston marriage. Given the lower frequency of sex between lesbian couples and the number of lesbians who are celibate, the Boston marriage is by no means rare. The partners of a Boston marriage meet many of one another's needs. Nevertheless, the reasons for the absence of sex and the possible nonreciprocity of sexual attraction need to be examined.

It is difficult to describe a relationship for which there is no clear definition, and we, the authors, were surprised to find that our individual inclusion and exclusion criteria for this type of relationship were somewhat different from one another, although there was considerable overlap. Kathy argued strongly that our case example should be one of a lesbian couple that was sexual for a period of time before drifting into a Boston marriage, as this was the more typical scenario. Esther, on the other hand, felt that the true Boston marriage was one in which the couple had never had sex and thus could not use the "legitimizing" presence of previous sexual activity to define their relationship. We decided to use the former scenario since we felt that therapists (like the lesbian community) would be more likely to discount the more "extreme" latter scenario. We would be interested to learn whether readers would have felt differently about Hilary and Anne's relationship and implications for therapy had we described them as never having had sex.

We also differed in our degree of acceptance of the Boston marriage, and our ambivalence is reflected in this chapter. On the one hand, we state repeatedly in this chapter that our society (including the lesbian community) should not define relationships solely by the presence of sexual activity. On the other hand, we also state that therapists need to examine the reasons why the members of the Boston marriage are not sexual, which implies that this is a problem that needs to be remedied. We have deliberately chosen not to take a position on this dilemma. Rather, we would like readers to consider the Boston marriage as a reality in the lesbian community that needs to be acknowledged and discussed.

Because the topic of the modern-day Boston marriage has not, to our knowledge, been described in the lesbian literature, we were not sure how others would react to this topic. Our imposter feelings were exacerbated when several lesbian therapists expressed ignorance of the term "Boston marriage" and its description. Interestingly, upon reading earlier drafts of this chapter, they asked for additional copies to distribute to clients who they now realized fit our criteria!

Finally, our conversations were often humorous as we realized that we had very different ideas about components of such relationships. We expect that many readers will find our conceptualization somewhat different than theirs and urge them to contact us with their own thoughts and experiences of modern-day asexual but romantic relationships among lesbians.

REFERENCES

1. Becker, C. S. (1988). *Lesbian ex-lovers*. Boston: Alyson Publications.
2. Blumstein, P., & Schwartz, P. (1983). *American couples*. New York: William Morrow.
3. Faderman, L. (1981). *Surpassing the love of men*. New York: William Morrow.
4. Faderman, L. (1983). *Scotch verdict*. New York: William Morrow.
5. Gawain, S. (1986). *Living in the light: A guide to personal and planetary transformation*. San Rafael, CA: New World Library.
6. Grumbach, D. (1984). *The ladies*. New York: Fawcett Crest.
7. Loulan, J. (1988). Research on the sex practices of 1,566 lesbians and the clinical applications. *Women and Therapy, 7,* 221–234.
8. Miller, I. (1969). *Patience and Sarah*. New York: McGraw-Hill.

17

MICHAEL SHERNOFF

Eight Years of Working With People With HIV: The Impact Upon a Therapist

Tony was a 33-year-old attorney whose response to the sudden and unexpected breakup of his seven-year relationship was to call in sick to work and spend a week drinking, using drugs, and having anonymous sex several times daily. One morning, frightened that he was placing his job in jeopardy and feeling that his entire life was falling apart, he called me to discuss beginning therapy.

During our first session, Tony complained of feeling depressed, hurt, and afraid. Initially, treatment involved listening to Tony's feelings and establishing a relationship with him that helped ameliorate a small part of the loneliness he'd been experiencing since the breakup. He berated himself for having been so trusting of and dependent upon Angelo. Over the course of several months, as he began to recognize that he was angry as well as sad, Tony became very confused. He had to deal with a feeling—anger—that hadn't been permitted in his family.

Tony was the only child of first generation, Italian-American parents whose other children were all stillborn. As a result of his parents' disappointment at not having more children, Tony assumed an importance in their lives that he described as "stifling." Though he had recognized that he was gay in high school, Tony never had sex, other than masturbating, until he graduated from college.

Because of his Catholic upbringing, his feelings for other men caused him shame and guilt. He kept hoping that if he never acted on his feelings, they would eventually go away. He knew that if his parents found out he was gay, they would be very upset. For most of his life, Tony believed that being gay meant he would always be lonely and unable to have a significant relationship or lead a happy and meaningful life.

Then Tony moved to New York City to attend law school and began to meet fellow students who were openly lesbian and gay and who introduced him to New York's gay community. Tony described that period as the first happy time in his life and the first time he stopped viewing his homosexuality as a handicap. His feelings of loneliness decreased as he began to make friends, "homo-socialize," and have sex with other men. He was so happy just dating and having sex that he had no interest in falling in love.

Tony met Angelo in his last year of law school. Angelo pursued and courted him and was the first man Tony was ever interested in dating for more than sex. Nonetheless, there were difficulties in developing the relationship because Tony, though he really liked Angelo, also wanted to continue going out with other men. He explained that once he began having sex at age 24, he felt hungry to make up for what he had deprived himself of for so many years.

Tony and Angelo never lived together. When I explored this with Tony, he at first explained that since neither he nor Angelo had ever told their parents that they were gay it seemed easier that way. But in continued sessions, Tony finally admitted that his need to have sex with other men was the primary reason he did not feel ready to even discuss living together with Angelo.

Despite the fact that they did not live together, after a year of dating they defined themselves as lovers, spoke daily, and spent several evenings a week and most weekends together. The relationship was explicitly not sexually exclusive. Tony said that this suited him perfectly because, although he loved Angelo and valued their commitment to each other, they both still wanted the option of having sex with other men. Tony would regularly have such outside encounters, yet he prevented any of them from developing into an affair. He would simply stop seeing anyone he felt would be a threat to his relationship with Angelo. Until the time that Angelo broke up with him, Tony assumed that Angelo was conducting himself in the same manner.

One day, to Tony's astonishment, Angelo announced that he had been having an affair with another man and was in love with him. He wanted to end his relationship with Tony so that he and this other man could seriously pursue their relationship. Tony was shocked, felt betrayed, and became very depressed.

Early in treatment he had no awareness that Angelo might have felt dissatisfied with their relationship. Tony never wanted a monogamous relationship. As this was explored, it became clear that Angelo saw the openness of their relationship as a barrier to their becoming more committed to each other.

By the time he and Angelo began to go out, Tony knew about and practiced safe sex, but he had spent the previous two and a half years having unsafe sex. Tony was diagnosed with Kaposi's sarcoma two years after beginning therapy. His diagnosis was a complete surprise to him because he had been feeling terrific, doing good workouts at the gym, and had no symptoms of any kind of immune deficiency until he discovered a lesion on his foot. His initial reaction to the diagnosis was a combination of denial—"I was usually the top man during intercourse"—and highly intellectualized problem-solving that was very functional and adaptive.

Within a month of receiving the diagnosis, anger became one of Tony's major coping strategies, and he immersed himself in political activity through involvement in the direct action group AIDS Coalition to Unleash Power (ACT-UP). His activities with ACT-UP fulfilled a variety of needs. Tony knew that participating in ACT-UP meetings, committees, and demonstrations were powerful ways for him not to feel overwhelmed, helpless, or powerless about having AIDS. "I'm not just passively sitting around," he would say, "doing nothing to help myself or other people with AIDS." At meetings, Tony met men he could socialize with or date who were not put off by his having AIDS.

AIDS activism provided Tony with a creative and healthy outlet for his anger. He dove into researching AIDS treatments and devoured everything he could read about his condition. He soon became so knowledgeable that he was corresponding with some of the world's leading medical researchers and treatment experts as a member of ACT-UP's treatment and data committee. I viewed his responses as very appropriate since they enabled him to mobilize himself into self-empowering action and prevented him from becoming socially withdrawn or depressed.

Over the course of three years, Tony lost over 40 pounds and became disfigured due to edema and lesions. He was not openly gay at his law firm and told people there that he had a form of cancer. This was the same story he told his parents. As his identity as a person with AIDS and an AIDS activist grew, Tony would spend a lot of time in therapy discussing the inconsistencies of publicly hiding both his sexual orientation and his diagnosis. When his lesions spread to his face and arms, he used makeup to hide them, and he rarely discussed dying or feelings about his worsening condition. Since he was following the advice of his physician regarding treatments, I did not see any denial this may have represented as maladaptive, so I rarely confronted it.

One day Tony did not show up for his regular lunchtime appointment. When I called him at his office to ask why he had missed the session, he sounded confused. He said that he was certain that our appointment was the next day. I assured him that today was Tuesday, the same day we had been having our sessions for the past two years. This caused him to become afraid. He admitted that he had recently noticed other indications of memory loss and a growing disorientation.

We rescheduled the session for the following day, and I got Tony's permission to telephone him a couple of hours before the session to remind him about it. During the session, I asked him his feelings about my having to call. He expressed anger about having AIDS and the growing realization that he was losing control of his body and mind. Eventually he burst into tears, pounded the couch he was sitting on and told me, "I know that for the past 30 years I've known the name for this thing I'm sitting on, yet for the life of me I can't remember what it is called. I can't really continue to practice law since I'm not even aware that I'm missing important details in contracts I read."

After consulting with his primary care physician about the memory loss, Tony was referred for a neurological evaluation that showed he had HIV encephalitis. For three sessions after he learned the result of that examination, we discussed his stopping work and going on disability. The following month Tony stopped working and began to collect disability income.

The week after stopping work, Tony was hospitalized for intense diarrhea and dehydration. We attempted to continue doing weekly therapy over the phone, but instead, Tony requested that I come to the hospital. He was losing his hearing due to a combination of opportunistic infections and the drugs being used to treat them and could not hear well enough to make good use of telephone sessions. I continued to make hospital visits for five weeks.

During the fifth hospital visit, Tony confided that he was ready to "give up" and wished he had the means of killing himself. He said this literally as the session ended. I was annoyed with him and glibly replied, "I can understand why you would feel that way," and left after telling him I'd see him the following week.

Immediately after I left the hospital, I had a regularly scheduled appointment with my supervisor during which I reported on my session with Tony. My supervisor asked why I had not inquired into Tony's feelings of depression and then asked me how I felt about working with Tony.

Initially, I resisted telling my supervisor my feelings about Tony. My work with him had been challenging and frequently difficult, even before he became ill, as his intellectualized ways of responding to situations were similar to my own. I was angry and sad that he had AIDS because I really liked and cared about him a great deal. After his diagnosis, I often felt relieved when he did not want to discuss his deterioration or dying because this provided me with a much desired reprieve from facing my own feelings about his illness and ultimate death. As his illness progressed, my anger at him increased.

I was embarrassed by some of my feelings about Tony. Each week that I had a hospital visit with him, traveling made it the time equivalent of a double therapy session. Since Tony's only income was disability, he was no longer able to afford my full fee and I agreed to accept the 50% his insurance company reimbursed me. At first, I tried to ignore my resentment at being so poorly paid for this emotionally draining and time-consuming work. Eventually, I realized that it was easier for me to focus my resentment on the fee than on my feelings about Tony's deterioration and the fact that he was going to die.

When I left the hospital, I was unaware that I had given Tony permission to kill himself, but during supervision this became clear, as did my guilt over what I had done. Feeling clearer about my feelings, I returned to Tony to correct my earlier mistake.

When I entered Tony's room he looked understandably surprised. "I've been thinking a lot about what you said to me while I was here earlier and realize that I never asked why you were having those feelings. I would like to hear what's going on that's made you feel this way." With a mischevious smile Tony replied, "I did think it was pretty strange that this was the one time in our work together that you didn't ask why I was feeling that way."

He explained that he had been told he was going to be discharged from the hospital soon, that he was no longer in need of acute medical care even though his diarrhea was uncontrollable. He was worried because he lived in a fourth floor walk-up apartment with an unsupportive roommate who had never even visited him in the hospital. It was a long apartment with his bedroom at one end and the bathroom at the other. He was afraid he would not be able to get up the stairs or even get to the toilet. He was regularly incontinent, even in the hospital, and dreaded the indignity of soiling himself at home or in public.

Tony did not kill himself. He died a few days after our conversation and before being discharged from the hospital. But his case made a lasting impression on me that has taught me several things about what happens when I stop paying attention to how I am feeling about treating a person with AIDS.

Tony had been a strikingly beautiful man when he first entered treatment. By the end of his illness, he had lost 40 pounds and his face and neck lesions had fused into what looked like leather armor. I had secretly wished that Tony would die so that I would be spared the ordeal of having to continue to work with him, look at him, and feel powerless to change the outcome of his illness. I was exhausted by the work with Tony as I had not been keeping on top of exactly what all of these feelings were. It was painful to look at Tony because his disfigurement caused him enormous physical pain as well as emotional suffering.

When Tony talked to me about suicide, I was unconsciously relieved and hoped that he might die soon. Regrettably, by saying that I could understand his feeling the way he did, I implicitly suggested that he kill himself, thereby ending our work together and relieving me of facing my conflicting feelings. At that point in Tony's treatment, I was feeling particularly overwhelmed by AIDS. My best friend Luis, who was also my business partner, was being treated for pneumocystis pneumonia (PCP) in the same hospital as Tony. Thus, every time I went to the hospital to visit Luis, I was reminded of Tony, and, conversely, every time I had a hospital session with Tony, I'd think of Luis. I was emotionally and physically drained by the stress caused by Luis's illness. In addition, Tony was not the only person with AIDS I was working with at that time.

PERSONAL RAMIFICATIONS

I have been in private practice in Manhattan, almost exclusively with gay men, since 1975, and I began to treat people with AIDS in late 1982. Since that time, I have often felt like a soldier on the front lines of a war in terms of how AIDS has shaped my life. Four years ago, I tested positive for the HIV-antibody. Thus, I have no personal respite from AIDS and certainly very little professionally in a psychotherapy practice filled with men who are sero-positive, who have AIDS, or who are mourning friends or lovers who have died.

The countertransference issues of doing this work and living with the knowledge that I, too, could one day become sick, are pervasive. Each time I work with a patient who has progressive HIV illness, there is a moment when I think to myself, "Will this be me someday?" A major task in working with HIV-infected patients is to use my feelings about being infected with HIV as a means of empathizing with them, but at the same time, I cannot allow myself to drift off during their sessions into thoughts about my own condition. One way I accomplish this is by continuously exercising my observing ego to distance myself from the difficult feelings, without distancing myself from the patient who is discussing and eliciting those feelings.

Confronting Mortality

It has taken me several years of working with people with AIDS to realize that simply spending time with a person who is dying can be emotionally draining and exhausting. There are several reasons. The first is that it is painful to be near someone you have grown to care about who is critically ill and has no chance for recovery. The second is that working with terminally ill people forces the therapist to directly confront his or her own mortality. Obviously I have known for some time that I am not immortal, but prior to doing AIDS work I never had to face this reality several times daily. Since I am infected with HIV, this is an especially poignant and, at times, difficult realization. Being close in age to Tony, I often identified with him. His condition would trigger fears and concerns about my own health. All of these issues contributed to my being angry with Tony. Until I had told him to go ahead and kill himself, I wasn't even aware how any of these feelings were influencing my work.

The analogy between working as a psychotherapist during the current AIDS health crisis and living in a war zone will become clear when I describe what happened when Luis, my business partner, was first hospitalized with PCP. After he was admitted to the hospital, I called his patients and canceled their appointments, telling them that Luis was ill. The next week I called them again to tell them that he would not be working for the rest of the month and asked them if they wished to make an appointment with me to discuss their feelings about this. About ten of his patients chose to schedule sessions.

During each of these sessions, I encouraged Luis's patients to discuss how they were feeling about Luis's being unable to work with them. It seemed remarkable to me that, though I had told them he had been hospitalized, not one of his patients asked whether or not he had AIDS. They each expressed anger at his not being there, fear that perhaps he was seriously ill and would not be able to return to work, and uncertainty about how this would affect their treatment. Some, but not all, discussed fears for his well-being. For some men, Luis's illness precipitated renewed fears about their own health and mortality. For each of them there was a lot of sadness about Luis's not being well and available.

These sessions were the most difficult of my entire career, because I was also experiencing every feeling I was encouraging these men to express. I have never felt, before or since, such a total lack of therapeutic distance between what clients were discussing and what I was feeling. During each session, Luis's patients were articulating all of my own feelings. I felt that there was no opportunity for me to form scabs over my fresh emotional wounds, because Luis's patients needed to express the very feelings that shaped my pain.

In my own therapy, I was discussing all the emotions that Luis's patients were expressing. I was worried about whether or not he was going to survive. I was pained to see him so critically ill and frightened. I was angry that such a vibrant, creative, and young man's life was going to be shortened. I was sad that our friendship was going to be so brief.

The last thing I wanted to do was to listen to other people telling me their feelings about Luis without being able to share my own pain with them. I felt an obligation to Luis to make sure that his patients were well taken care of during his illness. I knew that if the situation had been reversed he would have seen my patients. Yet, I often left these sessions feeling angry. It was my job to take care of these people, but I was feeling personally depleted. It took nearly all of my energy just to take care of myself and be there for Luis and his lover, let alone see 30 patients a week. The only way I was able to get through that period—and give good treatment—was by going to three therapy sessions a week in addition to my group supervision.

One year before I began working with Tony, my own brother died from Kaposi's sarcoma. Before becoming ill, he lived in San Francisco.

After having ARC for many months, he decided to return to New York where all of our family is. He moved into my apartment and for the next 14 months I was his primary care partner. Henry and I looked very much alike, thus I often felt like I was watching myself die as I watched him waste away. At times, Tony reminded me of Henry insofar as they both fought their illness with an incredible amount of bravery and dignity. Sometimes, looking at Tony, I would see Henry. This created an additional level of countertransference that had to be monitored and worked through.

IMPACT OF AIDS ON MY PRACTICE

In the past seven years of practice I have been therapist to 60 people with AIDS. As of this writing, only five are still alive. Prior to the AIDs health crisis, I had never had a patient die. Many patients with AIDS will suddenly discontinue treatment due to being hospitalized in an emergency that results in their dying. Several times I have gotten a call from a lover or friend of one of my patients informing me that my patient is in the ICU or on a respirator, or has died. Each patient's death takes a toll on me. It is especially difficult when we have not had the opportunity to wrap things up, terminate, and have a clear "good–bye."

HIV illness looms over approximately half of my current practice. In addition to patients who have full-blown AIDS, some are HIV positive and worried, though still in good health, others are contemplating whether or not they should be tested, many have a friend or friends who are ill or sero-positive, and still more are mourning the death of a lover, sibling, or child who has died from the disease. Thus every day I repeatedly confront the realities of AIDS.

As a result of working intensively with people with AIDS, my practice has changed. I now routinely do telephone sessions with clients who are hospitalized with AIDS-related conditions or who have moved back to their parents' homes in other cities. Hospital and home visits have become a regular part of the work. Listening to men who are my own age or even younger discuss their worsening physical and mental conditions leaves me with a powerful sadness. I feel helplessness, hopelessness, and an inability to improve their situations in any way except by listening intently and caring about them.

Another way that AIDS has affected me professionally is that there is now much less financial security and stability in my practice than there was prior to the health crisis. I consider it unethical and unprofessional to terminate a patient's treatment before it is completed just because he can no longer afford my fee. Thus I often work for reduced wages. My income is also negatively affected when people get ill or are hospitalized and must miss sessions or are too sick to continue any treatment at all. The economic insecurity involved in this work creates a very potent form of anxiety for a therapist faced with maintaining an overhead. The only way I can contain this anxiety is to work several hours more than I would wish to each week, in order to build a financial cushion for those times when patients unexpectedly leave treatment due to their illness, or are no longer able to afford to pay for therapy that they wish to continue.

LESSONS LEARNED

What have I learned after eight years of working with patients whose lives have been disrupted by AIDS? The most important thing is not to forget that I am a person with feelings, too. I have learned it is not in the best interests of either myself or my patients to deny that I am profoundly affected by the AIDS crisis. I have also learned ways to prevent emotional burnout. The first is by constantly monitoring my feelings about what's going on in my life and how it affects my work. For me, this means participating in individual psychotherapy, group supervision, and a support group with other health-care professionals who do AIDS work. Prior to each session, I spend a few minutes reflecting and asking myself, "What about this session is likely to be particularly difficult or painful?" Then I am somewhat prepared for what might be discussed during the session. The second way is by nurturing myself. I make a special effort to spend quiet time alone, get together with friends, do things I enjoy, and take plenty of vacations away from the practice.

Becoming Less Anesthetized

I've learned how to recognize when I'm feeling particularly stressed, vulnerable, sad, angry, or just overwhelmed. At times, I have a tendency to completely shut down feelings of sadness and loss about someone who has died.

It frightens me when I realize how numb I can become. I'm afraid, because shutting down my feelings hinders my ability to empathize with my patients, and my work suffers for it. Obviously, I cannot shut off only feelings of sadness and loss. I begin to shut down other feelings too and, as a result, feel very removed from people and life in general. Much of my own therapy has been about becoming less anesthetized. I find myself in personal and professional situations where it would be much easier not to have any feelings, yet to acknowledge my feelings is absolutely necessary. Staying aware of this conflict is a constant effort.

THE DEATH TOLL

I often feel as if I were in a state of "bereavement overload" since so many friends, clients, and aquaintances are now dead from AIDS. In a conversation I had with my mother, prior to her death at age 75, I realized that I had more peers who were dying or who had died than she did. The sheer numbers make it increasingly more difficult to mourn any one particular person and process reactions to any one death.

Sometimes it is difficult not to keep myself emotionally distant from a new patient who has AIDS. It is easy to rationalize that he is dying anyway, so why allow myself to get close to him? When I have not allowed myself to empathize with a new patient in this situation, the result has been that he feels as isolated from me within the therapeutic relationship as he has from all the people in his life who are keeping their distance in his personal relationships. If I am not able to correct my behavior quickly, the patient rightfully leaves treatment.

By focusing on how I'm thinking and feeling about a new patient, I've come to learn whether or not I should begin working with him. I have occasionally begun discussing a new patient during supervision by saying "A new person with AIDS has begun treatment." When my supervisor would request more clarifying data, I would repeat what I had just said instead of giving him the person's age, race, presenting problem, and preliminary dynamic formulation. If I am unable to see a person with AIDS as a unique individual with special issues and ways of relating to the world and his illness, it clearly indicates to me that I should not begin working with that person and need to refer him to a colleague.

Yet, I am always ambivalent about referring a person with AIDS. Accepting that there are limits to how many people with AIDS I can work with at a particular time shatters my illusion of being 'super shrink." I ask myself, "Am I shirking my professional responsibilities to my own community by not seeing this person?" even though I know I am not the only good therapist in Manhattan who is experienced in working with people with HIV. If the person seeking treatment is a former patient who has just been diagnosed or whose lover has just been diagnosed or died, the decision about whether or not to take this person back into treatment can be particularly difficult and full of conflict.

I sometimes question whether the strains of doing psychotherapy with people who have AIDS are any different from other psychotherapists' stresses. As therapists, we always run the risk of having to listen to things that are painful or difficult for us, or that we are facing in our own lives.

Yet being gay, infected with HIV, surrounded by friends who are infected, sick, or dying, and working with a large number of patients with AIDS-related concerns creates an urgency during treatment that I had never encountered prior to the onset of the AIDS health crisis. As I learn to recognize and tolerate the discomfort that arises from doing psychotherapy with people with AIDS, I continue to grow as a person as well as a therapist.

I have become aware of a unique paradox that is a direct result of this work. When I am able to not close off my feelings, I feel more alive than at any other time in my life. Experiencing and learning more about the variety of my feelings has resulted in an improvement in the quality of my life and of the therapy I do with all my patients. Largely this is due to my being able to empathize with more of what my patients are discussing. My awareness of when I drift off from what my patient is saying and begin to think about my own situation is heightened. Thus, I am able to quickly refocus my attention and be completely present during sessions more often.

It is difficult to listen to people talk about illness and dying so much. It requires a lot of discipline not to become preoccupied during a session with my health status or friends who are ill or who have died. Yet I remind myself I must be doing something right since so many people are allowing me to accompany them through this final phase of their lives. It is difficult to know so many people who are sick and who have died, especially when I am also infected with the virus that is making them ill.

Yet today I am not sick. My life is rich and interesting, full of wonderful creative people. My work is important, meaningful to me, and challenging. I am forced to savor and appreciate the ever increasing quality of my own life, even as I recognize how much sadness there is in it. The duality of the richness and the sadness inherent in life creates a potent awareness that flavors all aspects of my life and work. Working in the field of AIDS continuously reminds me how fragile and brief life is. Thus at 38 years old, I no longer take it for granted that I will have enough time to do all that I want. I have consciously begun to focus more on the quality of my life instead of the length of it. I work with my patients to try and help them achieve this perspective.

I do not believe that there are any "silver linings" to AIDS. I can't stand it when some people talk about AIDS as a gift. Yet experiencing the way that life continues and even flourishes in the midst of so much suffering has been the most bizarre and surprising outcome of living and working through all of this.

18

CHARLES SILVERSTEIN

When the Therapist
Is More Anxious
Than the Patient

ALAN IS A 32-YEAR-OLD gay man who selected me to be his therapist after he had completed a residence at an institution for substance abuse. As he explained to me at our first meeting, he wanted an older, established therapist. He found my voice over the telephone to be mature and masculine, just the features he was searching for in a therapist.

Alan is over six feet tall and well built, with a slightly stooped posture, as if he's always ducking his head to fit beneath low door frames. He has an attractive face with a warm smile, and he immediately makes good social contact. As he sat down, he gave the appearance of being relieved to be able to talk about his problems.

PRESENTING PROBLEMS

Alan presented four therapeutic issues. The first was continuing his abstinence from drug abuse. For the past two years he had abused cocaine and crack-cocaine. After leaving the residential institution, Alan had entered its aftercare group program, in which he was still participating. Now, in individual therapy with me, he hoped to learn why he had sought drugs as a means to deal with his emotional problems.

Alan also questioned his capacity to love. Although he had been sexually

My thanks to Gerald Perlman and Greg Lehne, who reviewed an early draft of this paper.

active for many years, he had never sustained a love relationship for more than a few months. He felt he wanted a lover, but didn't know why he had been unable to find one. Nor did he understand why no one had ever sought him out as a lover.

A third problem was Alan's overly close relationship with his mother. He complained that he was always furious with her, yet he spoke to her daily and sought out her advice. He recognized that he was both dependent upon her and, at the same time, angry at her. He gave every indication of being in a rubber band relationship with her, first pushing her away, then snapping back. He clearly described that each of them was hostile-dependent toward the other.

The final problem Alan mentioned was his sexuality, which he described as "compulsive." He was quite upset by it. His sexual complaints took two forms. The first was "compulsive" masturbation. Alan stated that he masturbated a few times a day, and that he was able to fondle his penis for hours without ejaculating. He also judged his sexual contacts with other men as being compulsive "because of their frequency and their quality of impersonality."

Alan expressed a great deal of anxiety and guilt about his "compulsive" sexuality. He said he wanted it to stop. A friend had advised him to join a group for "sexual compulsives," and at our first session he wanted my opinion about whether he should. I asked him not to join such a group. In the first place, I thought it would be inadvisable for him to split his therapeutic alliances between an individual therapist and two separate groups, the aftercare group and a "sexual compulsives" group. The second reason was my belief that participating in such a group would be counter-therapeutic. Briefly stated, my perception was that Alan was already rid-dled with guilt about his sexual behavior. The last thing he needed was to join a group that reinforced his feelings of guilt and shame. I did not agree with him that his sexuality was compulsive and, while he said he didn't understand my explanation of all this, he agreed not to participate in the second group.

Alan left the initial session much relieved and said so. This session had reaffirmed his belief that he had chosen the correct therapist, and he wanted me to know that. It was quite clear that the transference was already strong by the time he left the initial session. In fact, the transference probably had taken shape a week earlier when he talked with me over the telephone.

PREVIOUS EXPERIENCE IN THERAPY

Alan has had many therapists. While he was an undergraduate, he saw a college counselor to whom he had gone because of ego-alien homosexual feelings. He described the therapist as "just sitting there" and providing little feedback. He found it unsatisfying, didn't confide much of his inner life, and soon terminated.

At the age of 21, Alan sought out a behaviorist to "cure" his homosexuality. While he was in therapy with the behaviorist, he read about aversion therapy and asked if it might help him. He was then referred to a therapist who used electrical aversion techniques to "cure" homosexuality. What followed was one of the most traumatic and scarring experiences of his life. In Alan's words:

> He would put electrodes on my arm. Then he would do this hypnosis, relaxation thing on me. Then he would have me imagine having sex with men, and he would shock me. Sometimes he would show me these pictures of these really gross men. He would tell me that that's what I do. They were older, ugly men.

The therapist turned the "shockers" to the maximum level, he added, making the experience extremely painful. At times Alan wanted to cry, but he controlled himself and never screamed out because of the pain. It was a battle of wills, he said. Alan believes that the therapist used electrical shock to punish him as a form of sexual sadism, and that the therapist was turned on sexually by the experience. He believes that while he was in pain, the therapist had an erection. There is no way to confirm this, of course. I suspect it was a wish turned into a projection. Alan also asserts that his S&M fantasies began immediately after aversion therapy.

While he was in aversion therapy, a gay friend took Alan to a few places where gay men meet. Alan told his therapist that he liked meeting them and intended to continue. The therapist responded to this challenge by making an extraordinary statement. "When you get older," the therapist said, "in ten years, and you're no longer attractive, you'll cut your dick off."

Shortly thereafter, Alan met a young man, a hustler with whom he had sex. He terminated aversion therapy and began to participate sexually in the gay scene, both by buying hustlers and hustling himself.

Two years later, when he was 23, Alan became disillusioned with his homosexual life and once again tried to change. This time he tried primal therapy, in which the patient was instructed to scream at fantasized images of his parents. During the next year and a half he stopped all homosexual contacts while he participated in the therapy. Then he left because he felt the therapist wasn't interested in him.

By age 26, Alan's S&M fantasies had increased considerably. He was using drugs more often and was fully involved with the hustling scene, both as buyer and seller. Then he joined Aesthetic Realism, an organization whose philosophy includes the "curing" of homosexuality. A friend claimed that he had been cured of his own homosexuality by the group, which, it later turned out, was untrue. Alan liked Aesthetic Realism's belief in the dualities of mind, because it appealed to the feelings of good and evil in him. He studied with them for the next four years, and during that time he made every possible attempt to suppress his homosexual feelings. He left the group because he found that he was living a lie. His sexuality hadn't changed.

When he was 32, Alan entered the residential institution to end his drug use. Once he left, he entered its aftercare program and began individual therapy with me. It was clear from Alan's therapeutic history how often he had conspired to be abused in therapy. At the same time, I believed that his frequent excursions into therapy were an indication of his difficulty in establishing a long-lasting intimate relationship with a man.

FAMILY HISTORY

Alan perceives his mother as "a mean lady who would really beat the shit out of me." While it is true that his mother occasionally hit him on the bottom with her hand or with a Ping-Pong paddle, Alan was not a physically abused child, but his words are useful metaphorically: There was a battle of wills between mother and son. Each used the weapons at hand. Mother used coldness and withdrawal to its maximum effect. When Alan was about five or six, she caught him masturbating and threatened to pull out his penis "by the roots." Her toughness was still evident in her later years. When she visited Alan at the residential treatment center last year, the other residents nicknamed her "Mrs. Rambo."

Alan responded to his mother's coldness by turning into a provocative child. If his mother was talking to a friend on the telephone, he would scream at her, hoping the friend would hear and that his mother would be embarrassed. He also had temper tantrums in public if he didn't get what he wanted. For instance, while they were shopping together in a supermarket, Alan would start screaming that this woman wasn't his mother and that she had kidnapped him. He did everything possible to humiliate her in public.

Even in his early thirties, Alan alternates between feeling the most intense anger toward his mother and the greatest need for her love. He still discusses almost all aspects of his life with her, and he manages her finances.

Alan's father died of cancer when he was nine, and the death was a central event in his life. The relationship between them had been good. His father entertained him with stories about his own childhood. From Alan's accounts he was a pleasant man, but he apparently had one peculiarity: He was opposed to wasting water, and he always instructed his son never to flush the toilet after urinating, only after defecating. When Alan violated this rule, he was criticized for flushing the toilet "needlessly."

When Alan was eight, an uncle died of bleeding ulcers. "Daddy," Alan asked, "are you going to die of that?" His father responded by saying, "I'll probably die of you aggravating me to death." It was later that year that the father fell ill and lay sick for about five months. Alan was told almost nothing about the illness and remembers being told sometimes that his father had ulcers and, at other times, that nothing was wrong. One morning he learned that his father had died during the night. Alan does not remember, but his mother reports that he responded to the news by yelling that he had killed his father and then fainting. He was prohibited from going to his father's funeral even though he desperately wanted to. He still feels resentful that his mother forced him to stay at home during the funeral.

After his father's death, Alan turned off emotionally. He distrusted people and lost his zest for living. He constantly feared that if he got close to anyone, particularly a man, the person would die. This began a period of intense loneliness, relieved only briefly by his frequent sexual episodes.

EARLY SEXUAL LIFE

Alan began masturbating in his early teens and developed two unfortunate behavior patterns associated with it. First, he coped with stress, no matter how slight, by masturbating and therefore ended up masturbating many times a day. Second, he learned how to maintain his sexual arousal without ejaculating, so that he could masturbate for hours. These habits ultimately led to a finely tuned masturbatory ritual that brought Alan extreme pleasure. Yet the quality of the pleasure was so solitary and idiosyncratic that one wonders whether another person could provide Alan with as much sexual pleasure. The men in his masturbatory fantasies were mainly rough-looking, streetwise boys wearing black leather jackets. Alan fantasized that they were weak and that he had power over them.

His first sexual contact was at age 19 with a male hustler. He continued to pay for sex until, one day, while cruising a hustler, another man propositioned him. When Alan hustled, he would be "top," but when he bought sex himself, he wanted to be a "bottom."

ANXIETY AND THE THERAPIST

Alan gave every indication of being pleased with his therapy with me. He was trusting and was willing to discuss any fantasy or behavior. He was occasionally upset about his feelings, especially about his anger at his mother, but in general he was not a particularly anxious or defensive patient. The same claim could not be made for his therapist—me.

My own anxiety arose during a session when Alan began to discuss an old sexual experience. I was expecting to hear something about hustling and S&M, but that day Alan decided to confide another dimension of his sexuality that he had not yet revealed to me. It began when he was 26. One day he bought a "heavy-duty" S&M hustler and brought him home, where the hustler started to beat him. He then ordered Alan to "rim" him. While Alan was doing this, the hustler, quite unexpectedly, defecated into his mouth. Alan found it exciting and, in fact, described it as "magical," a word that would hardly have occurred to me as I listened to his account. He said that after the experience, he began to fantasize about masculine men defecating into his mouth. If the men weren't masculine-looking, Alan would fantasize defecating on them. It was very clear that power relations and feces were strongly related.

After this revelation, Alan fell silent, and it was during that silence that my own anxiety level rose. Alan was testing me. He wanted to know whether he could talk to me about scatological sex. He was waiting for some kind of response and hoping it would be a permissive one.

I failed the test. Internally, I was beset by a jumble of conflicts and fears. I felt repulsed by the scatological scene that Alan had described. Voluntarily allowing someone to defecate into one's mouth felt offensive to me (to say nothing of paying for it). I was also painfully aware that Alan hadn't finished describing the sexual scene; he had ended it with the hustler defecating into his mouth. I didn't ask, nor did I want to know, what had happened next, and Alan was gracious enough to spare me the imposition of a truth I was not yet prepared to accept. I must have sensed that the revelation was only a crack in the door, and that beyond it lay quite a number of other scatological experiences—and heaven knows what else. I had also not lost sight of the fact that my patient was describing a six-year-old experience, and that the intervening years may have provided an ever escalating series of scatological adventures. While appreciating the trust that Alan placed in me that day, I had no intention of listening to any more sexual adventures that would further disturb my usual placid therapeutic style. I therefore shut him up by acting "professional."

By "professional," I mean a demeanor of cold impersonality, which is often described as "objective." It is a primary technique for therapists to create emotional distance between themselves and their patients. Being "professional" has one primary purpose: to punish a patient for having the audacity to disturb the therapist's psychological equilibrium. There are a number of punishing techniques available to the therapist. One can change the topic or ask for irrelevant facts or information. That avoids affect. Ignoring, that is, not saying anything about the revelations of the patient is also a good punishing technique. It can be combined with looking at one's watch, touching an appointment book, and, in general, performing any behavioral action that will lead the patient to conclude that what he's saying is boring (that he's a boring person).

Stronger measures are needed if the patient doesn't take the hint, or if he or she is insensitive to the therapist's narcissistic needs. The patient then must be punished overtly and firmly. "That's disgusting," would be the crudest example (although a soft "ugh!" would do as well). One hears much these days about the need to be "honest" with a patient, which usually means that a therapist is about to deliver a particularly brutal blow.

My "professional" behavior with Alan was to remain silent. I was well aware that it would stop him from divulging more information about feces and sex. As an experienced therapist, I knew that he wanted to discuss his conflicting feelings about scatological sex, which were, on the one hand, disgusting and, on the other, exciting. He could hardly have known that his therapist was as conflicted as he. But Alan took his cue from me and stopped discussing feces. In the sessions that followed, he would, from time to time, mention scatological experiences. He would begin with a tepid review of a sexual adventure over the weekend and then fall silent. I would respond with silence and shortly thereafter we were engaged in another topic, one (any one!) less likely to arouse my always unarticulated anxiety. Yet I gave constant thought to my feelings about Alan's scatological sex.

I knew a number of things that could not explain my reaction. I was not afraid that Alan would release long repressed scatological desires in me. Nor did I fear an upheaval of S&M fantasies from my unconscious. My own sexual fantasies, quite "vanilla" by comparison, had been welcome companions for decades. I did not believe there were dangerous incubuses to be let out of my unconscious.

Nor did my feelings of disgust explain all my behavior. Yes, I react emotionally when I hear a patient tell me that he allows other men to defecate in his mouth. I cringe a bit when he says that he eats it and/or smears it over his body. I feel offended to hear about parties consisting of dozens of men orgiastically defecating upon each other after carpeting the floors with rubber sheets. (These are things Alan told me about later on, when I was prepared to hear them.) But, over the course of many years, I have worked with gay men who are heavily involved with S&M sex and with paraphilias. So I came to believe that my countertransference involved not simply Alan's scatological experiences, but something more important that they evoked in me. I sensed that my emotional reaction to Alan's sexual adventures was a cover-up for deep-seated personal feelings.

Listening to Alan each week made me aware of how unconventional a person he is, and how different he must feel in our society. He is, first of all, homosexual. He's been addicted to cocaine and crack. He's participated in the hustling scene for years as both buyer and seller. He takes pride in and talks about his large penis and how he attracts other men with it. He participates regularly in S&M sex, including ritualized scenes in which needles and nails are thrust through nipples. And of course, there is the scatological sex. Alan's ability to violate (I am tempted to say obliterate) social standards is remarkable. He even remarked one day, while discussing sticking needles into a man, "I liked doing things that were so against the way I was brought up." He was still being the provocative, horrendous little boy.

Painfully, I began to understand that Alan's unconventionality made me aware of my own conventionality. While I am also homosexual, I am quite ordinary in most other ways. In childhood, I learned that I could please my parents, particularly my mother, by being good. I learned that pleasing her was the ultimate good and resulted in rewards of love. But sexuality was definitely not on her list of good behavior. People who expressed themselves sexually were always bad in her eyes. For instance, the Italian boys on our block were bad for a lot of reasons. First of all, they didn't listen to their mothers. They were poor students and behavior problems in school. They walked around bare-chested in warm weather, and they constantly touched their bodies. They rubbed their genitals, fingered their nipples, and exuded a lusty sexuality in their play that frightened me. I envied these "bad boys" because they did all these bad things. I envied them because they looked like they were having fun. Those bad Italian boys are still favored sexual fantasies for me.

I cannot imagine myself being as "bad" as those Italian boys from my youth. Nor can I imagine myself being as "bad" as my patient, Alan. I suspect that, like many of my colleagues, I demonstrate my goodness by performing the meritorious social function of being a psychologist. Yet underneath my professional demeanor must lie a magnetic attraction toward those who have, for whatever reasons, violated parental rules. I'm not suggesting that I need to be "bad" in order to help people. Nor do I pine away at home wishing I could be as "bad" as Alan. But the fact that I do not want to participate in such sexual adventures is quite irrelevant. What is important is my awareness of a feeling of deficiency in me and my envy toward Alan's ability not only to be "bad" but to glory in it. By becoming aware of my deficiency of badness, I allow myself to develop empathy both for the excitement of Alan's lust, as well as for his pain. To argue that his badness gets him into psychological trouble is also irrelevant, because I had been viewing him through my childhood eyes.

My conclusion was that I prevented discussion of Alan's sexuality for two reasons. First, I was disgusted hearing descriptions of the sexual scenes and feared that I would convey that feeling to my patient. Second, I was upset by my awareness of my own conventionality, and I envied his lusty "badness." It was as if there were a split in me—on the one hand I was playing the professional who is accepting and objective about Alan's sexuality while, on the other hand, I was experiencing powerful emotions of my own. Until I experienced the awareness I have described, I was asking Alan to integrate his emotional world, a task I had not yet accomplished myself.

CHANGES IN THERAPEUTIC INTERVENTIONS

Armed with my new knowledge and feeling more relaxed, I waited for Alan's next reference to feces. When it occurred (it was a masturbatory fantasy), I jumped right in and inquired into the most minute actions in the fantasy. For the first time, I could hear the dynamic meaning of the fantasy in which Alan feels physically connected to another man. In fact, his feelings about the fantasy suggest (as we later learned) an infantile wish to be reunited with his mother. Alan's scatological fantasies invariably led to images of a baby being fed via an umbilical cord to its mother. These fantasies were like a life force, a sense of connectedness that served as a palliative to his inability to get close to people in real life.

Alan's sexual fantasies of being reunited with his mother suggest an infantile fear of being abandoned by her. It seems that the early conflicts between them were caused by the fact that he refused to allow her out of his sight. He followed her around constantly, and his incessant demands that she talk to him was a neurotic need to be reassured again and again that she wouldn't leave him. "That's what made her crazy," Alan said. I suspect that a hernia operation that Alan was subjected to at the age of six months contributed greatly to his childhood fear of abandonment by his mother. The hospitalization was probably handled poorly, and his mother still refuses to discuss it with him. The death of his father when Alan was nine was the final shock that deepened and perpetuated his abandonment fears.

After the session in which I was at last able to encourage Alan's references to feces, he started to discuss the importance of defecation in his family. His interest in feces turned out to be an exaggerated and eroticized reflection of the importance of feces to his mother. While he was growing up, everyone in Alan's family complained of being constipated, and the minutely described circumstances of one's daily bowel movement was the barometer of health. At family gatherings, discussion inevitably turned to bowel regularity. Parents, uncles, and aunts were all addicted to laxatives, prune juice, or an endless variety of homemade potions made in the blender.

"My mother was a shit reader," Alan says. "She always wanted to look at my shit so she would know how I felt physically." Alan's mother wanted to know if the feces were "floaters" or "sinkers," by which she meant whether the bowel movement was firm or not. Even though he resented his mother's intrusion into his privacy, Alan notes that there was "something magical about taking a doody. Your health was how you shit." I had the impression that his mother was better able to respond emotionally to a symbol of Alan (his defecations) than to Alan himself. Certainly he associated her warmest expressions of acceptance with those occasions when he produced the kind of bowel movements she approved.

I was amazed at how much information about Alan's life emerged after

I came to terms with my own conflicting feelings. There is no doubt in my mind that he recognized the change in me and responded appropriately by developing a greater sense of trust and rapport.

THE EARLY EFFECTS OF THERAPY

My openness to discussing scatological sexuality produced changes in Alan's life. He reduced the frequency of masturbation. He also severely curtailed his daily, impersonal sexual encounters and stopped hustling completely. He's also better able to delay gratification, so that slight social frustrations are less likely to result in long masturbation sessions or impersonal sex.

Two types of behavior have replaced the previous obsessive sexual conduct. In the first place, he participates in a social network, hoping to meet and date other men. This is a new and frustrating experience where potential relationships are egalitarian and where rejection is possible—a great contrast to the clarity of the power differential in the hustler relationship and in his impersonal S&M sex. For instance, Alan recently told a man that he liked and cared about him and then asked for a date. This was the first time in his life that Alan expressed those sentiments to another man. The advance was rejected, and he felt all the more lonely afterward. Whether he will be able to withstand the frustration involved in dating and intimate relationships remains to be seen.

Alan, along with many men with paraphilic problems, cannot yet integrate sexual excitement and emotional attachment. It's not that they can't love, but that the men they do love are a different set from those they have sex with. They question whether it's possible to integrate such high degrees of lust and excitement into a humdrum love relationship. Psychotherapy doesn't yet have a good answer to the question, either.

The second recent change in Alan is an increase in the number and the intensity of his scatological fantasies. Some inexperienced therapists may believe that repressed (or suppressed) sexual fantasies vanish after they have been verbally expressed by a patient. These practitioners operate from a drive-reduction model, under which the sexual excitement ostensibly decreases with the tension reduction of telling the fantasy. It has been my experience that what really happens is quite different. In a permissive atmosphere, the patient opens his self-imposed psychological gates and feels the intensity of his socially condemned fantasy life. Tension is increased by expressing the fantasies to a therapist. When there is a permissive therapeutic environment, acting out the fantasy in real life is *more* likely to occur with regard to sexual behavior, particularly paraphilic sexuality.

Both changes in Alan are therapeutically positive. But why have they occurred? There are at least two reasons. Alan had always had a strong transference to me as his therapist. With my new empathy toward his sexual fantasies and experiences, the transference relationship became even stronger. There was no longer anything about himself that he needed to hide from me. He even commented on how active and assertive I had become during our sessions. The second reason for the changes is that Alan doesn't have to expend psychological energy covering up his scatological fantasies. By allowing himself the freedom to indulge them without guilt or anxiety, he has become less defensive in the task of understanding their psychodynamic meaning.

The new trust between us allowed Alan to discuss his conflicting feelings about scatological sex as well as his fears of loneliness. He talked more about forms of communication between members of the coprophilic underworld. "Hey, I'll get you lots of patients into shit," he said to me one day. The statement shocked me until I realized it was merely his way of thanking me for caring about him. But it also amused me because it sounded so "bad."

CONCLUDING NOTES

I noted earlier that most therapists are conventional or what I have pejoratively labeled "good." I know that I am. In our society, feces is objectionable and, therefore, disgusting to discuss. For Alan, and with respect to all the paraphilias, the initial disgust becomes transformed first into an attraction, then into lust. The patient's feelings of lust may then collide with the therapist's feelings of repulsion.

In general, there are three kinds of patient sexual behaviors that are likely to create emotional problems for a therapist: self-injurious behavior, behavior injurious to others, and behavior that is socially perceived as offensive. Extreme examples of self-injurious behavior are eroticized hanging, the insertion of foreign objects into the body, and masochism that leads to physical injury. Behavior injurious to others includes rape, child molesting, and sadism so extreme that it results in hospitalization and perhaps death. Patient behaviors perceived by the therapist as offensive would include coprophilia, erotic urination ("water sports"), and spanking.

Injurious behavior, whether to others or to oneself, generally presents no *conscious* countertransference in the therapist. Usually the patient has already judged the behavior as ego-dystonic, and the therapist agrees to a contract to help eliminate the offensive behavior. In such a case the therapist usually takes on an attitude of self-righteousness, which reinforces feelings of guilt and shame in the patient. The obvious danger is that the therapist may end up being perceived as both the symbol of society and as its punishing agent. In this situation, a subtle, but powerful sadomasochistic (and parent/child) relationship develops that inevitably dooms any hope of effective psychotherapy. This occurs because the therapist is likely, at some point, to punish the patient through anger or the withdrawal of love, in the same way a parent might.

A different dynamic is created when the patient behavior is perceived as merely repulsive. In this case, the therapist is aware of his or her countertransferential feelings. Since therapists are supposed to be good but, in this situation, feel repulsed by the patient, the therapist ends up feeling bad. Ultimately, the therapist feels guilty for his or her feelings and then resentful toward the patient for exposing the therapist's weakness.

I have suggested that envy is an elusive but powerful feeling that can result in therapeutic countertransference. Envy on the part of a therapist toward his or her patient isn't limited, however, to sexual behavior. A therapist has merely to feel deficient in some vital way for the seeds of envy to grow. If the envy goes unexamined, the therapist is likely to play the moral judge who prevents successful treatment by diagnosing the patient as "bad" and him or herself as "good."

19

EDWARD J. TEJIRIAN

The Symbol of the Destructive, Phallic Male

IN THE BALLCOURT AT THE ruins of Chichen Itza the great Mayan-Toltec city in central Yucatán, carved reliefs depict two opposing teams of players lined up and facing each other. The finely chiseled reliefs permit us to make out the details of a drama enacted at least seven hundred years ago in the brilliant Mexican sunshine. The athletes are lithe under their protective padding, and one can imagine the colors of their plumed head-dresses flashing contrasts against the deep blue of the sky. At the head of the line depicting one team, the athlete-warrior is holding a broad, double-edged sword. In his other hand, he holds the head of the captain of the opposing—and losing—team. It has the handsome profile of a young man, whose strong—but headless—body still rests erect on one knee. From its neck, jets of blood in the form of snakes fan upward to form the shape of a graceful fountain. Between the two teams, a large, ball-shaped object rests, enclosing a profiled skull within its outlines. This Toltec version of the Mesoamerican ballgame—part sport, part ritual—incorporates what appears to be a powerful theme in male-to-male psychology: confrontation with an adversary in lethal competition.

In the core fantasy around which his sexual life has been organized, Len, the subject of this chapter, has been, nightly, the helpless victim of a merciless seducer. In his fantasy, he is always a boy, usually adolescent, occasionally younger. Although he is straight to begin with, he cannot resist seduction by the powerful, phallic male who penetrates him at will, usually mocking him with demeaning epithets. This man, often old enough to be the father of the boy whose role Len is taking, is the instrument by which the boy is changed from straight to gay. In some versions of the fantasy, after "breaking in" the boy, the man turns him over to other men to be used sexually.

The similarity between the fantasy of a 20th-century urban man and the deadly ritual of an almost entirely extinguished culture is the confrontation with destructive male power. The Toltec captain holds the sword with which he has decapitated his losing opponent. The man in Len's fantasy uses his phallus like a sword to destroy the boy's budding masculinity—for that is Len's view of the meaning of being turned from "straight" to gay. Paradoxically, however, the exercise of this destructive, phallic power is intensely erotic for Len. It is so charged with excitement that it is even superimposed on sexual encounters with actual people. In such an encounter, his partner may have no inkling that, for Len, the sexual transaction is between a boy, typically blond, whose persona Len has temporarily borrowed and a destructive, phallic, and more powerful male. The fantasy is so compelling that, though Len is in his fifties, it has emerged even when the actual partner has been a much younger man.

For Len, as for many heterosexual men in our culture, to be penetrated by the erect penis—the phallus—of another is to suffer a fatal blow to his masculinity. For these other men, the repudiation of any possibility of gay feeling within themselves guards their sense of masculine identity. For Len, paradoxically, the destruction of his masculinity, when he is in the role of the fantasy boy, is an intensely erotic experience. The destructive, phallic man is a powerful symbol, and the fantasied submission to him is a compelling symbolic experience. I am using the terms "symbol" and "symbolic" here to designate an image or an experience that is powerfully expressive of meaning and deeply evocative of feeling. It is important to add that it is not necessary that these meanings or feelings be capable of being put into words. Let me also make absolutely clear that I do not use "symbolic" in a way that opposes it to "real." On the contrary, symbolic experience can intensify and focus the experience of reality, especially the reality of inner life, in a way that is almost impossible to match through other means. Sexual experience, whether in the heterosexual or gay modality, is one of the most important, and usually necessary, forms of symbolic experience. Sexual imagery and action both express and bring people into touch with their deepest emotional needs and express meanings central to the individual's psychological life. One of the important goals of psychotherapy is to help the person to find and use those symbols, including sexual symbols, that work for him or her and that allow him to experience important meanings and feelings.

THE CULTURAL SYMBOL OF THE DESTRUCTIVE, PHALLIC MALE

Across the spectrum of human experience, through an evolutionary process that is poorly understood, culture reacts selectively, and often capriciously, to certain potentialities of human nature. Some are idealized, others condemned. Certain widely prevalent aspects of human nature become the focus of intense preoccupation, while others may, by comparison, be de-emphasized. The destructive aspect of male human nature seems undeniable. Both history and newspaper headlines testify to its reality, both at the individual level and on a global scale. The individual's life history inevitably exposes him to both the positive and negative sides of male nature. Competition and cruelty are hard to avoid. And this is true in that most intimate male-to-male relationship, that between son and father.

The image of the destructive male, then, inevitably confronts men – whether gay or heterosexual – because it is rooted in the realities of male human nature and the experience with that nature. However, regardless of individual life experience, the destructive, phallic male is a powerful and omnipresent cultural symbol in various permutations and guises. In my book dealing with these and other issues (Tejirian, 1990) I tried to show that not only has our civilization emphasized the destructive meaning of phallic action, *but it has also made the phallus – the erect penis – symbolic of the destructive side of the male character*. I believe the phallus has the inherent potential to be symbolic of this destructive meaning. This meaning is underscored in rape. But it can, equally, be symbolic of other, quite different and more positive meanings – for example, primal, generative strength. Hinduism reverses our emphasis, with the *linga*, the abstract sculptural form of the phallus, being emblematic of Shiva, who is one of the two male deities (the other is Vishnu) most widely venerated by Hindus. However, since our civilization long ago paired the symbol of ultimate, cosmic evil with phallic power, for us, the Devil is the quintessential image of the destructive, phallic male. In my earlier work, I presented the analysis of a young man who obsessively feared that he might be possessed by the Devil. This young man longed for male love, and this longing was so intense that it urgently pressed forward to express itself symbolically in sexual terms. However, because of our cultural emphasis and his own individual life experiences, the sexual contact he desired also symbolized enslavement by a cruel and evil force and the consequent dissolution of his (heterosexual) identity. That young man, although he came to accept his sexual feelings for men, remained heterosexual in his life, primarily because there were powerful emotional needs towards women that he could not relinquish. Len, however, became gay and placed the destructive, phallic male at the center of his erotic life.

PARENTS AND FAMILY

A bleakness seems to have characterized Len's relationship with both his parents. Reflecting what must have been an oppressive control, his mother would not let him run around when he was a child and became anxious if he sweated. She would make him stand in the corner, where he was forbidden to cry, adding emotional to physical control. Nevertheless, he once said that he had never felt part of his father's body, but rather his mother's. He believes his father was affectionate with him while he was still a baby, but most of his memories are of a profound silence between them. He does recall, however, that it was his father who had forbidden him to come into his parents' bed. He believes his father was illiterate and, even before Len became the accomplished writer that he is, he felt superior to his father while simultaneously feeling guilty about that feeling. He learned little from him, bitterly remarking that his father had never told him what to do with his penis. As a deeply troubled adolescent, he had once come at his mother with a knife when she nagged him about getting a job. Speaking of that incident once, he said, "It was the first and last honest feeling in my life." And, in a quite conscious reversal of Freud's classic formula for the Oedipus complex, he remarked, "I wanted to kill my mother and sleep with my father." In fact, at the climax of his most common sexual fantasy, he has said, "Oh, Daddy. . . ."

There were two older sisters; a brother, who would have been the oldest sibling, died in early childhood. His childhood memories of his sisters suggest that they were, for the most part, affectionate and protective of their younger brother. Some sexual play initiated by the younger sister left him with residual feelings of anger and guilt. He looked up to his older sister a good deal and felt upset when she began to date and then felt deserted when she left home to get married. One of the first males he felt strongly attracted to was the boyfriend she eventually married.

I first began to see Len when his mother was in a nursing home upstate. Len, who was then in his mid-forties, felt compelled to take the bus trip every Sunday to see her. I did not have the impression that these visits were ever enjoyable. It was about that time that he had left behind a promising career as a playwright to turn to another literary genre, poetry. Years later, he reflected with bitterness, "I didn't have to give up my career to see her." At that time, I was unaware of any such connection. Perhaps this is a connection that he has only inferred retrospectively.

BEING GAY

Len has been deeply ambivalent about being gay. In the past, he has made such statements as, "My homosexuality is my anger;" and "If I didn't hate myself, I wouldn't be gay." He has also remarked that only heterosexual man are "real" men, and he once said that he came for *my* penis since neither he nor any other gay man had one. Consistent with these feelings, he had once been angry with a friend of his for pursuing an 18-year-old "straight" boy. He has since repeated that he feels it would be wrong to take a straight boy and turn him gay, which is precisely what occurs in his core sexual fantasy. He has defined a "faggot" as someone who longs for a man that he cannot have.

"IS THIS LOVE?"

Len once described a scene from his youth. He was with a man, a casual pickup, who grabbed his testicles and seemed to want some kind of sado-masochistic scene. Len was disturbed by this and, as they parted, he asked, "Is this love?" The theme of love seems to run a tortuous and convoluted path through Len's sexual fantasies and his life. Initially, he said he wanted someone to love him but this, somehow, had been lost. Before I knew him, Len had fallen in love with a young man who was acting in one of his plays. The attempt to consummate this love left Len with painful feelings of remorse. As Len described the scene, he pulled down the young man's pants and put his finger into his anus. Whether because of physical pain, psychological pain, or both, the young man started to cry, and the attempted sexual intimacy ended with Len's feeling that he had raped him. Paradoxically, some time later, they met in the street, and the young man remarked wistfully, "You don't love me anymore." Many years later, they again met by chance in the street, and Len realized that the young man had wanted a father in Len, adding, "And that's why I loved him."

Since I have known Len, his sexual experiences have largely been anonymous encounters. Before the health crisis, these took place at the baths and, more recently, in movies and places where young male dancers strip and perform. Some years ago, a younger friend, a fellow writer who was married, approached Len sexually. He really liked Len, both as a friend and physically, and wanted to perform oral sex on him. Len allowed this but with much ambivalence and discomfort. Afterwards, the image rose up in his mind of this man coming at him with a knife.

POLARITIES

It has gradually become clear that Len's feelings about men are polarized. The man to whom he is attracted or whom he loves is also the man who is profoundly dangerous to him. Several years ago, and for the first time since I knew him, Len fell in love, genuinely and strongly, with a man about 25 years his junior. This younger man, David, was artistically and literarily inclined and seemed to like Len and to appreciate Len's interest in him. He invited Len over for his birthday, with some other close friends. Len went, bearing an interesting pair of gifts—a poem written expressly for David and a set of porno magazines. A few days later, they spoke, and David told Len how much he liked his poem. About the magazines, he said that, after Len had left the party, he and some of the others had gotten sexually excited by the pictures and had sex together. He then said to Len, "I still feel hot," and, in an obvious invitation, suggested that Len come over. Len declined, with the excuse that he had to work on some writing projects. Nevertheless, at the end of the conversation, he said to David, "I really like you," and David replied, "I really like you too." Within a few days of this exchange, Len dreamt that he was with a young man who tries to attack him with an axe. He runs into the bathroom. The young man tries to get in. There is another young man in there who tries to help Len keep the other one out.

The young man with the axe must have been David, who Len feared would hurt him if "let in." These images of being attacked were, however, not consciously associated with David. What he consciously felt with David was a sense of paralysis. He told of how, one day, when he met David, who looked wonderful, "poured into" his jeans, he could not say anything to him about his feelings. The first time David invited him up to his apartment, which was soon after they met, it was a hot night, and David lay back on the couch clad only in shorts, as if to invite Len to make a move—one that he could not make. In these early stages of their relationship, Len was intensely aware of his feelings for David. What he found himself wanting to do was to hug him and kiss him all over. Yet he did not dare. When David would call to see about making plans, Len would put him off.

The imagined scenes of tenderness seemed somewhat removed from Len's usual conceptions of sexuality. More indicative of those was his comment when David was going away on a beach vacation. Len said to him, "Send me a used jockstrap." But when I asked him what he actually imagined doing with David, he only thought of holding him, touching him, being nice to him. Sometimes it felt unbearable not to be able to do this.

Later in their relationship, Len would bitterly reproach himself for not having taken more sexual initiative with David who, he was sure, would have been receptive to it then, as he proved not to be later. But the perception of David as potentially hurtful seemed to be lying just below the threshold of consciousness and prevented him from taking action. The young man with the axe in the dream already mentioned was obviously David. But the perception of David as hurtful also came into consciousness when he had the obsessional thought that David would call up his place of work and say invidious things about him.

It seems to me that it was the expectation that his feelings would be harshly rejected by David that both accounted for Len's paralysis in expressing his feeling for him and for the images of a hurtful David, whether thinly disguised as in the dream or all but admitted in the obsessional thought. The expectation that his tender feelings would be rejected also accounted for a shift in his fantasies about David towards the kind of stereotyped and commercially pornographic images to which Len was accustomed to masturbate. One night, David telephoned him from the bathtub. They talked for a while and Len, who felt there might have been some kind of a sexual invitation to this, reproached himself for not saying, "Are you getting your ass all nice and soapy for Daddy?" Later, when he was telling an old friend about this call and the missed opportunity, he cried. By now, a little more than a year after their initial meeting, he was persuaded that David liked and expected to be approached forcefully and brutally "fucked." He reproached himself with failing to play his assigned role in this scenario. It seems that the tender feelings for David, which he anticipated would be rejected, had been replaced by something else which he felt David would accept—brutality. Sometimes in fantasy, he would imagine scenes in which he would tie David up and rape him. However, his tears after the telephone incident hardly seem to have been those of a sadistic rapist; rather, they were indicative of someone deeply but hopelessly in love.

TRANSFORMATIONS

Freud (1926, p. 48; 1930, p. 13) points out how love (Eros) attempts to abolish the boundaries between the self and its object. Opposite-sex lovers can feel a sense of merging and unity, a feeling of oneness that can be experienced in a heightened way through sex and through other means as well. For people of the same sex, love and a sense of oneness may be heightened even more because of the similarity in gender. For a boy, the desire to be like his father coexists with and is heightened by the existence of a loving relationship between them. In Len, the process of identification with the loved other was carried to such extremes that the end result was a kind of transformation. In fantasy, Len would become, not just *like* someone else, he would become that other person entirely. Len himself would disappear.

The way in which this process of transformation could take place was illustrated in a complex set of reactions that Len described to me in relation to a handsome young ballet dancer that Len greatly admired. Having seen him perform previously, he looked forward so seeing him again when the company returned to New York a year later. As he watched him dance again, Len found that tears came to his eyes. In answer to my query, he said that he thought this was a reaction to the dancer's youth and beauty. Afterward, however, a reverie began in which the young dancer was the only member of the company who was not gay, but was forced by the choreographer to have sex with him. Later that evening, Len became this young man in fantasy and was raped. I said that it seemed paradoxical that he would subject the person he had felt such obvious love for to this kind of treatment, even in fantasy. In reply, he said that he could not imagine his feelings for him being accepted. So, maybe the rape was a revenge for that.

It seems Len did not feel that, as himself, he could have this young man. Therefore, he became the young man. This form of abolishing the boundaries between self and other contrasts with sexual union, where the identity of both partners is maintained even while symbolically merging with the loved person. I think Len selected this route because of the conviction that he did not have an identity worth keeping or being wanted for. Through the transformation he could, for a time, feel young, handsome, and desired.

Some time earlier, Len had related to me that he had seen a television interview in which a young man told of how he had killed the father who had raped him when he was a teenager. The story had moved him to tears of sympathy. It seems both perplexing and ironic, therefore, that the fantasy I have just described, a variation of the core fantasy, resonates with the elements of father-son rape. However, the emergence of this fantasy seems to follow the same sequence of emotional events that occurred with David. An initial impulse of tender love evokes the fear and expectation of rejection. In this instance, the image of Len himself in a tender and sexual liaison with the young dancer did not emerge even briefly into awareness, as it had with David. Instead, it yielded immediately to the sadomasochistic fantasy. In the case of David, Len's frustration and anger found some expression in his taking on the role of the brutal aggressor. However, in the fantasy with the dancer, Len is entirely identified in consciousness with the masochistic role. Whatever anger he feels for the expected rejection of his feelings by the young man is only vicariously felt through an unconscious identification with the choreographer who forces him to submit.

The relationship with David had ground to a halt in a crushing disappointment a little over a year before this time. After the initial charge of erotic potential, it had evolved, for David, into a literary friendship in which he looked to Len for advice and guidance for some of his own writing aspirations. For Len, it became a mixture of altruistic satisfaction in trying to help David and a source of frustration because, despite David's friendship and gratitude, Len had come to serve not only as literary mentor but also as something of father-confessor for David's love affairs with others. When, after more than a year, he finally told David of his sexual desire for him, David harshly replied, "I don't find you attractive."

OLDER AND YOUNGER MALES

One of the most widespread patterns of male-to-male sexual relationships, historically and across cultures, is the older male's attraction to or love for the youth. Freud's concept of the negative Oedipus complex refers to that part of the sensual current between father and son that flows from son towards father. Since our culture holds the adult male's sexual interest in the adolescent boy to be immoral (from a psychiatric point of view, it is a perversion) little attention has been paid to the reverse flow of sexual desire from older man to youth or from father to son. The older man's desire for the youth symbolizes, in a manner I believe to be normal in male psychology, the father-son relationship. While in consciousness, the older man is more closely identified with the role of the father, he can also vicariously identify with the role of the son.

Silverstein (1982) has documented the not infrequent occurrence of conscious sexual fantasies about the father by boys who later became gay men, as well as evidence of sexual responses of fathers toward sons. His research also attests to the existence of long-term relationships between men of the same age. But that is not the pattern to which Len is primarily drawn. It is the intergenerational relationship which is electric for him. For the past year, he has gone with some frequency to venues where young men dance and strip for an audience consisting largely of older men. For a fee, these young men can be privately engaged in the back room. At first, he was hesitant to do this, but with some encouragement from me, he allowed himself to explore those avenues of satisfaction. The role of prostitute, however, is not conducive to the experience of the kinds of loving feelings which seem to be struggling to find expression in Len. Rather, they tend to lend some force to the rhetorical question that Len put to me not too long ago: "What does love have to do with sex?" The answer to this question was forthcoming in a fantasy whose emergence into his consciousness shocked and embarrassed Len. In this fantasy, all the dancers in the show were his own father's sons, whom he spanked, while also sucking their cocks. Embedded in the desire to have the father sexually, I believe, is the need to have his love. In the fantasy, the father expresses his wish for closeness with the son by taking his penis into his mouth, and this same gesture acknowledges the son's masculinity. Simultaneously, however, and in seeming contradiction to this, the son is also a child who can be spanked by the father, whose power is thus upheld.

It is only recently that Len told me of an incident that occurred when he was a boy, probably even before adolescence. He had gone to the RCA building to see if anyone would give him a free ticket for a radio show. A man offered him one and took him into the building and through some offices to a hallway. There, he started talking with Len about how his son masturbated. Taking out his penis, he asked Len to show him how he held his own. Len recalls being frightened at the size and color of the man's erect penis. He thinks he was brought to an orgasm as well. Reflecting on that incident, he said, since that time it has been important to be someone's son in a sexual sense.

BEING HURT AND HURTING

It appears that not only can Len see the person he desires as hurtful, but he can also feel the desire to hurt him. In the case of Brian, a heterosexual young man at work whom Len found attractive, a pattern of verbal sparring verging on sadomasochism had been established. Brian would remind Len that, though he knew Len wanted him, he would never have him. One day, as Len was leaving, Brian remarked aloud, "Look at how he's carrying that bag, just like a woman." Following Brian's last taunt, Len had the fantasy of slashing Brian's body with a knife, adding that he had no sexual fantasies about him. When I asked him what he *was* able to imagine with Brian, the image that came to him was, paradoxically, to hold him and caress him tenderly.

It was striking when, a few months after the incident described above, Len told of a fantasy in which he was slashing his *father's* hands. He made the connection between this fantasy and a memory of his childhood. He was walking with his father on the street, and he reached up to take his father's hand, only to realize that it was the hand of a stranger. He became frightened and cried. That incident had come to symbolize abandonment by his father and the fear and grief it provoked. Later on, as a teenager, he was sometimes afraid to go to sleep at night, lest his father come to his room and kill him. It seems that, alongside the erotic current symbolizing his need for love from his father, another current existed, consisting of hatred and fear. In the core fantasy, these two currents seem to have blended into an eroticized sadomasochism. However, in the work situation, the feelings of hatred and fear were sometimes experienced in virtually pure, unalloyed form, as when he imagined slashing Brian's body or when he feared physical violence by one of the men.

Len had recently said he cannot associate love with eroticism. He had also once said that he could only fall in love with a straight man, never a gay man. His falling in love with David belies both these assertions. I think it is closer to the truth to propose that he is deeply fearful that his need for love will be rejected in any relationship with a man, and that this expectation generates intense anger with the man from whom he antici-pates disappointment.

In a recent sexual encounter at the movies, a younger man seemed to be attracted to Len. He blew Len and kissed him lightly on the lips. Afterward, Len wished he had said to the young man, "Daddy wants you to suck his cock, you little cocksucker." The imposition of the father-son scenario on the real life situation testifies to the tremendous emotional charge it has in Len's feelings. However, I think its sadomasochistic tone also has a second function: the denial of the need for tender feeling that the young man's actions expressed on his own part and threatened to evoke in Len.

LOVE AND POWER

In my discussion of the issues raised by my patient with the devil obsession, I tried to show how, for men, the themes of love and power are interwoven in the fabric of their emotional and sexual lives. The need for love seems to me to be the most important component, though not the only one, in generating sexual imagery and desire. The abolition of the need for love and tenderness from consciousness through repression or denial cannot, I think, disable the operation of such a fundamental human motivation. However, its repression can emphasize, as it has for Len, the component of destructive power in male sexuality. The wish to feel powerful seems an inescapable part of male human nature. For many men, to feel powerful is an erotic stimulus, and in sex one can feel identified with male power through the effective operation of one's own phallic power. When this occurs in a sexual relationship where love is simultaneously felt, the overall experience can have a tremendous incandescence, merging pleasure in the self with pleasure in the other. Len's reactions to power in other males has seemed balanced on a virtual knife-edge, with the desire to bond with it through his body on the one hand, and a deep hatred and mistrust for it on the other.

Our culture has decreed that when the penis of another male is received into oneself, its power always operates as a force destructive to one's own masculinity. In spite of the anxiety and conflict this formulation can and does cause, it *is* possible for men to enter into sexual relationships that are not experienced in destructive terms. For Len, however, this has seemed almost impossible. And yet, in a moment of introspection, Len recently wrote, "At the moment of orgasm, the boy feels bodily that he has the love of the father, who accepts him just as he is."

OUR RELATIONSHIP

Ours has been a long relationship, something like 15 years. However, in my notes from as recently as six years ago, I have recorded a remark of Len's that, of course he had wanted me to fall in love with him, but he must mean nothing to me. One of the frustrations I have often felt is that my quite real liking and respect for Len could not seem to get through to him.

Not too long ago, Len quipped, "I don't want to have sex with you but you'll be sorry." More recently still, he said, "Don't you realize you're the man I care most about?" And a few days later, in discussing some of his troubles with people in authority at his work place, he said to me, "Aren't you an authority?" His last query helped to raise my consciousness, even after so long, about an aspect of our relationship that had been nagging at the back of my mind without my having quite put it into words. There was an aspect of a sadomasochistic father-son game in our relationship. It came out in a sort of verbal sparring in which I was allowed to have the upper hand. Just as Len's sadomasochistic erotic fantasies served to deny the danger posed by his need for love, our sadomasochistic "game" has, I believe, protected both of us from having to deal with his need for sexually expressed love from me. Len protected me from his anger over my failure to meet this need by directing his sarcasm as much towards himself as towards me and by ensuring that I had the last word as therapist and "authority." All this prompted me to mention something which Len did so frequently upon leaving at the end of a session that it had become a ritual: He would make some kind of remark, often lightly sarcastic or self-deprecating, that seemed to say, "Nothing serious happened here," and that had an emotionally distancing effect.

Len recently asked me about my own father and, letting down my guard, I talked with him about that. There has been a shift, it seems to me, even after all this time, to more genuineness in our relationship. Hopefully, this shift will help us in the work we have yet to do, including the exploration of the sexual tensions in our relationship.

THE DESTRUCTIVE, PHALLIC MALE –
FINAL REFLECTIONS

Our dominant culture conceives of male-to-male sexual relations in sado-masochistic terms because the male who undergoes phallic penetration suffers the destruction of his masculinity. But when the need for love is directed at another male, it ultimately leads to the wish for contact with that part of him—the erect penis—that symbolizes his power and his passion. While the need for male love might draw the man who identifies himself as heterosexual to an obsessive fascination with "homosexuality," the fear of degradation by the destructive, phallic male accounts for a large measure of his revulsion against it.

For the man who has accepted that his sexuality revolves around the male, our culture provides a ready-made set of symbols through which he can continue to experience what he is doing as destructive and degrading. The consciousness-raising and liberation movements of the past two decades have helped to provide men with alternative emotional contexts for their sexuality, alternatives that stress friendship, affection, and love. However, the personal life history of the individual will, I think, influence to what extent a man's sexual images and actions symbolize the destructiveness of male power or the extent to which, resisting cultural definitions, the experience of this power will be centered in feelings of love, received or given.

For Len, as for most boys, his father was the most important man in his life and also personified masculinity. Masculinity was experienced by Len as being characterized by rejection, silence, and unavailability. Neither Len nor I will ever really know why his father, after some initial reaching out to his little son, withdrew from the fragile and tender bond that had developed between them. However, in a scene of immense poignancy, Len related how his father, who was dying of cancer and was in his last hours, turned to Len and said, "Hold me." Len started to comply but his mother hysterically intervened and prevented him. Len was then in his twenties, and perhaps the embrace would have helped to bridge the frozen gulf that had separated them for so long. Even if it had, I do not know if it would have changed the course of Len's emotional life, which had become stuck in that most inexplicable of human compulsions, the need to repeat the pain suffered at the hands of the one from whom love had been sought. Through the symbol of the destructive, phallic male, both the need for love from his father and the pain of rejection by him were recreated.

For some men, as for Len, the symbol of the destructive, phallic male is at the center of their emotional lives and lends a powerful vibrancy to their sexual experience. I think it should be repeated that people have the right to choose their symbols for themselves. Yet, as a therapist, I do have questions. Although I can vicariously feel the excitement in humiliating another, I cannot endorse those feelings in myself, nor, in all fairness, could I work therapeutically to reinforce sadism or masochism in someone else. Len has sometimes accused me of not accepting the boy or child in him. I would probably have to admit to an inability to accept a fixation at a stage that negates all the qualities of sensitivity and intelligence which Len possesses. In one of our recent sessions, we were discussing the fantasy of the beautiful boy and comparing him to the person Len actually is today. Yet, he said, he most definitely had the wish to be accepted for just who and what *he* actually is. Since the disappointment with David, Len has met people who seem to accept him just that way, including sexually. When I told Len I was writing a chapter for this book, he pointed out that we were not finished therapeutically. I agreed but replied that life itself is a work in progress. The symbol of the destructive, phallic male is embedded in male psychology and is a powerfully reinforced cultural symbol. For Len, as for many men, it may always retain a certain electricity. However, I am optimistic that Len will be able to discover other symbols that enable him to integrate the needs of the boy that he was without negating the needs of the man that he is, and that incorporate rather than exclude his need for tenderness.

REFERENCES

1. Freud, S. (1926). Inhibitions, symptoms, and anxiety. In J. Strachey (Ed. and Trans.), *The standard edition of the complete psychological works of Sigmund Freud* (Vol. 20, pp. 77–175). New York: Norton.
2. Freud, S. (1930 [1929]). Civilization and its discontents. In J. Strachey (Ed. and Trans.), *The standard edition of the complete psychological works of Sigmund Freud* (Vol. 22, pp. 59–145). New York: Norton.
3. Silverstein, C. (1982). *Man to man: Gay couples in America*. New York: Quill.
4. Tejirian, E. J. (1990). *Sexuality and the devil: Symbols of love, power and fear in male psychology*. New York: Routledge.

Index